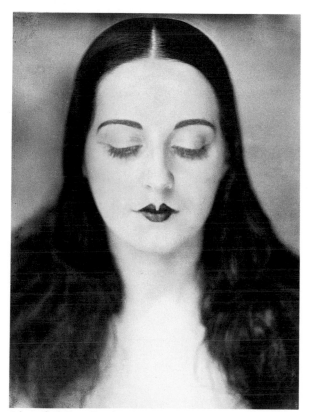

Solange by Jacques-Henri Lartigue – page 177

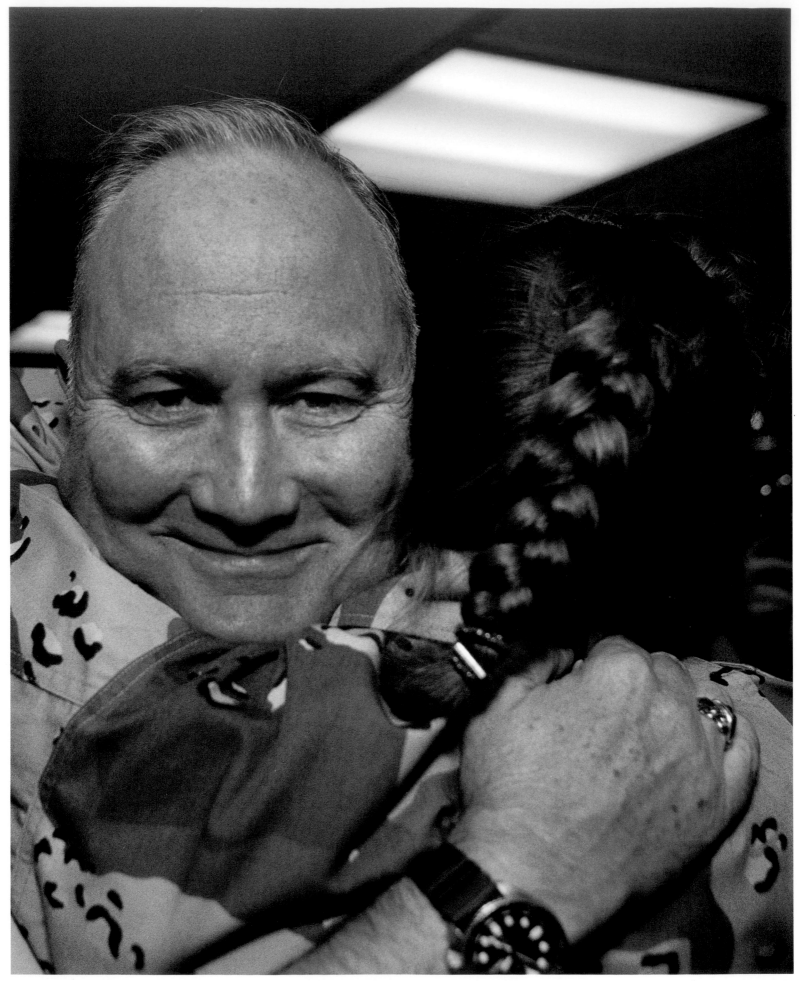

H. Norman Schwarzkopf by Harry Benson – page 172

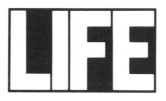

FACES

Commentary by John Loengard

A BOB ADELMAN BOOK

DESIGNED BY BOB CATO

Macmillan Publishing Company / New York
Maxwell Macmillan Canada / Toronto
Maxwell Macmillan International / New York Oxford Singapore Sydney

Picture Research: *Gretchen Wessels*
Text Editor: *Morin Bishop*
Copy Editor: *Amelia Weiss*

ACKNOWLEDGMENTS

A number of people were instrumental in the creation of this book. At Macmillan Publishing Company, Wendy Batteau has been remarkably encouraging and understanding. At The Time Inc. Magazine Company, I am especially indebted to Richard B. Stolley, Katherine M. Bonniwell, James R. Gaines, Peter Howe and Roger W. Neal, who gave the project their support from the start.

It is impossible to work with photographs that have appeared in *Life* without getting invaluable assistance from Barbara Baker Burrows, Debra Cohen, June Omura Goldberg, Doris C. O'Neil and Beth Bencini Zarcone. Also: Marie Schumann, Deirdre L. Wilson, Mary Shea, Laleli Lopez, Joseph Aprea, Margaret Sedgwick, Kathleen Doak, Joan Shweky, George L. Zino, Gedeon de Margitay, Stacey Harmis, Roxana Lonergan, Helene Veret, Gail Ridgwell, Liz Corcoran and Maria A. Paul.

Hanns Kohl, John Downey and Eric Valdman with Luis R. Barrios, Victor Echevarria, Hieke Hinsch and Nihal Mahawaduge, made sure that the Time-Life lab produced the best possible prints and transparencies for layout and reproduction. I am also grateful to Russell Burrows, Elin Elisofon, Richard Pollard and Rebecca Spivak.

Most important, I want to thank the photographers and their representatives who were invariably generous with their time and their knowledge.

Macmillan Publishing Company
866 Third Avenue
New York, NY 10022

Maxwell Macmillan Canada, Inc.
1200 Eglinton Avenue East
Suite 200
Don Mills, Ontario M3C 3N1

Macmillan Publishing Company is part of the Maxwell Communication Group of Companies.

Library of Congress Cataloging-in-Publication Data

Faces/LIFE Magazine: commentary by John Loengard
 p. cm.
 Includes biographical references and index.
 ISBN 0-02-574043-1
 1. Photography—portraits. 2. Photojournalism. I. Loengard, John. II. Life (Chicago, Ill.)
TR681 . F3F33 1991 91-3863 CIP
779'.2'0822—0020

Macmillan books are available at special discounts for bulk purchases for sales promotions, premiums, fund-raising, or educational use. For details contact:

  Special Sales Director
  Macmillan Publishing Company
  866 Third Avenue
  New York, NY 10022

10 9 8 7 6 5 4 3 2 1

Printing: Dai Nippon Printing Co. Ltd.
Printed in Japan

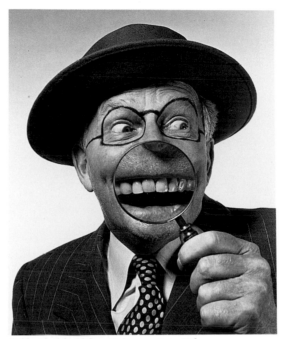
Bobby Clark by Philippe Halsman – page 126

This book is dedicated to the photographers whose understanding of the human face illuminates the printed page . . .

ALI AMIN	MARK KAUFFMAN	W. EUGENE SMITH
EVE ARNOLD	ROB KINNEAR	HOWARD SOCHUREK
ALEXANDRA AVAKIAN	WALLACE KIRKLAND	KEN SPENCER
BILL BEALL	J.A. KUMPF	TERENCE SPENCER
HARRY BENSON	BOB LANDRY	PETER STACKPOLE
MARGARET BOURKE-WHITE	BRIAN LANKER	STAN STEARNS
BRIAN BRAKE	JACQUES-HENRI LARTIGUE	JAN SVAB
MICHAEL BRENNAN	NINA LEEN	JOHN SWOPE
DAVID BURNETT	HANS LEURS	MILDRED TOTUSHEK
LARRY BURROWS	LOU LIOTTA	HENRI DE TOULOUSE-LAUTREC
ROBERT CAPA	RUTH HARRIET LOUISE	BURK UZZLE
HENRI CARTIER-BRESSON	THOMAS MCAVOY	H.M. VAN TINE
EDWARD CLARK	EAMONN MCCABE	GREY VILLET
HUESTIS COOK	LEONARD MCCOMBE	JURGEN VOLLMER
RALPH CRANE	DONALD MCCULLIN	HANK WALKER
BRUCE DAVIDSON	ANGUS MCDOUGALL	HANS WILD
LOOMIS DEAN	BEN MANCUSO	EMMONS WILLIAMS
D. DOWNEY	MARY ELLEN MARK	MADAME YEVONDE
W. DOWNEY	JOE MARQUETTE	
ALFRED EISENSTAEDT	GJON MILI	
ELIOT ELISOFON	FRANCIS MILLER	
J.R. EYERMAN	RALPH MORSE	*. . . and to their subjects*
ANDREAS FEININGER	ARNOLD NEWMAN	
HERBERT GEHR	JOHN OLSON	
FRANCIS J. GRANDY	MICHAEL O'NEILL	JULIA AARON
ALLAN GRANT	RUTH ORKIN	JINX ALLEN
PHILIPPE HALSMAN	LÜTFI OZKÖK	NICOLE ALPHAND
GUY HAYES	HY PESKIN	LOUIS ARMSTRONG
KEN HEYMAN	JOHN PHILLIPS	JOHN BARRYMORE
STOCKTON TODD HOLDEN	BILL REED	SAMUEL BECKETT
ALLEN HORNE	HERB RITTS	JIMMY BELOTE
F.L. HOWE	MICHAEL ROUGIER	ORLIN AND GLORIA BENEDICT JR.
BOB JACKSON	WALTER SANDERS	THOMAS HART BENTON
YALE JOEL	APRIL SAUL	M. AND MME. HENRI BERGERON
SVEN-GÖSTA JOHANSSON	DAVID E. SCHERMAN	BARBARA AND BETTY BOUNDS
HENK JONKER	PAUL SCHUTZER	MARLON BRANDO
YOUSUF KARSH	RAY SHORR	VICTORIA BROTKO
		YUL BRYNNER

GEORGE BUSH

MARTHA JANE CANARY

CHARLIE CHAPLIN

WINSTON CHURCHILL

BOBBY CLARK

ROSS CORBIT

BILL COSBY

BING CROSBY

MAURICE CULLINANE

JOHN DAMMEYER

BERNICE DAUNORA

CANDICE DE GRUCHY

DAVID DENNIS

ERNIE DESROSIERS AND SON, ZANE

DIANA, PRINCESS OF WALES

JIMMY DICK

JANE DILL

JOE DiMAGGIO

DAN DUKE

BEATRICE EDEN

EDWARD VII

EDWARD, DUKE OF WINDSOR

DWIGHT AND MAMIE EISENHOWER

GWYNED FILLING

STIG FORSBERG

CLARK GABLE

GRETA GARBO

GEORGE V

MEL GIBSON

JOHN GILBERT

MIKHAIL GORBACHEV

ULYSSES S. GRANT

SID GRAUMAN

WILLIAM RANDOLPH HEARST

JAMES HOFFA

AUDREY MAE HULSE

BLANCHE JENKINS

LYNDON B. JOHNSON

MRS. AUGUST KACHIGIAN

KAY KENDALL

JOHN AND CAROLINE KENNEDY

LARRY KING

ANTHONY KIRK

VERONICA LAKE

JUAN LARRA

LUGRASH LARRY

CAROL AND HENRY LARSON

GERTRUDE LAWRENCE

JAMES LEAVELLE

VIVIEN LEIGH

DAI LLEWELLYN

RICKY LOFY

DEBBIE AND MARY LOVE

MGM STARS OF 1943

SHIRLEY MacLAINE

BETTY McDOUGALL

RODDY McDOWALL

DOLORES MACIAS

MADONNA

HARRY MARTIN

LOUIS B. MAYER

LAURITZ MELCHIOR

MARILYN MONROE

KATHERINE MRZLJAK

MARJORIE MUNN

CARL NICHOLS

OLIVER NORTH

SEAN O'CASEY

LAURENCE OLIVIER

JOHN ORRIS

LEE HARVEY OSWALD

JACK PALANCE

SACHI PARKER

JOHN J. PERSHING

CHERYL POND

ELVIS PRESLEY

CECIL PRICE

ALICE PRIN

ERNIE PYLE

LAWRENCE RAINEY

MELISSA RATHBUN-NEALY

RONALD REAGAN

SYNGMAN RHEE

KANG KOO RI

GEORGES ROUAULT

JACK RUBY

DARLENE SCHALLER

JAN SCHLUETER

H. NORMAN SCHWARZKOPF

JEAN SIBELIUS

RAM PRAKASH SINGH

SOLANGE

JOSEPH STALIN

DENNIS STOCK

STUART SYMINGTON

EUGENE TALMADGE

ELIZABETH TAYLOR

DIANE TERDIK

SPENCER TRACY

HOLLIE AND CHEYENNE VALLANCE

QUEEN VICTORIA

KEITH WALKOWITZ

ALLEN WEAVER

CHARLES WELBERT

ORSON WELLES

WALTER WILLIAMS

WILLIAM WILLIS

PETER WITKUS

ANN ZARIK

INTRODUCTION

Imagine a world without faces, without expression, without tears, without smiles. Imagine a world where everyone looked exactly alike.

Or imagine if every face were round, young and innocent, and none were oval, wrinkled, closed, or even lifted.

Such a world would seem a wasteland to most photographers because faces fascinate them. Photographers have photographed more faces than any other subject. Indeed, since *Life* magazine began publishing in 1936, it has printed photographs of more faces than can be seen today in the state of Vermont—so choosing a few for this book from more than half a million required some criteria. Primarily I looked for an expression on the face that conveys the subject's feelings at the moment the photograph was taken. Or if the subject's feelings remain a mystery, I looked for a face that had been caught in a fresh or revealing light.

This book is not a collection of flattering portraits whose subjects have one eye cocked toward posterity. Most of the pictures are candid in their description of a person. Few were made in a studio. Many show people doing things that were more important than having their pictures taken.

These photographs were made for many purposes—as news, publicity or documentary pictures, even as informal snapshots. Some of the photographers who took them had artistic ambition; others did not. But all the photographs record a bit of the human condition, which is why they remain interesting long after the original reason for publishing them has been forgotten.

The five-and-a-half decades covered by *Life* are all well represented. Possibly overrepresented is the period between the end of World War II and the early 1960s, when television began dominating the news-in-pictures business. The '50s are considered the golden age of still-camera photojournalism, and the decade's rich legacy continues to demand attention. Underrepresented are the 1970s, when *Life* all but suspended publication for nearly six years.

Anyone who photographs people works quickly. (There are very few deadlines shorter than a subject's patience.) Some photographers spend hours before meeting their subject deciding where and how to take a picture. Others, after gaining rapport, spend days taking many photographs. Even so, expression comes when it comes, and it must be caught. The first exposure of an extended project may be as fine as the last.

When a photographer works in public, the subject is often unaware of being photographed. In private, things are different. No one looks at a painting and wonders if it was posed, but everyone notices when the subject of a photograph is self-conscious. For that reason, even the kind question of a willing subject may prove daunting: "Come in. What would you like me to do?"

A photographer might like to answer, "Please move into wonderful light and do something beautiful, meaningful and original," but things don't work that way. In such situations, photographers must draw their subjects out. They say, "I'd like to look around." Or ask, "What do you normally do?" and take time to study the subject and the light and the location.

While some photographers may spend time until their presence is ignored, others must get down to business quickly, and *they* use distraction to coax expression into flight. One clicks his teeth. Another fiddles with the lens as if something were amiss. A third asks a question...

Snap!

This book is a tribute to the art that results when photographers practice all the patient skills of their bloodless hunt.

Dennis Stock by Andreas Feininger – page 127

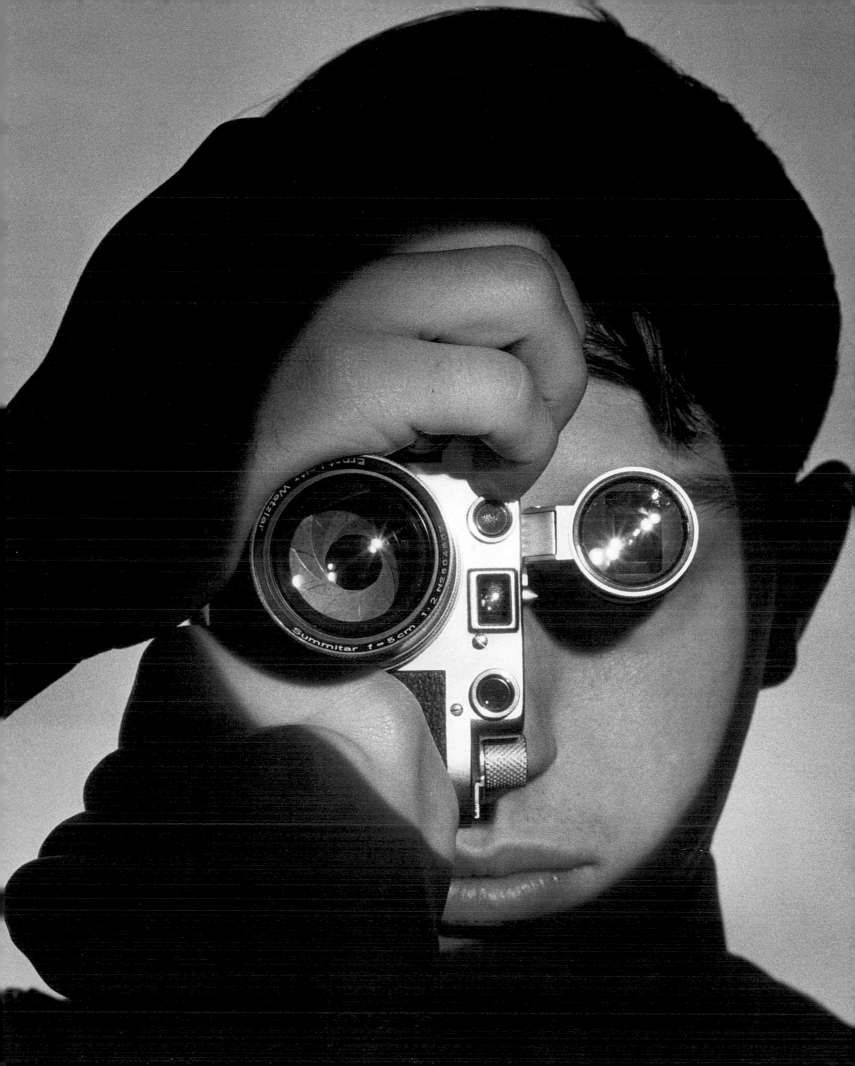

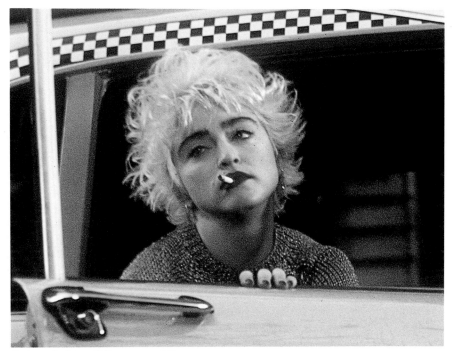

Madonna by Jurgen Vollmer – page 117

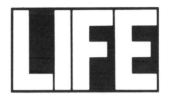

*The date under each title denotes
the issue of* Life *magazine in which the
photograph first appeared.*

FACES

Commentary by John Loengard

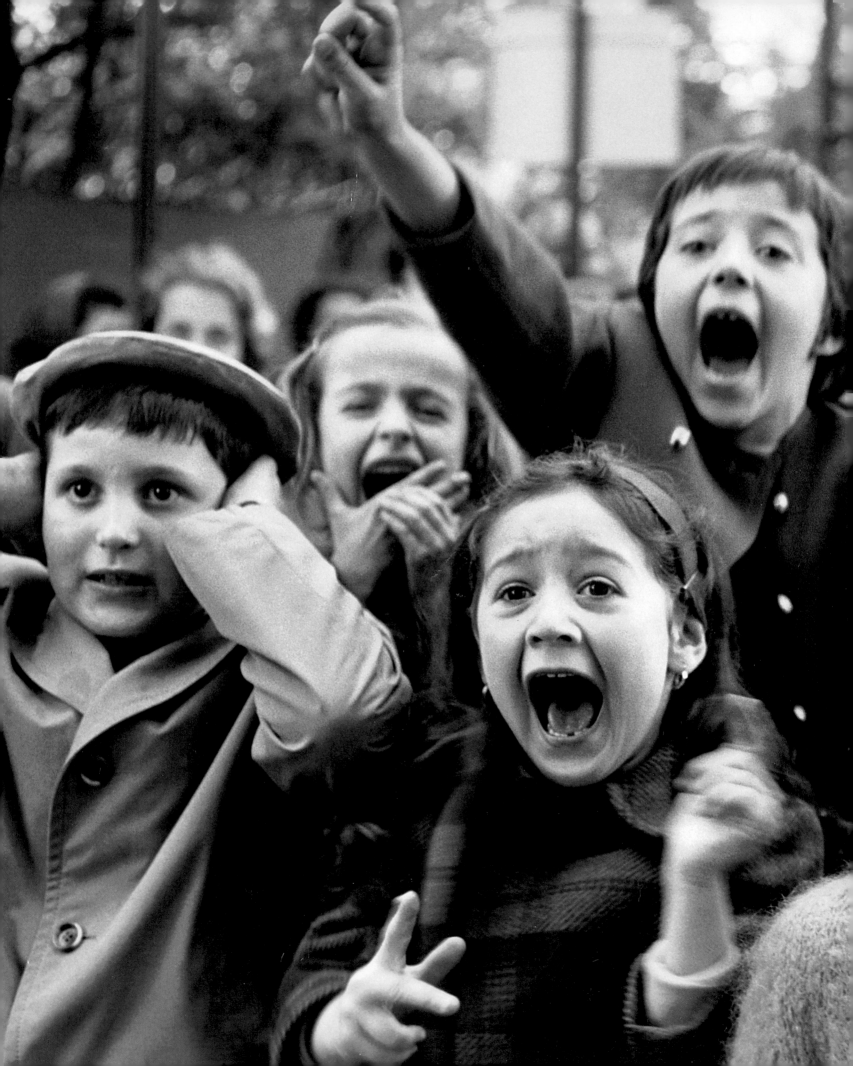

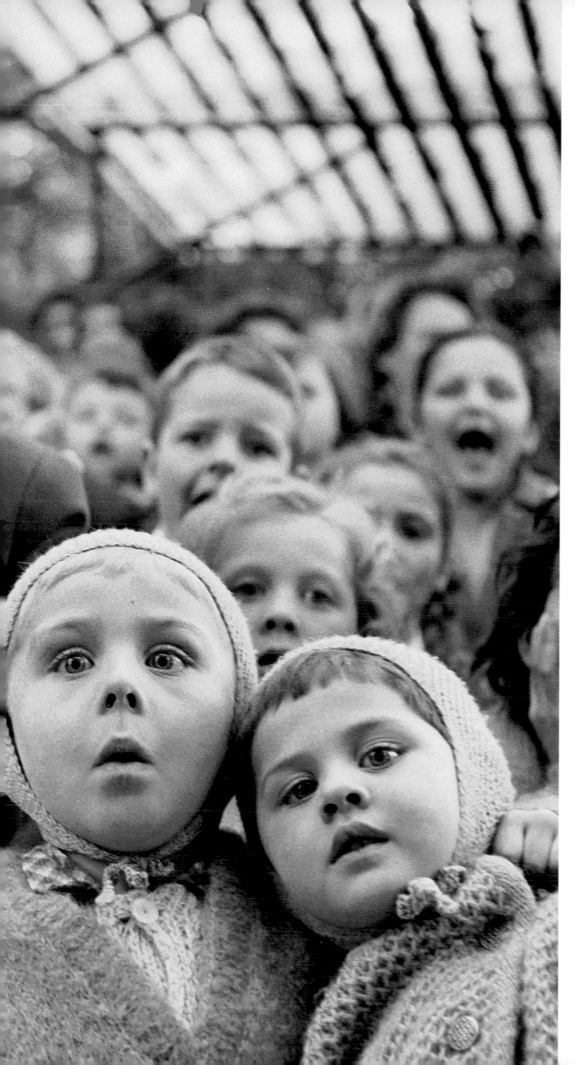

Puppet Show
ALFRED EISENSTAEDT
August 12, 1963
(International Edition)

"*Life* wanted me to photograph 'Eisenstaedt's Paris' after I did a story on monkey behavior in India," Alfred Eisenstaedt remembers.

"In some ways there wasn't much difference between the two assignments. Monkeys have to eat, and so do people. They drink, and so do people. Of course, monkeys also pick lice out of each other's fur. I never saw Parisians do that.

"It was a difficult story because Paris had been photographed so often. When I started, a very knowledgeable reporter worked with me. Every time I raised my camera she said, 'Oh, Capa has taken that,' or Cartier-Bresson, or some other photographer.

"Finally I told her, 'Look, I have to do it *my* way. For a story like this, I must look and wait, and that's something I do best alone. Nobody who comes with me ever understands what I'm doing.'

"In the Parc de Montsouris I discovered an outdoor puppet show, and then I found a little niche under the miniature stage, in front where a prompter's box might have been. It was wonderful watching the children's faces at the moment the bad dragon was slain. I shot almost two rolls." At 92 Eisenstaedt admits, "I have never made a better picture of expressions on the human face."

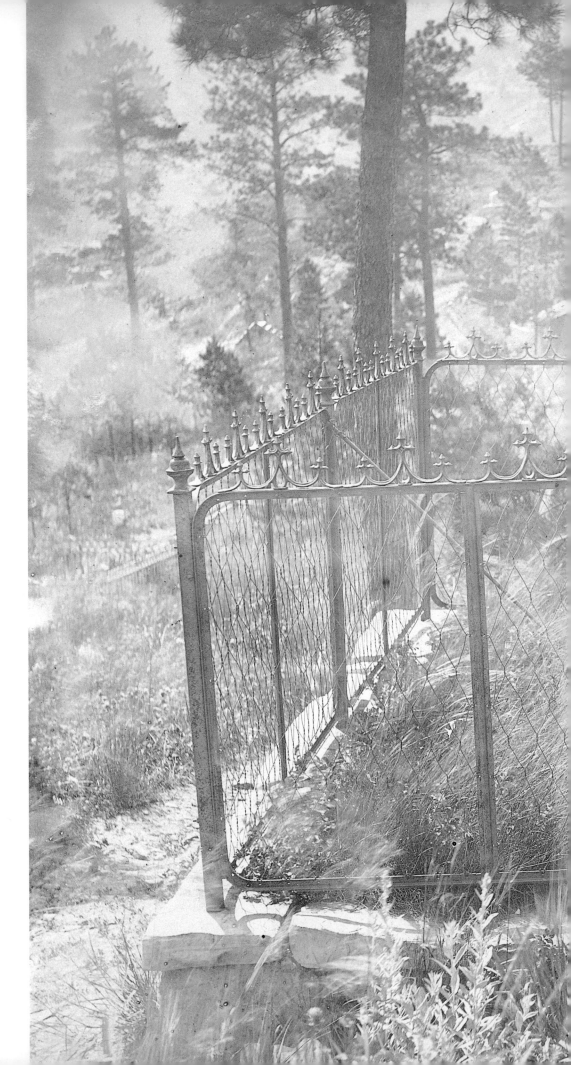

Calamity Jane
J.A. KUMPF
Remarkable American Women, 1976

"Nobody knows just why Martha Jane Canary came to be known as Calamity Jane," *Life* wrote. "According to one story, she used to threaten that men who dared offend her were courting calamity.

"Born around 1852 in Missouri, she spent most of her life drifting through the West, attaching herself to construction gangs and periodically being locked up for drunkenness and prostitution.

"She liked to wear men's clothes, cuss, chew tobacco, and—when liquored up—howl like a coyote and fire off her rifles. She also had a gentler side: when a smallpox epidemic broke out in South Dakota, it was Calamity Jane who volunteered to nurse the victims. Occasionally she would settle down with a man and call him her husband."

One such husband was Wild Bill Hickok, whose grave in Deadwood, S. Dak., she visited a short time before being buried beside him in 1903.

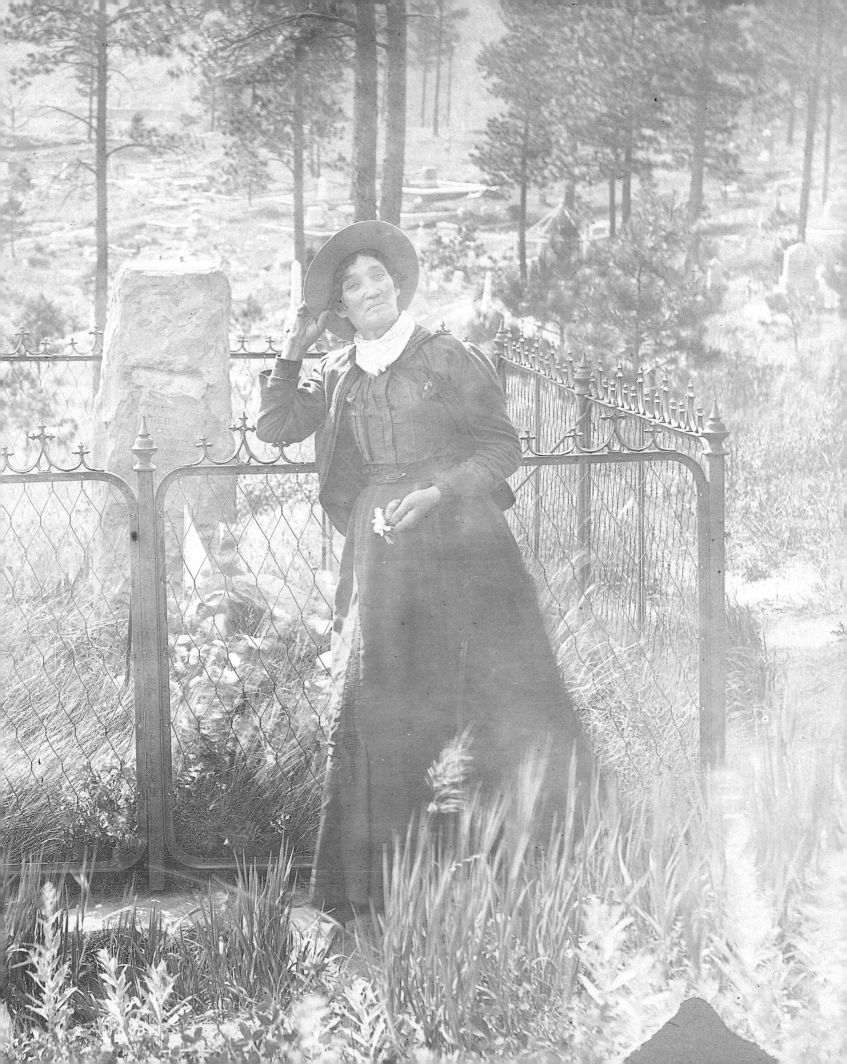

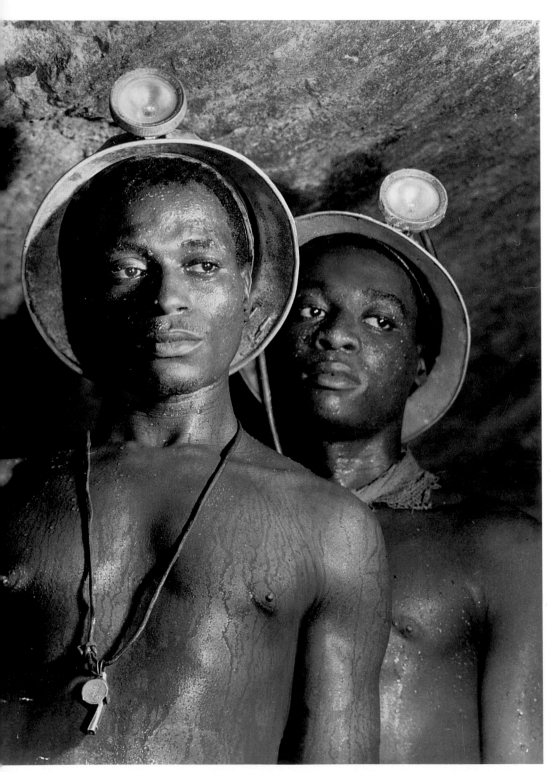

While taking pictures in South Africa, Margaret Bourke-White photographed the weekly tribal dancing of miners at the Robinson Deep mine, outside Johannesburg. Afterward, she asked permission to photograph two of the dancers where they worked below the earth's surface.

"When we reached the little sloping point where the two men were assigned, I could hardly recognize my dancers," wrote Bourke-White in her autobiography, *Portrait of Myself.* "With rivers of sweat pouring down their bare chests, and with sad eyes and perspiration-beaded faces, they hacked away. I was in the midst of making photographs when a strange depression and lassitude came over me. I could hardly raise my hands; I had lost the power of speech."

Recognizing the symptoms of heat prostration, a supervisor quickly took Bourke-White nearly two miles up to the surface. "I left the mine realizing that I had spent only four hours underground," she later wrote. "But these men, who had danced so gaily and happily in the upper air, were destined to spend the better part of their waking hours underground with no hope of escaping the endless routine."

Lieut. Colonel Oliver North
HARRY BENSON
January 1988

"**I** wanted to see the goodness, the pureness and self-righteousness of America in uniform," says Harry Benson, who grew up in Scotland and now lives in New York. "How could this man ever lie? He looks like what anyone would like their son to look like. I know it's how my mother would like me to look.

"I liked him. He looked me straight in the eye. Of course, any policeman will tell you that's not always a criterion of being honest. Scotland's biggest mass murderer, Peter Manuel, looked me straight in the eye. He was the last man to be executed in Scotland.

"I was visiting Glasgow when I learned I would photograph North. That night I phoned a man in London who paints my backdrops. I said I wanted storm clouds and thunder and lightning. He had the canvas ready the next morning when I changed planes in London. The paint was still damp.

"I had very much wanted to photograph North at home, where there would be opportunities for unposed photographs, but he had said no. The pictures had to be taken in his lawyer's office. I think he thought nothing could go wrong there."

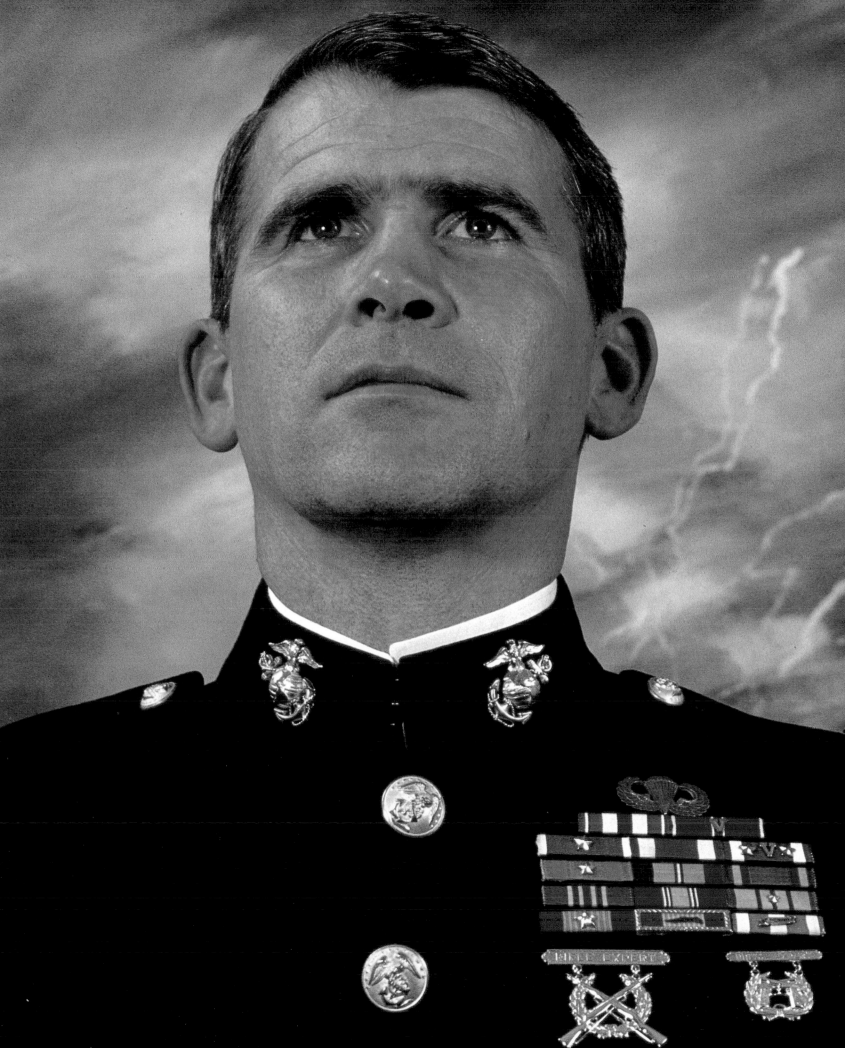

Mrs. Anthony Eden
MADAME YEVONDE
April 8, 1940

Elvis in New York
BEN MANCUSO
March 1985

Society ladies do the oddest things! In March 1940, the *Tatler* magazine in London printed this portrait of Beatrice Eden taken by Yevonde Cumbers, a successful Mayfair portrait photographer and the daughter of a prosperous printing-ink manufacturer. Madame Yevonde, as she called herself, had asked more than 20 socialites to dress up as goddesses. Mrs. Eden, her hair curled with white liquid paste, posed as "the goddess of history" appearing, *Life* thought, "in startling dishabille."

Mrs. Eden's 43-year-old husband Anthony had surprised the world by resigning as Foreign Secretary two years earlier, to protest Neville Chamberlain's policy of appeasing Adolf Hitler. After World War II started in 1939, he hoped a new Prime Minister would give the job back to him. Winston Churchill soon did just that.

In 1957 a movie magazine asked Ben Mancuso to cover Elvis Presley, who was in New York City to make his third appearance on Ed Sullivan's TV show. After taking some photographs in the singer's hotel room, the two went down to a coffee shop for a chat. On their way back upstairs, Elvis killed time (or avoided further conversation) by considering his reflection in the elevator lobby mirrors. Mancuso, who had his Speed Graphic camera in hand, remembers, "I was struck by the fact that in spite of all his fame and all his fans, this was a very lonely guy."

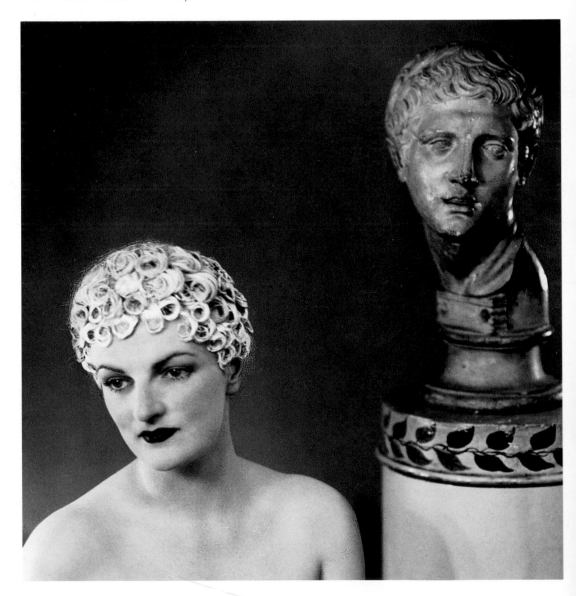

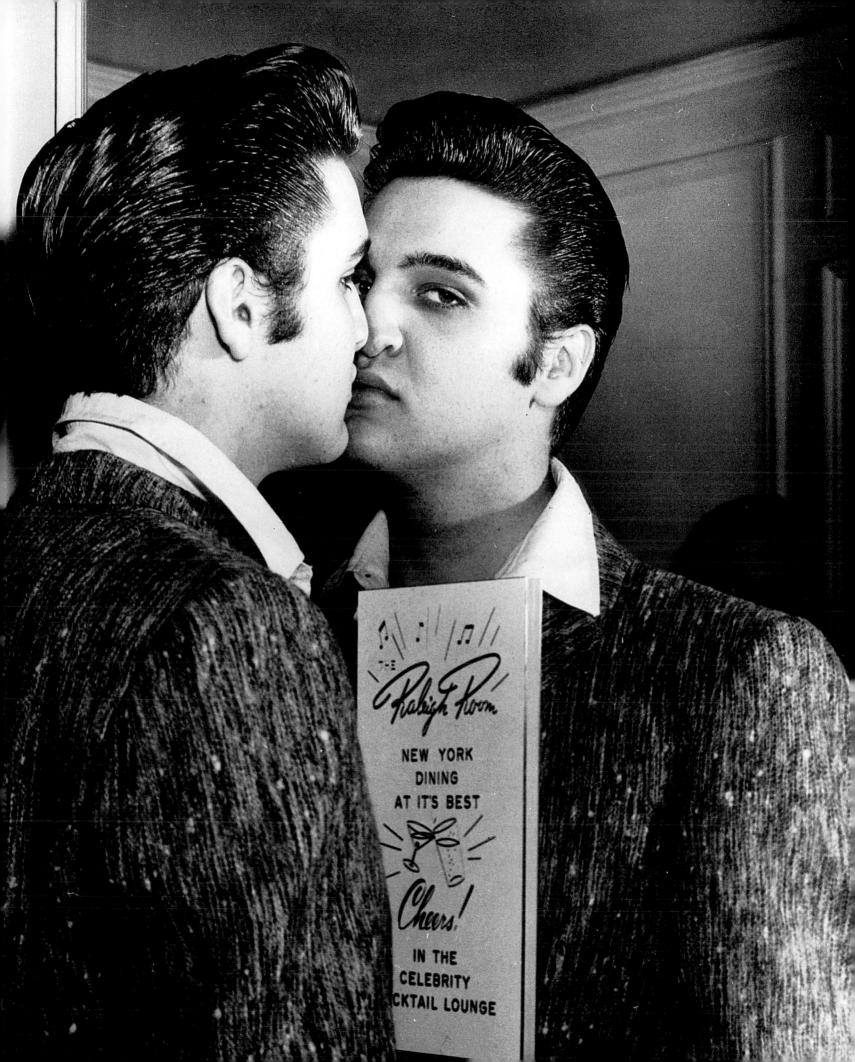
The Raleigh Room

NEW YORK
DINING
AT IT'S BEST

Cheers!

IN THE
CELEBRITY
COCKTAIL LOUNGE

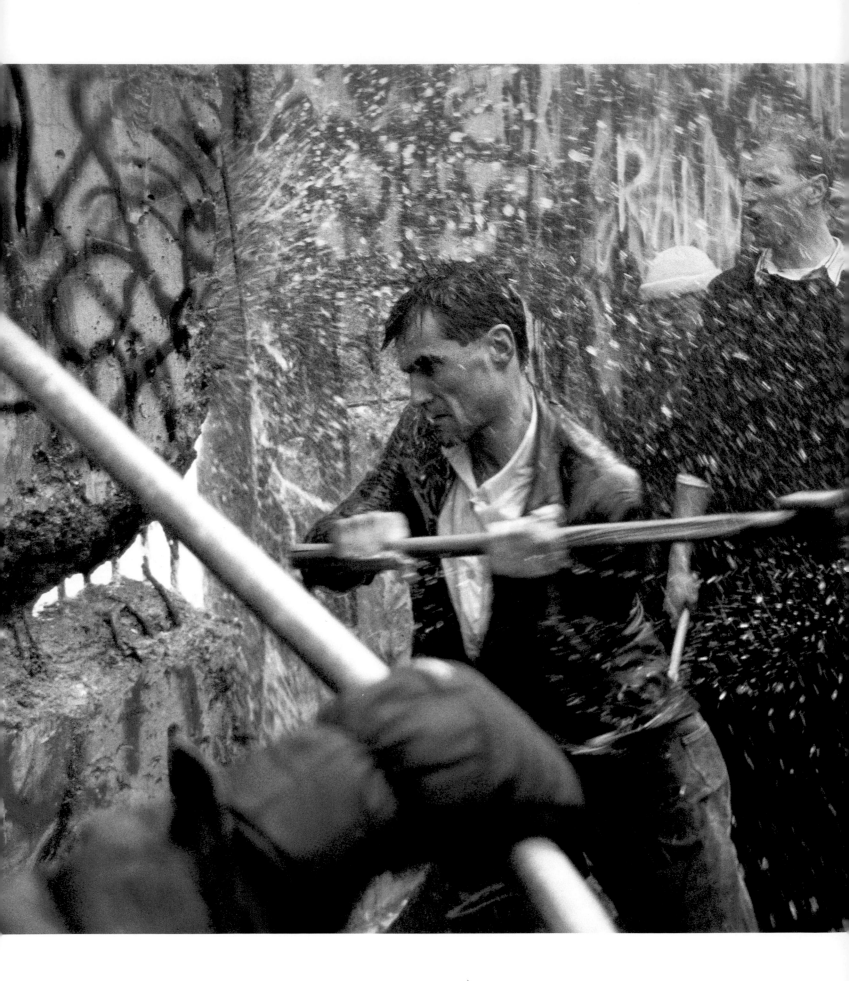

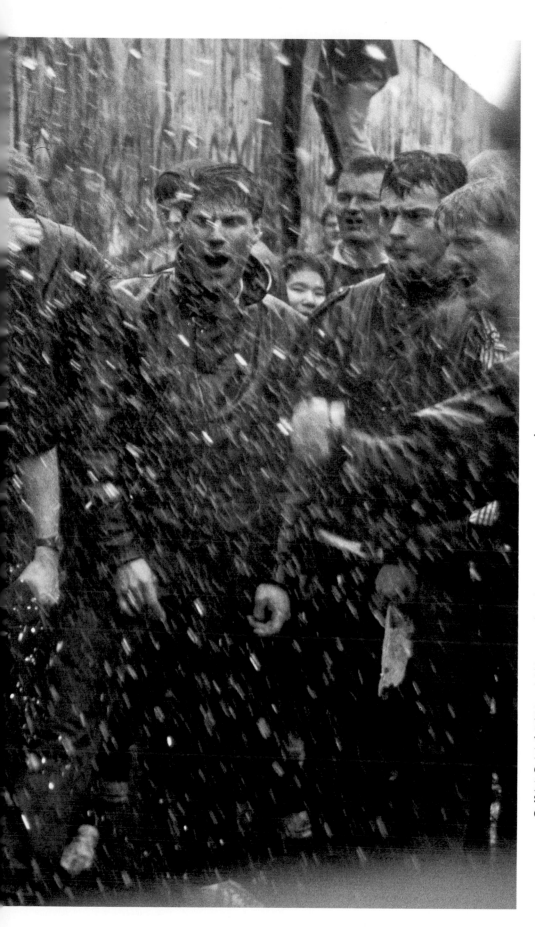

Berlin Wall
ALEXANDRA AVAKIAN
January 1990

In the evening at the Hotel Hervis, near Checkpoint Charlie, a rumor circulated that young men from the neighborhood would tear down a section of the Berlin Wall at dawn. Shortly after 6 a.m., 10 minutes' walk from the hotel, Alexandra Avakian found them.

"I saw this guy hitting the wall. He looked absolutely determined, absolutely serious," says Avakian. Climbing a ladder, she looked over to East Berlin and saw policemen bringing up a water cannon and, further back, amid some trees, troops ready with machine guns.

As the young man attacked the wall, water from the cannon sprayed through the holes. Finally, a section of the wall came down.

When it did, the tension curiously evaporated. Surly East German border guards became friendly, but there was no celebration. The isolated event was over, and people drifted away. Everything had happened, and nothing had happened. That evening, however, the idea spread. Thousands of jubilant East Berliners joined those from the West swarming over the wall, and began its complete destruction. Overnight the cold war ended.

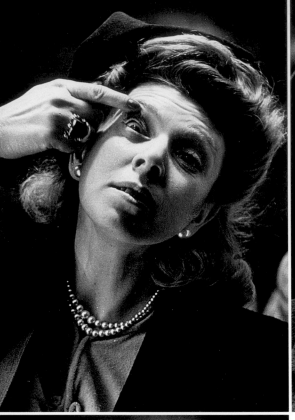

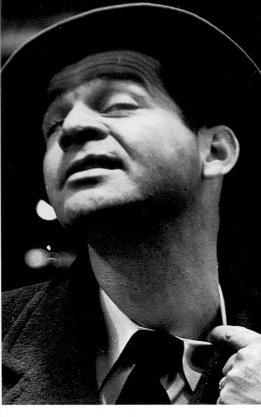

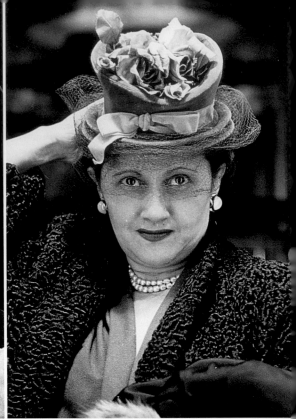

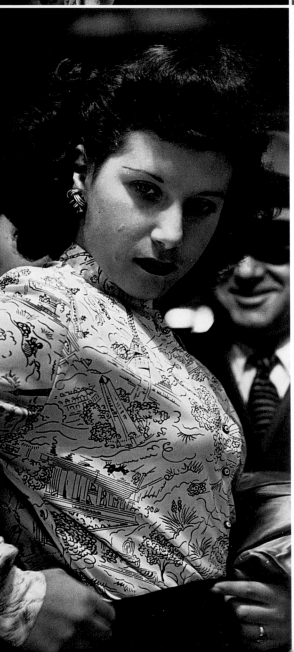

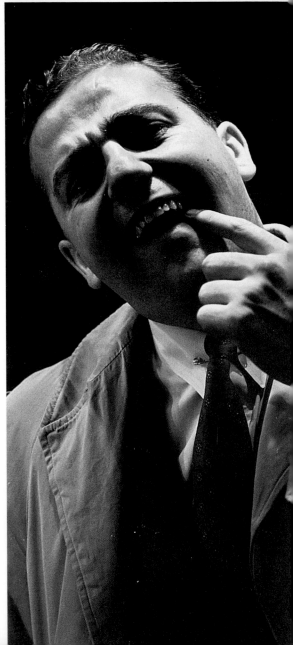

One-Way Mirror
YALE JOEL
December 16, 1946

It's not clear who came up with the idea (*Life* or a press agent), but the result was that a Broadway movie house built a booth with a one-way mirror on one side and put it in the theater's lobby. Inside, Yale Joel could sit unseen, with his camera on a tripod, and photograph the patrons as they made sure they hadn't grown an extra head or something. Joel spent 13 hours doing so.

"People looking at themselves in a mirror in a public place don't reveal deep, dark secrets," notes Joel, pondering the moral implications that might be raised by this kind of work. "It's not the same as looking through a peephole into a room where people think they are alone."

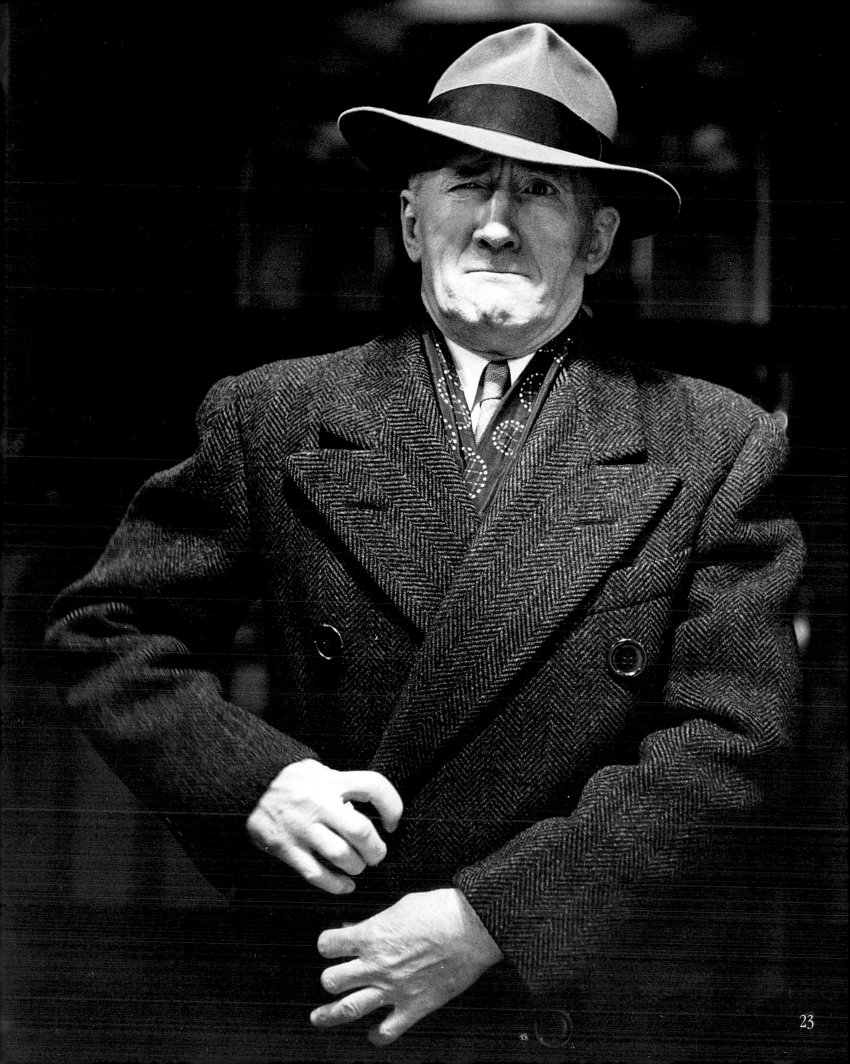

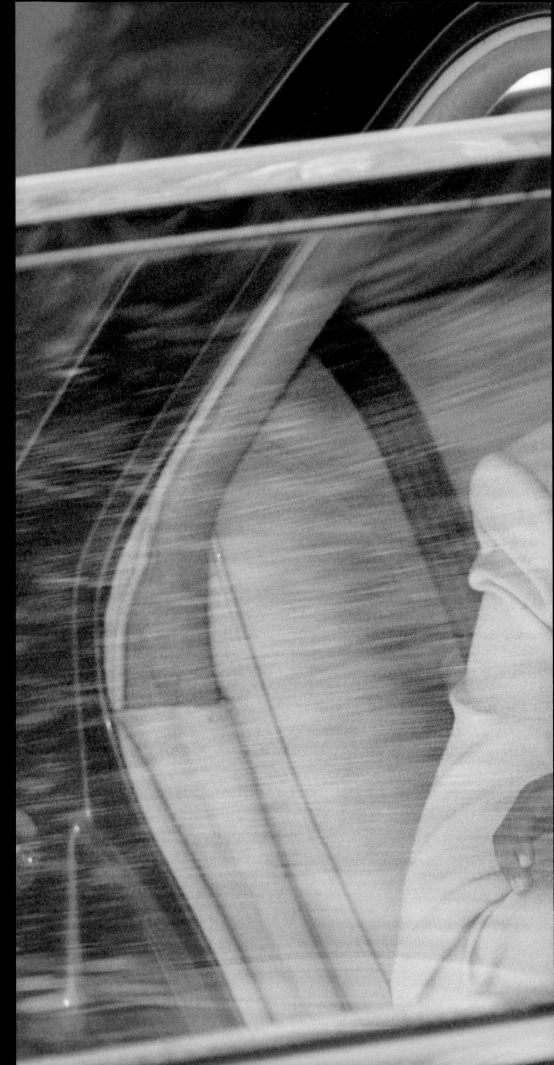

Princess Di
MICHAEL BRENNAN
December 1990

"When the embassy's dark green Rolls-Royce pulled up, the first thing I saw was a small black hand," says Michael Brennan.

Diana, Princess of Wales, had gone out the back door of Grandma's House (a refuge in Washington, D.C., for children with AIDS) and been driven around the block to the front steps to be greeted by the mayor's wife (a royal tour is a very complicated business). One three-year-old girl living at Grandma's had asked for a ride and been granted her wish.

"I'm not a great lover of the royals," says Brennan, who has concentrated on stories for the British press since he moved from London to New York 20 years ago. "Still, the woman broke completely with formality. It was a mother's instinct, wasn't it? She took the time to do this for that child. It makes all the royals look good."

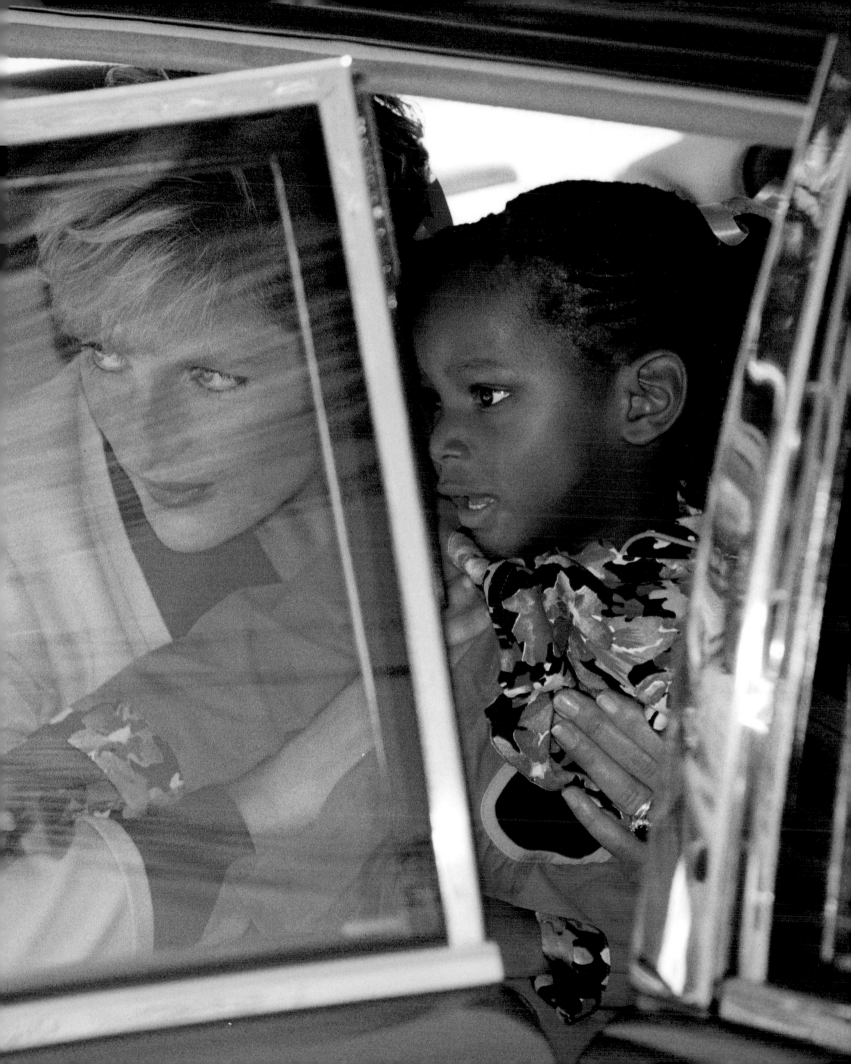

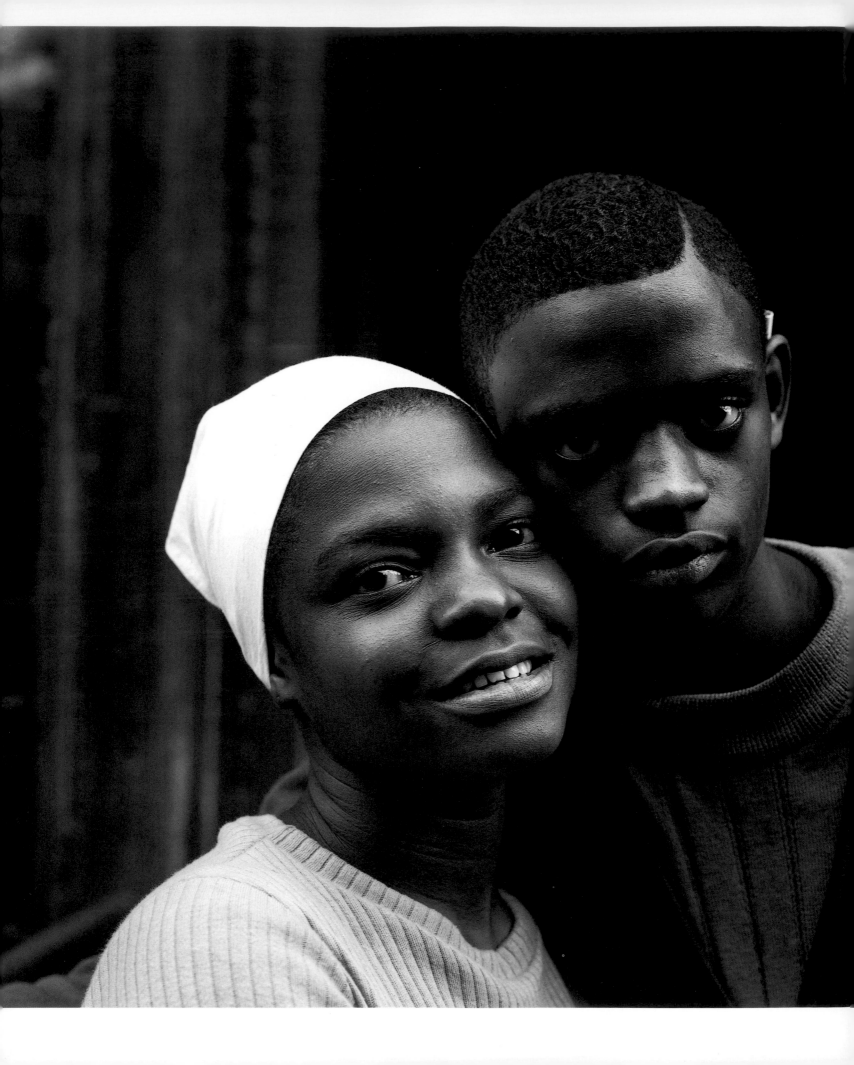

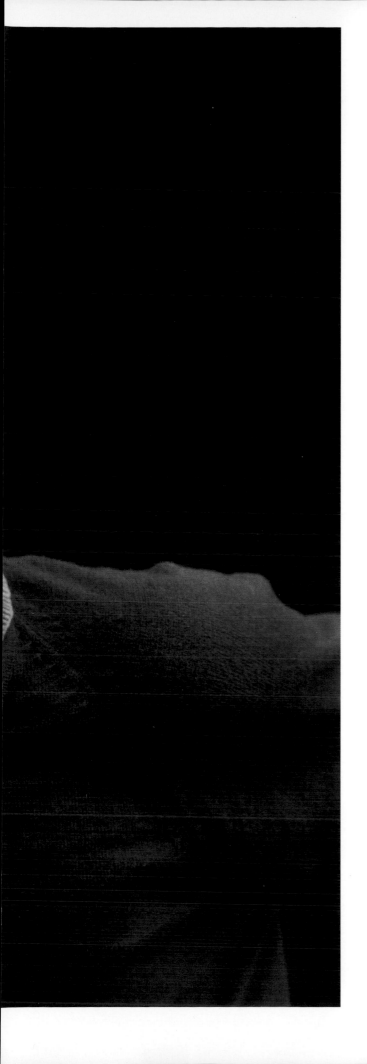

100th Street
BRUCE DAVIDSON
August 15, 1969

Bruce Davidson carried a large camera and a tripod into buildings on 100th Street between First and Second avenues in New York City, taking pictures of anyone who seemed interested in having him do so. In 1968, two years after he started the project, he'd given away 2,000 prints and collected enough pictures for a book.

"I wanted to dignify the act of photography," says Davidson. "I didn't like the idea of *stealing* pictures. We all do that, of course, but with the big camera I felt I was one to one. Eye to eye. I was looking for a moment that was private, both for them and for me.

"These two teenagers were childhood friends. I think his mother cleaned a fashion photographer's studio downtown, but I never checked that out. They stood in the shade by a stoop on the street. Their faces were beautiful, open, hopeful. I began to understand something about the block just by looking at them.

"I was up there again, recently, and I recognized one of the guys I'd photographed. I'd taken his picture while he was dancing by a jukebox in a social club. 'How'd you recognize me?' he wanted to know. 'It was 20 years ago!'

"'Sure,' I said. 'But I've been looking at your picture for 20 years.'"

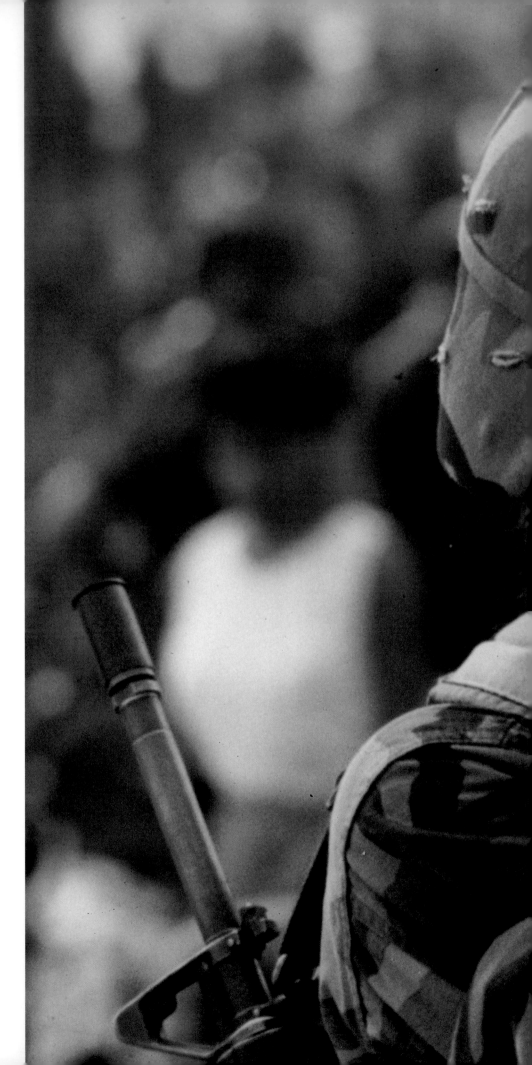

Hollie Vallance
ALLEN HORNE
January 1991

"They gave the troops a 10-minute break to say goodbye to their families," says Allen Horne, of the Columbus (Ga.) *Ledger-Enquirer,* who covered a ceremony at Fort Benning for troops leaving for the Persian Gulf. "I turned around and saw her walk up and grab her baby from her husband."

"It happens," was all Specialist Fourth Class Hollie Vallance, an Army medic, could say to describe her situation as she held her seven-week-old daughter Cheyenne. But the fact is America had never seen it happen before.

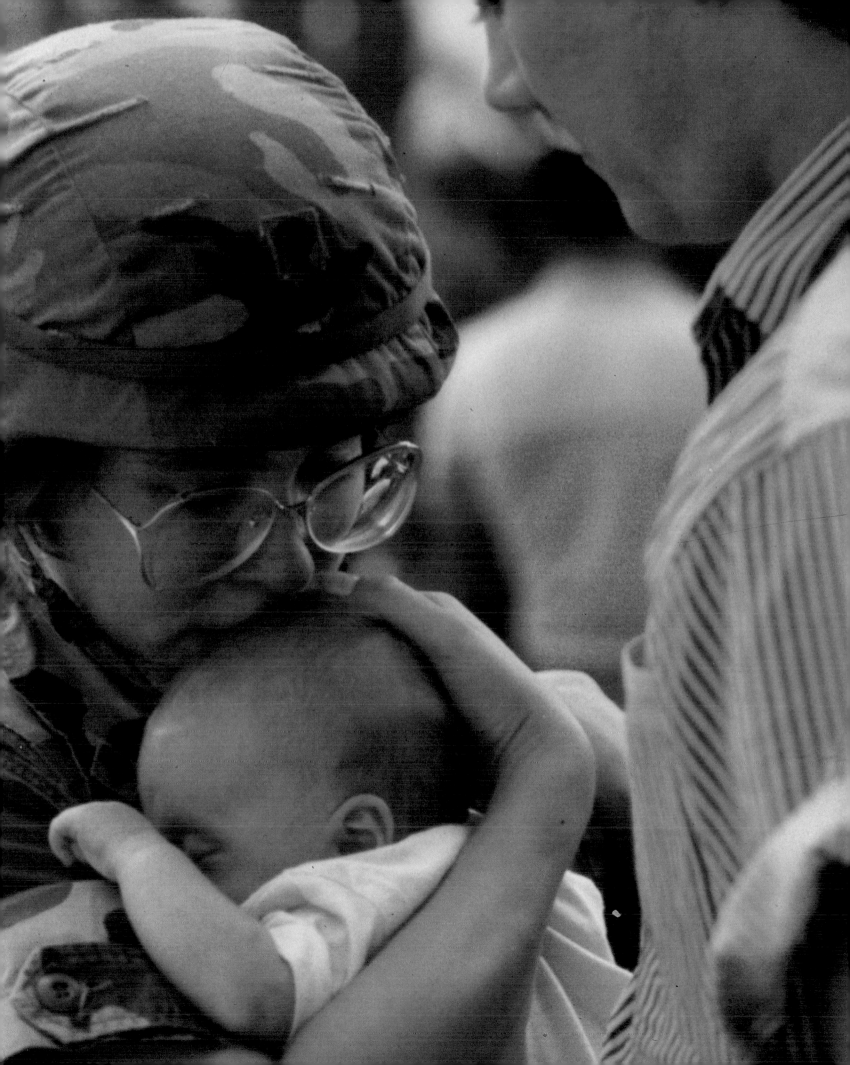

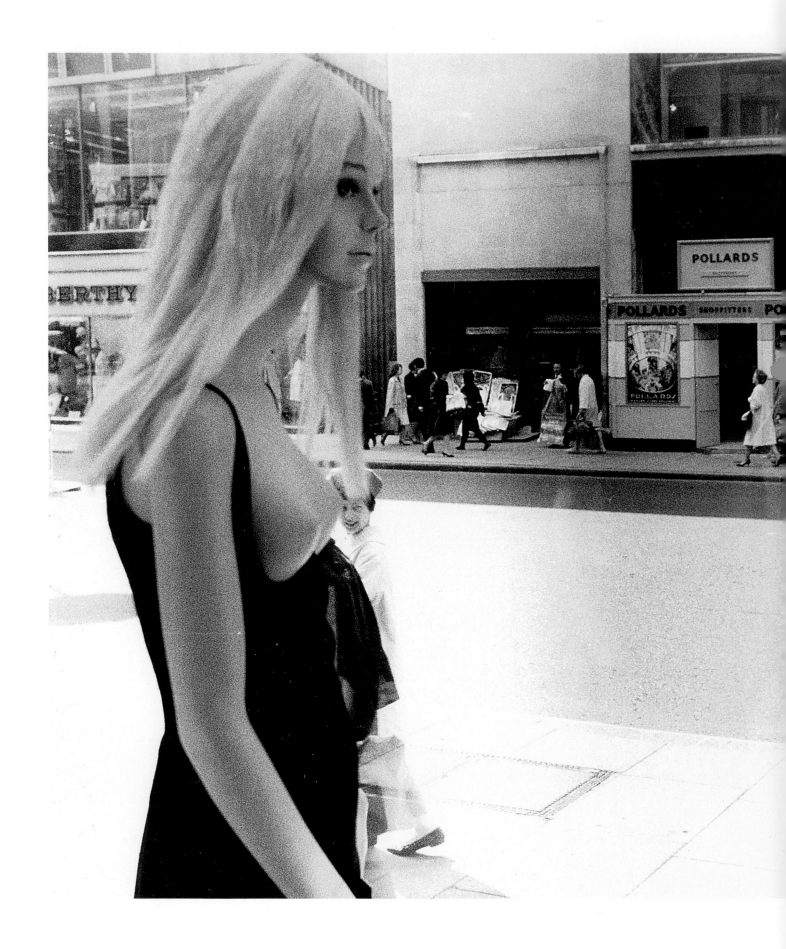

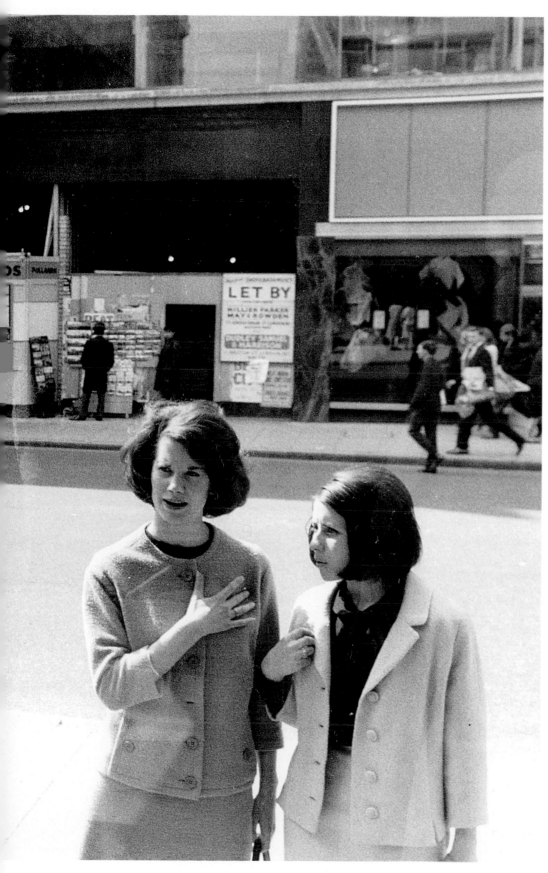

Topless
TERENCE SPENCER
July 10, 1964

In 1964 California designer Rudi Gernreich brought forth the first topless bathing suit for women and prophesied that swimwear would be bottoms only by 1970.

In London, where the topless concept encompassed evening wear, Terry Spencer put a camera in a shop window on Oxford Street. Working the shutter unseen from the back of the store, he recorded the reaction of potential customers. The wife of an architect actually bought the dress and, *Life* reported, "wore it to a party, where its merits and demerits were debated loudly all night."

In conservative New York, the same dress sold with a net fill-in, while from Los Angeles, writer Shana Alexander harrumphed about the beachwear, "Once you get over the shock, which takes about 10 minutes, the new suit begins to strike you as the most absurd garment since those two rascally weavers manufactured the emperor's new clothes."

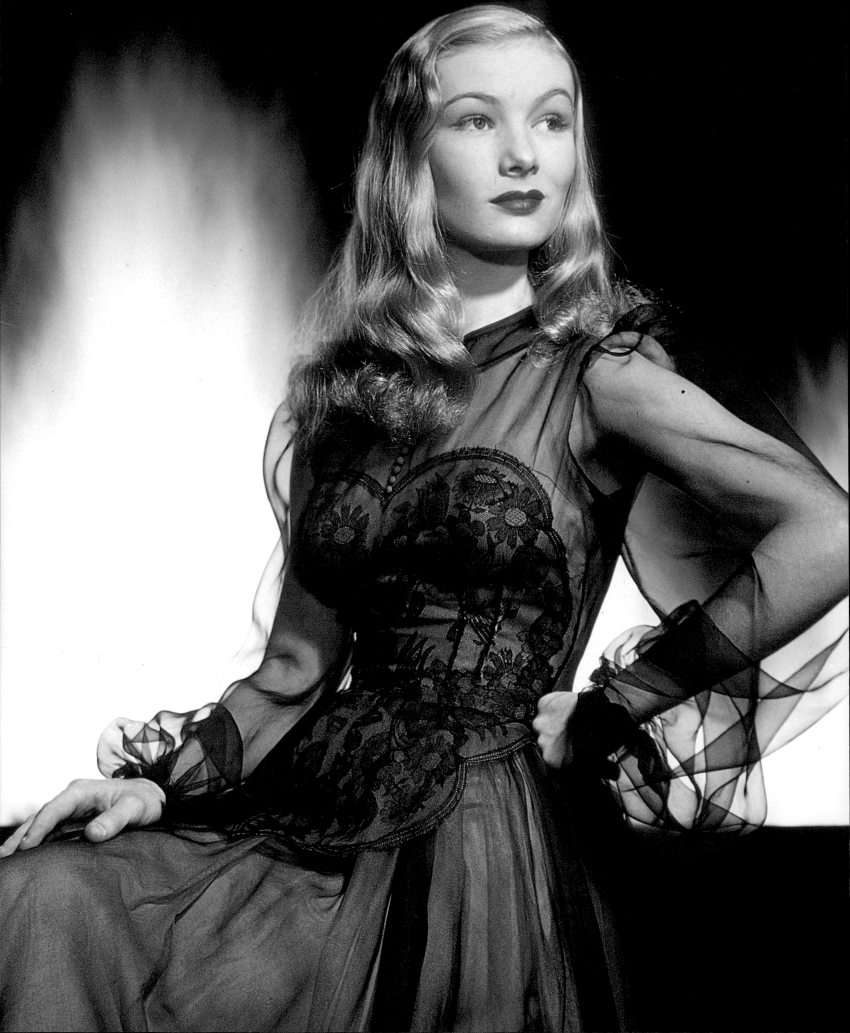

Veronica Lake
ELIOT ELISOFON
August 3, 1942

"Today there is a trend toward more purely female allure, because men at war want women to be attractive," *Life* claimed in the summer of 1942, describing Eliot Elisofon's portraits of top women movie stars. "To show how Veronica Lake preserves her cool personality in the midst of an inferno," *Life* said, Elisofon "posed Miss Lake so close to the wall of flame that he singed some of the priceless Lake hair, which was never insured against fire."

A Queen and Three Kings
W. AND D. DOWNEY
December 8, 1947

Edward, Duke of Windsor, noted in his memoirs, "The great Queen Victoria, who came to my christening, wrote: 'The dear fine baby, wearing a Honiton lace robe...worn by all our children and my English grandchildren, was brought in and handed to me. We were photographed, I holding the baby on my lap, Bertie, Georgie standing behind me, thus making four generations!'"

Writing later to her daughter Princess Victoria, Germany's Empress, the Queen added, "It seems that it has never happened in this Country that there should be three direct Heirs as well as the Sovereign alive."

The group, including young Edward Albert Christian George Andrew Patrick David, ruled Britain for 99 years as Victoria, Edward VII, George V and Edward VIII. If little David, as the family called him, hadn't got stuck on Mrs. Simpson and abdicated, his reign might have lasted till his death in 1972, 36 years longer than the 11 months it did.

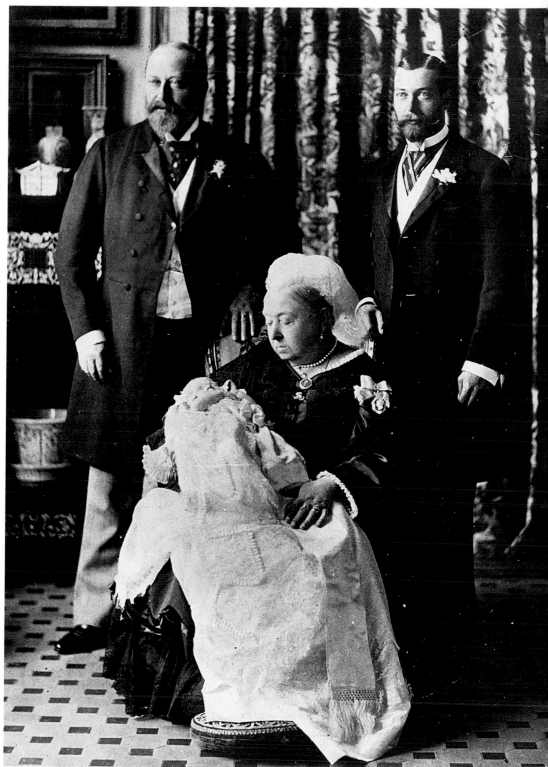

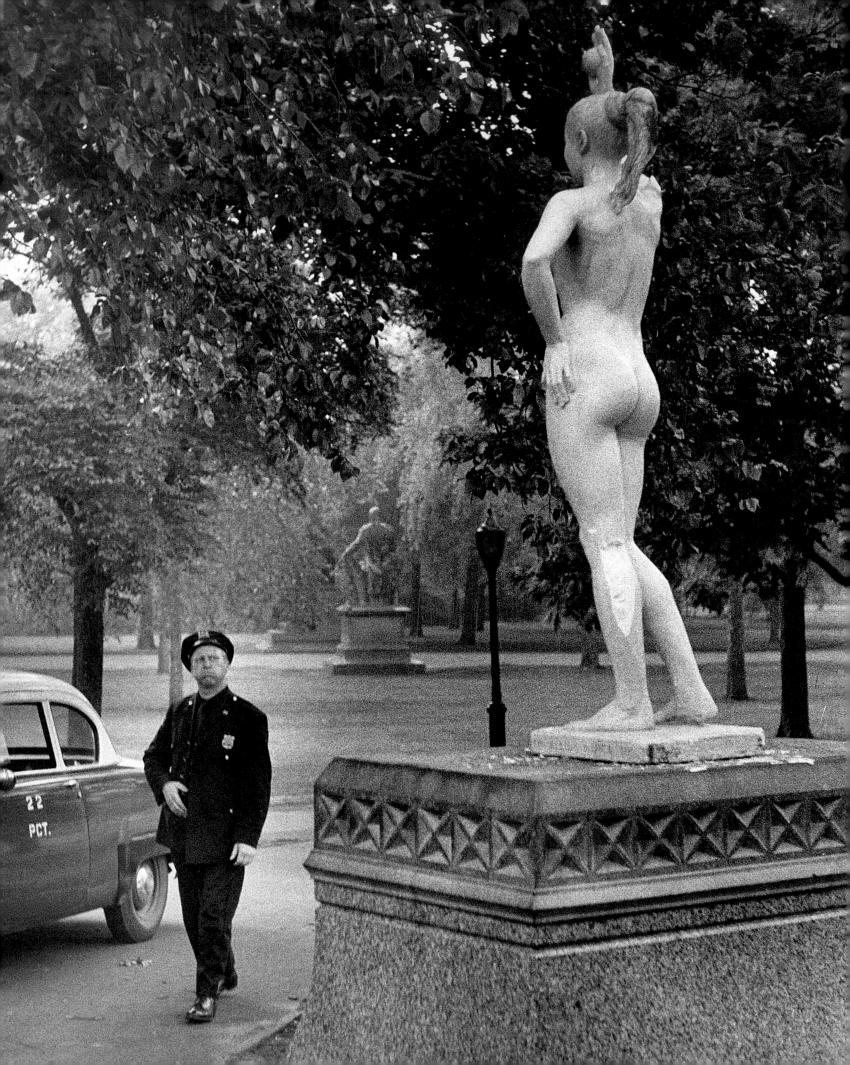

Up in Central Park
GREY VILLET
June 6, 1955

At dawn, patrolman Peter Witkus walked into a photo opportunity. In New York City's Central Park, where statues of literary figures such as Robert Burns and Sir Walter Scott stand, *Venus* had materialized overnight.

Nejla Ates, a Turkish belly dancer appearing in the Broadway musical *Fanny,* had posed for the statue's sculptor, Albino Marcus, and both were on hand for the unveiling. Also there, you can bet your boots, was the show's press agent who had arranged it all and alerted the press the night before.

"Hey, Mother!"
STOCKTON TODD HOLDEN
December 13, 1968

"Frankly I had the shots I needed in the can, so I drifted around to the back of the formation," says Stockton Todd Holden, who covered crime for the weekly paper *The Aegis,* in Bel Air, Md. As the front ranks of the Maryland State Police stood at attention for the colonel's inspection, trooper William Willis stood very much at ease. Spotting Holden, he turned and waved. "As he said, 'Hey, Mother!' I pointed a camera hanging at my waist and snapped the shutter," says Holden.

The editor of *The Aegis* apparently considered the issue of law-and-order too sensitive to joke about and refused to publish the picture. At the time, the nation was polarized over the police. Some attacked them as "pigs" and decried the use of excessive force against demonstrators at that summer's Democratic National Convention in Chicago, while others defended the police as the nation's last bastion against anarchy. Holden's photograph of pistol inspection was used instead.

Two weeks later, as Holden tells it, the news editor (who had views different from his boss's) slipped the picture into *The Aegis* when his superior was out having lunch. Readers, happy to see a human face on a cop, began calling to congratulate the paper as soon as the issue hit the streets.

None of this publicity harmed trooper Willis. The following year he became the Governor's personal driver.

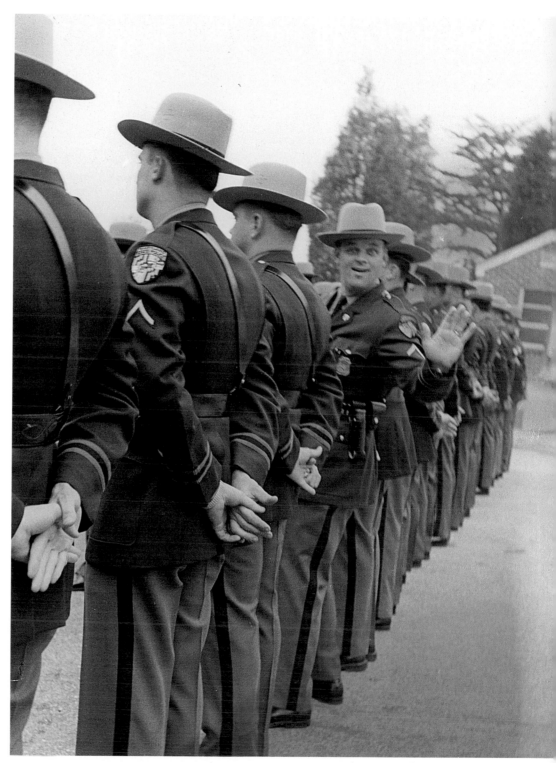

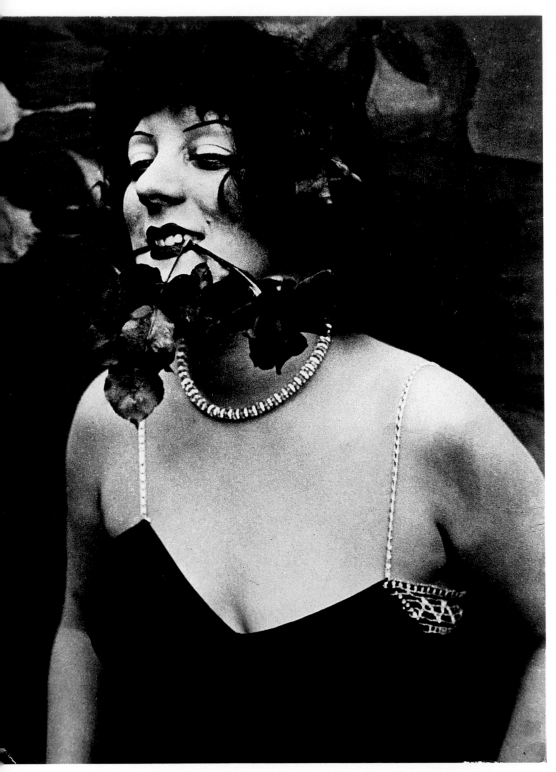

Kiki
UNKNOWN
June 29, 1953

Before her death at 51, Alice Prin looked back on her life and said, "We laughed. Mon Dieu, how we laughed."

By the time she was 17, Mademoiselle Prin was known in Paris as "Kiki of Montparnasse." A model, Kiki was an inspiration for many artists and the mistress of several, including Man Ray, with whom she lived for six years. Her high spirits fueled the gaiety of Paris in the 1920s. "When you knocked at Kiki's white, strong flesh," writer Kay Boyle recollected, "she opened wide her heart and moved the furniture aside so that you could come in."

Gertrude Lawrence
PETER STACKPOLE
June 13, 1938

Sometimes editors have to scramble to find a good cover subject for an issue. Peter Stackpole had photographed Gertrude Lawrence at her dressing table in a theater in Washington, D.C. During a slow news week in early June 1938, Stackpole's picture, taken several months earlier, looked as if it would make a wonderful cover. The only problem: there were no current pictures with which to make a story.

"Hearing that Miss Lawrence's *Susan and God* would leave New York," wrote the editors, referring to the play in which she starred, "*Life* sent Mr. Stackpole to her apartment overlooking Central Park. With furious energy and incomparable mimicry, she compressed into an hour for him the activities of a busy day."

Fine and good. Three pictures taken in the Central Park South apartment were used to make a one-page story. Miss Lawrence, the story said, was turning 40 and was probably the best actress on Broadway that season.

Apparently no reader complained that the story was less substantial than those from which *Life's* covers were usually chosen, but, Stackpole remembers, many found fault with the mimicry. A photograph described as showing the actress playing "a good hard game of chess with her secretary" did no such thing. The chess pieces, noted readers, were on the board in completely senseless positions.

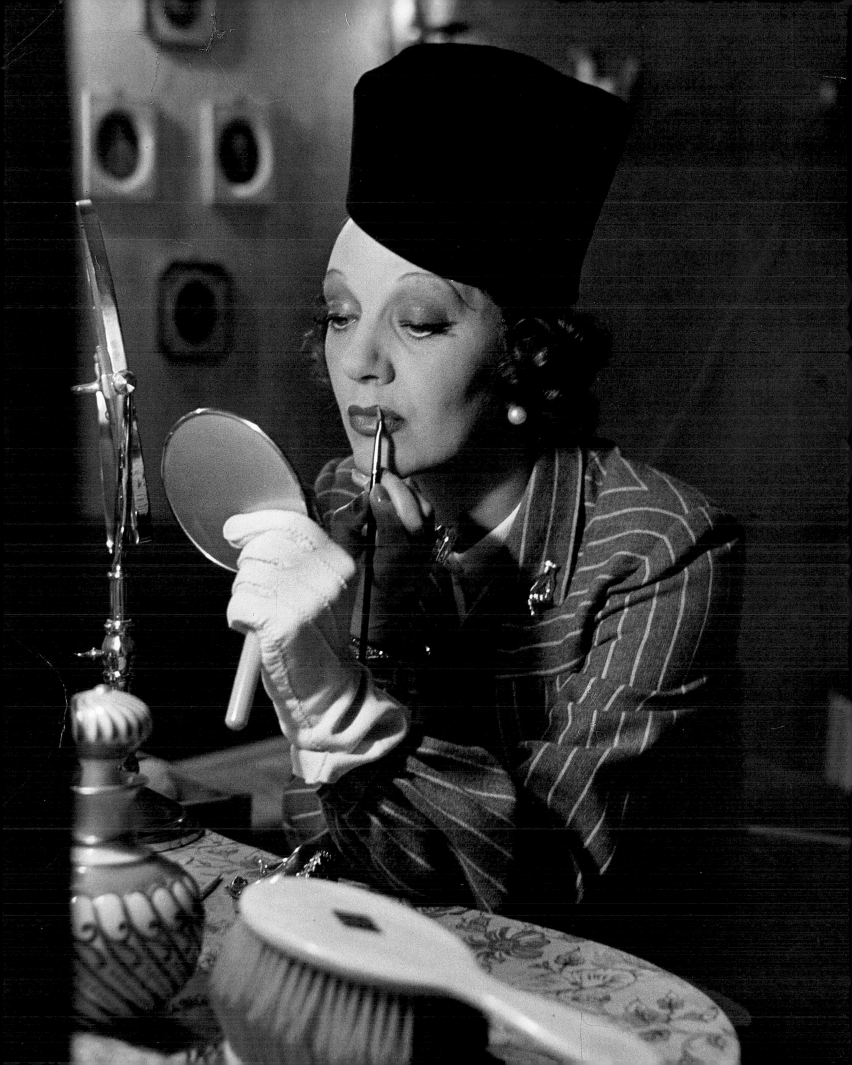

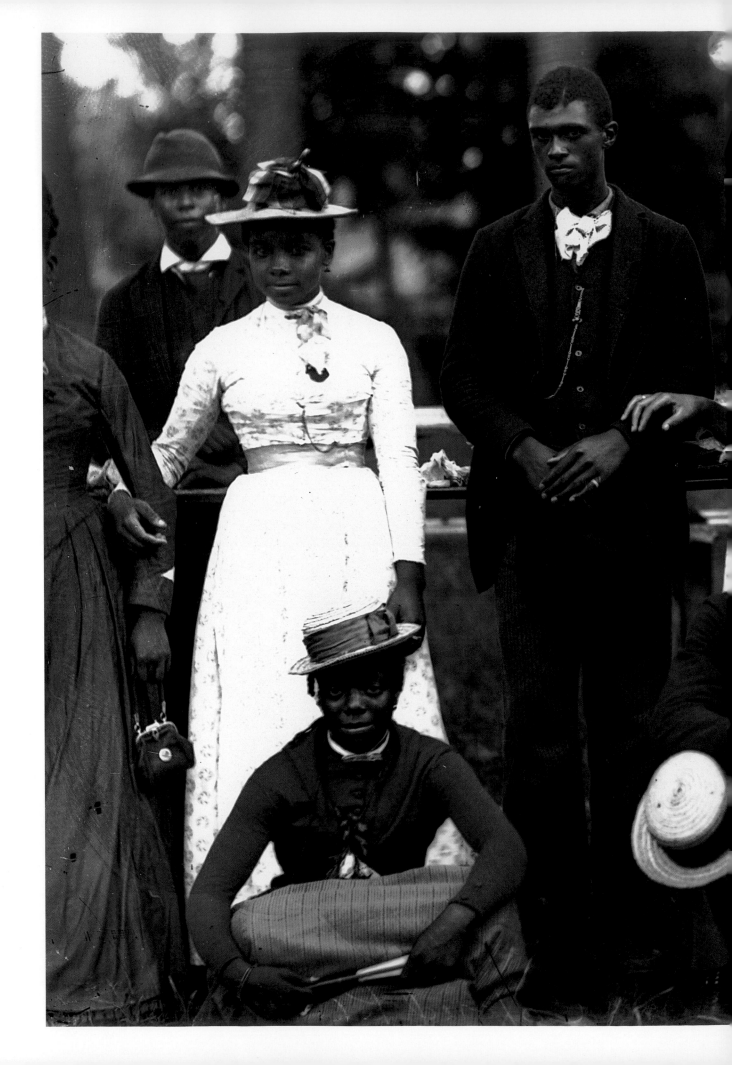

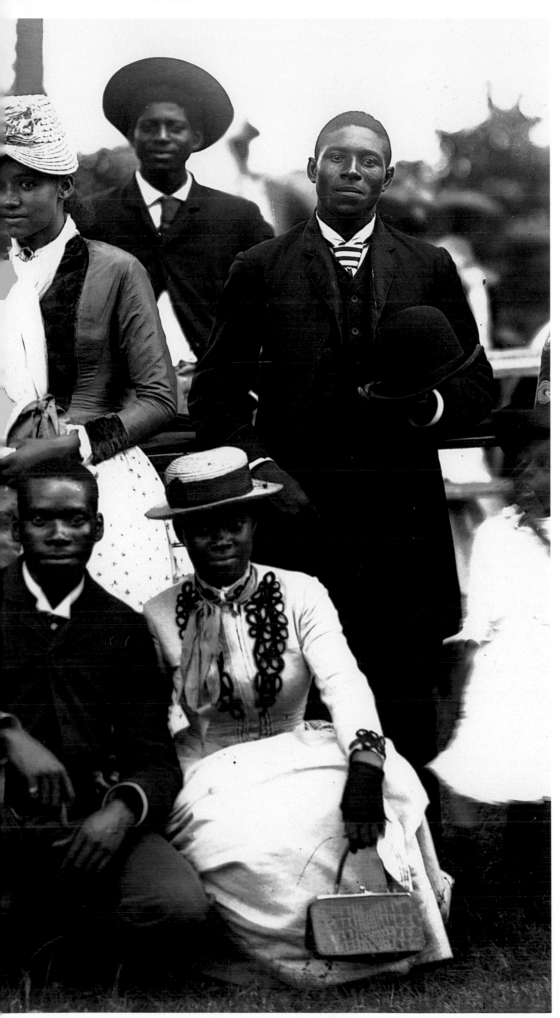

HUESTIS COOK
November 29, 1968

George S. Cook studied painting but took up photography as soon as it was invented. Moving from New York to Charleston, S.C., in 1849, he photographed the defenders of Fort Sumter at the beginning of the Civil War, going on to document the fighting in the South much as Mathew Brady's cameramen recorded it in the North. Fifteen years after the war, Cook moved to Richmond, Va., where in the late 1880s his youngest son, Huestis, joined the family business, taking one of his first photographs of this well-dressed group of Richmonders at a church picnic.

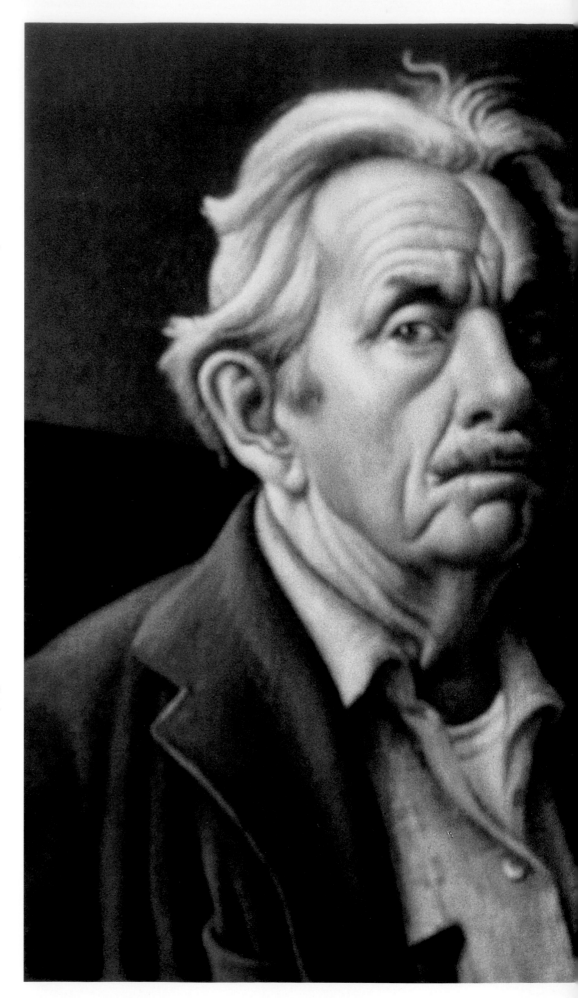

Thomas Hart Benton
ALFRED EISENSTAEDT
May 21, 1971

"Naturally he liked the idea. I photographed him almost every year," says Alfred Eisenstaedt (known as "Eisie"), who first photographed Thomas Hart Benton in 1937 painting murals for the legislature in Kansas City.

Benton, a crusty, independent man, was one of Jackson Pollock's teachers. Considered a regionalist painter, he proclaimed in the 1930s, "It's high time that native painters quit emulating our collectors by playing weathercock to European breezes."

"Benton had a vacation home on Martha's Vineyard, where I go every summer," says Eisie. "He was my friend, and I could do anything I liked with him. Of course, on the other hand, he is the only person who's ever called me Alfie."

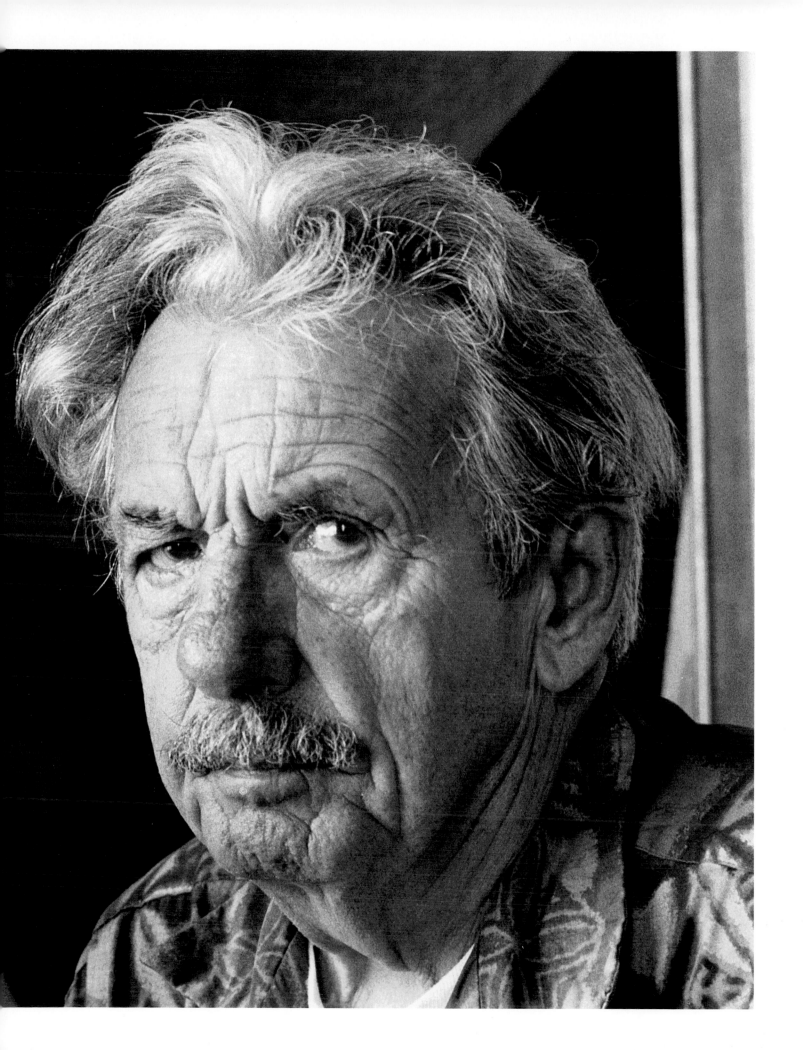

41

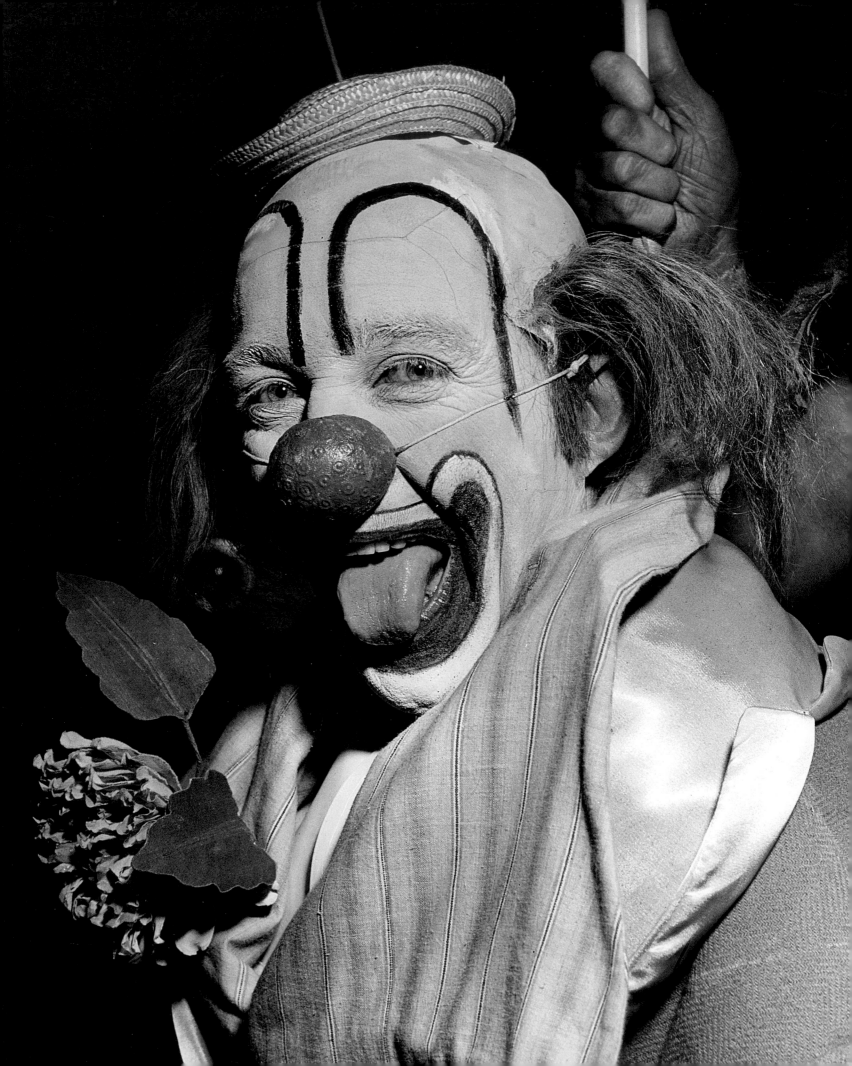

Bing Crosby
ALLAN GRANT
September 27, 1948

Ten thousand people went to a benefit performance of the circus in Los Angeles. Although movie stars mixed with the show's regular cast, Allan Grant thought this clown he photographed backstage was one of Ringling Brothers' finest. "I didn't know who it was," says Grant. "Then Bob Hope came over and started talking with him. *Then* I realized."

Winston Churchill
HANS WILD
April 14, 1947

Voted out of office four months earlier, in July 1945, Winston Churchill rested on a wooden bench beside the main house at Chartwell, his country estate. Wrote *Life* correspondent Eleanor Ragsdale in captions that accompanied this picture: "The big house is a rather stiff and forbidding red brick structure, but from this angle, with the vines, gables and cupola to break the lines, [it] has considerable beauty. During the war it has been largely unoccupied. However, since the election, it has been opened up a few weekends when visitors were invited to Chartwell."

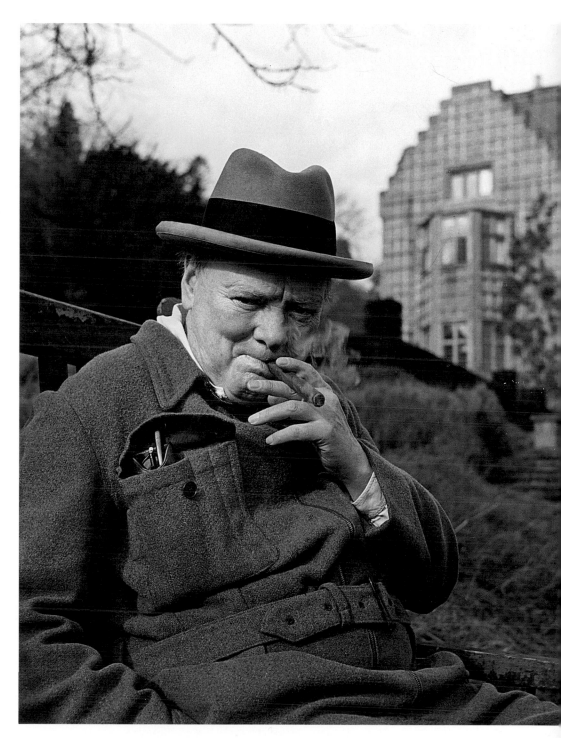

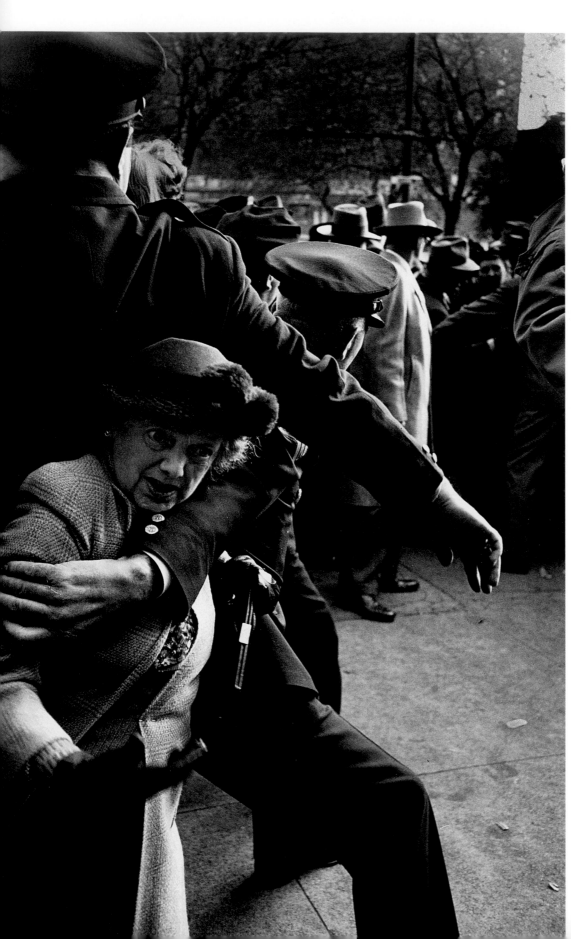

Mamie Eisenhower
MARK KAUFFMAN
November 3, 1952

The truth is, political campaigns are interesting to talk about and boring to look at. "During the last days covering the 1952 election," explains Mark Kauffman, "I decided to work around the edges of events, looking for unusual pictures.

"In Providence, Rhode Island, I had my foot on the step of the campaign train, ready to climb aboard the press car. Mamie Eisenhower appeared at the back of the railroad-station crowd. Policemen started to clear her a path. I sensed something marvelous, reacted, and felt very good in my gut, even though I could never have told you that a portrait of a little old lady caught in the confusion was what I'd got."

Free Fall
ALI AMIN
October 31, 1960

What would Pharaoh think? Seeking a visual record of where he'd been, Ali Amin, an Egyptian army sergeant and parachutist, carried a pack on his back and a lens on his shoe. Falling headfirst from a plane, he smiled at the camera, tripped the shutter with a wire he held in his hand, and then opened his parachute. This put him in an upright position, and as he glided toward earth, Sergeant Amin unbound the camera from his shoe to keep from damaging it when he landed.

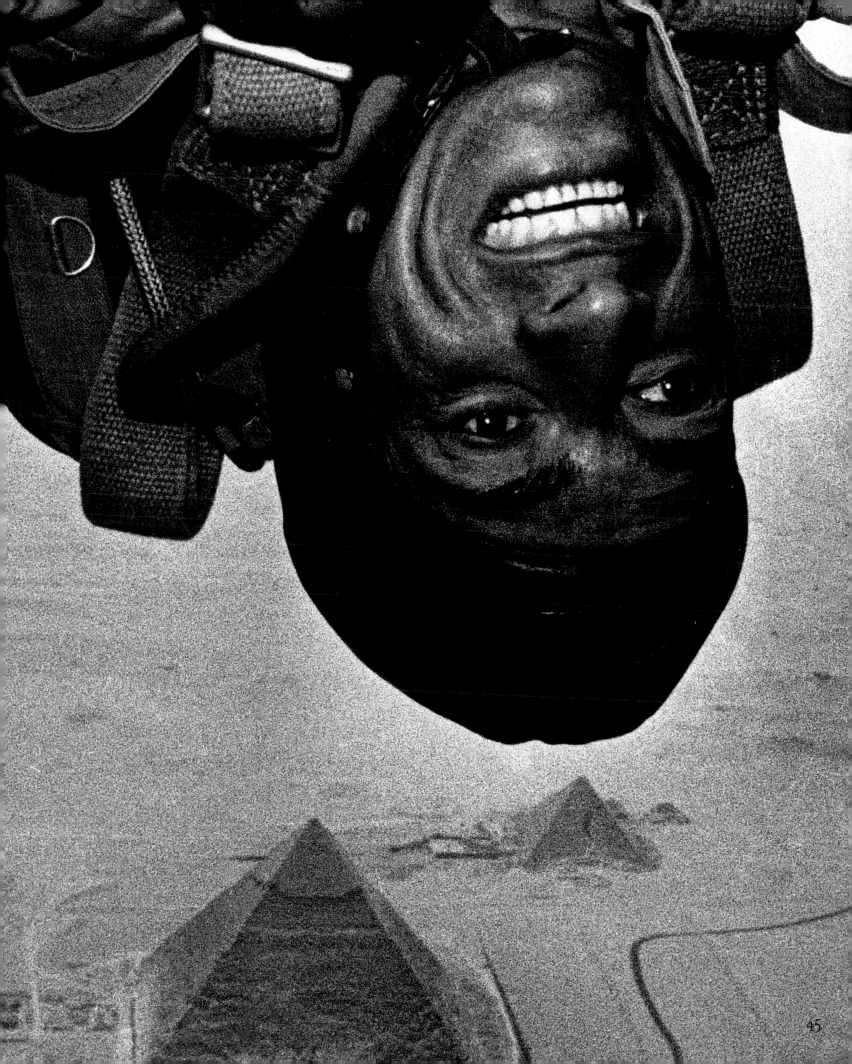

Korea
HANK WALKER
November 20, 1950

Hank Walker, a Marine combat photographer during World War II, was faring well as a freelance photographer in Washington, D.C., when the Korean War started. Asked by *Life* if he wanted to cover it, he said yes.

Walker was present for General Douglas MacArthur's landing at Inchon and advanced with U.S. troops to the Yalu River bordering Manchuria. At that time, the Chinese army suddenly entered the war—and with shocking force. Then, mysteriously, there was a two-week lull in the fighting.

Retreating with an Army unit along a road south of Kusong during this supposedly quiet period, Walker remembers, "I was in a little microcosm. I didn't know the big picture. First we got a lot of heavy artillery; then came mortar fire. I was taking pictures of soldiers lying with me in a ditch when I heard a lot of shouting and shooting. I looked up and saw a group of terrified Chinese soldiers being flushed from a house beside the road."

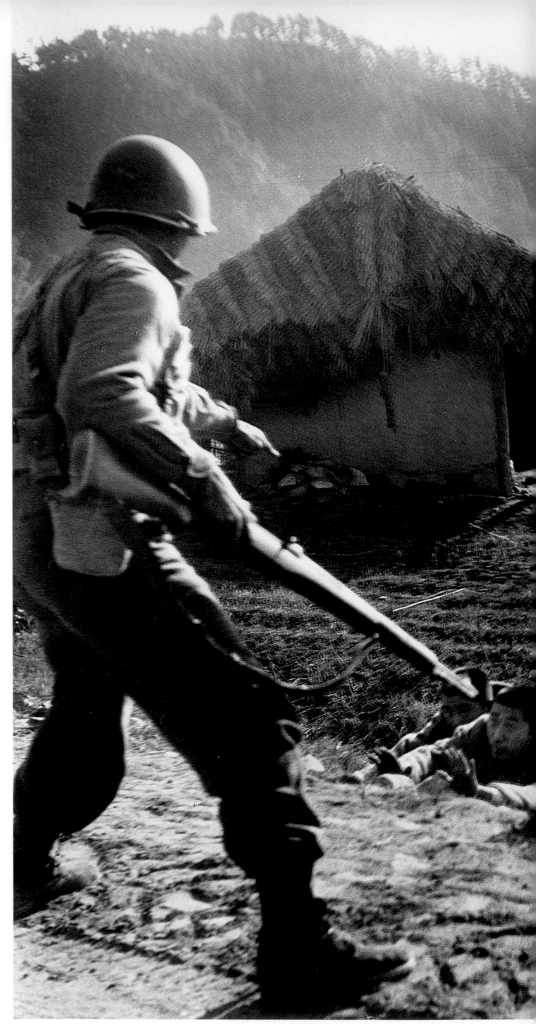

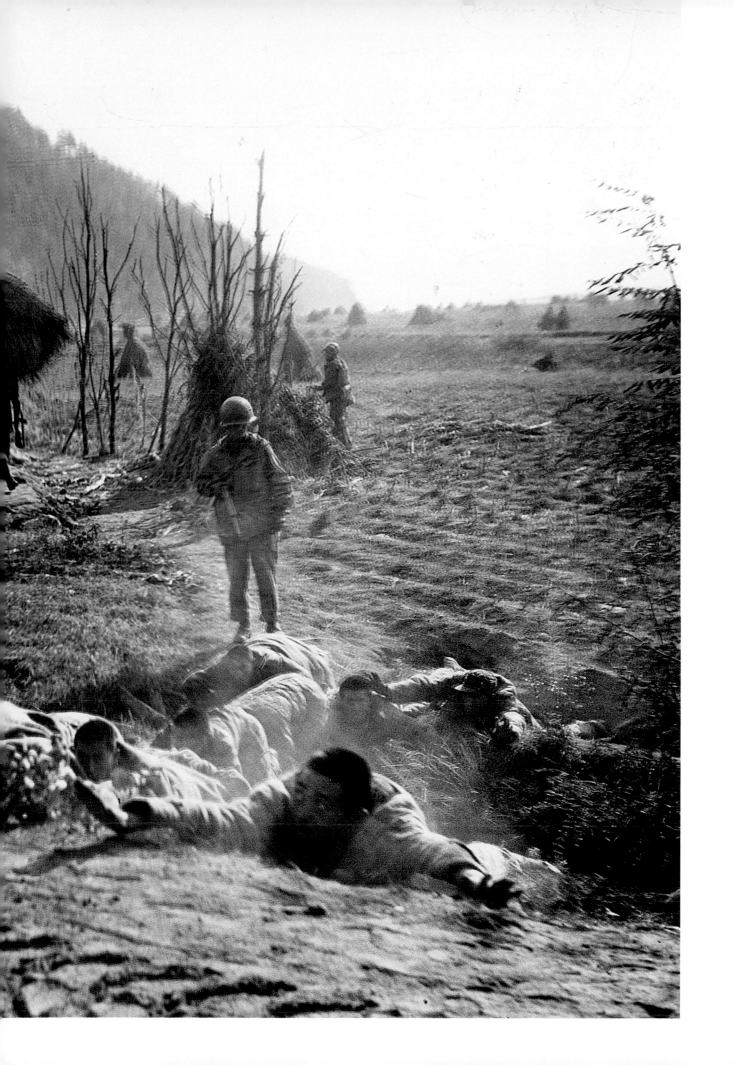

Valencia
HENRI CARTIER-BRESSON
December 5, 1955

"**I** prowled the streets all day, feeling very strung-up and ready to pounce, determined to 'trap' life—to preserve life in the act of living," wrote Henri Cartier-Bresson to describe his mood at the age of 24 when he switched from painting to photography. One year later, in 1933, he recorded this man at the edge of the bull ring in Valencia, Spain. "We photographers deal in things which are continually vanishing," he wrote, "and when they have vanished, there is no contrivance on earth which makes them come back again."

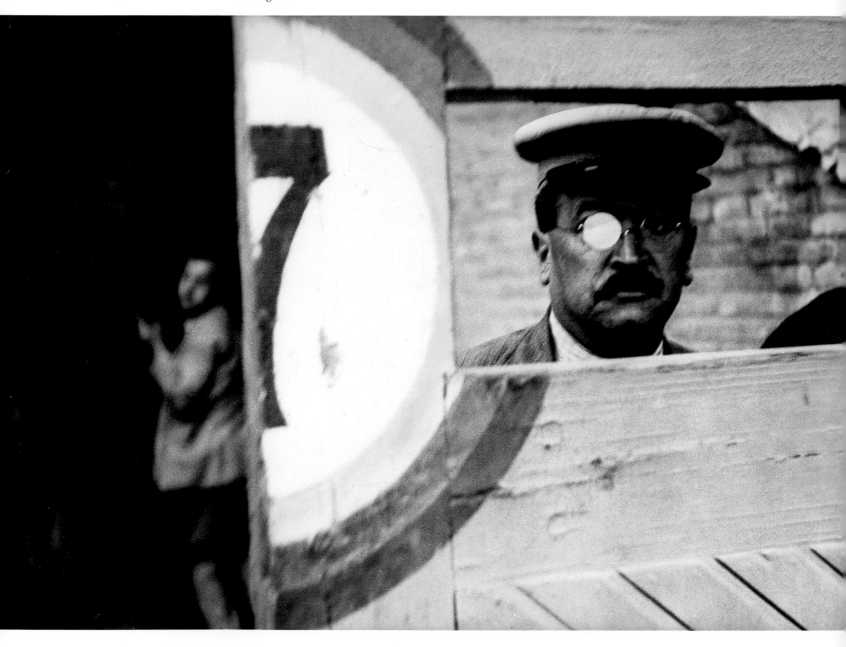

Roddy McDowall
ELIOT ELISOFON
April 14, 1958

"It is the most complicated portrait I have ever attempted," said Eliot Elisofon, who asked 11 stars to choose roles they dreamed of doing on Broadway. Roddy McDowall, who had played Ariel in a summer-stock production of Shakespeare's *The Tempest,* did his own makeup. Wearing a bathing cap, McDowall stood behind a scrim of blue and green gauze with spangles and rhinestones glued to it. The photograph was given a one-second exposure, wrote Elisofon, "so that any slight movement of the actor would add softness and mystery to the image."

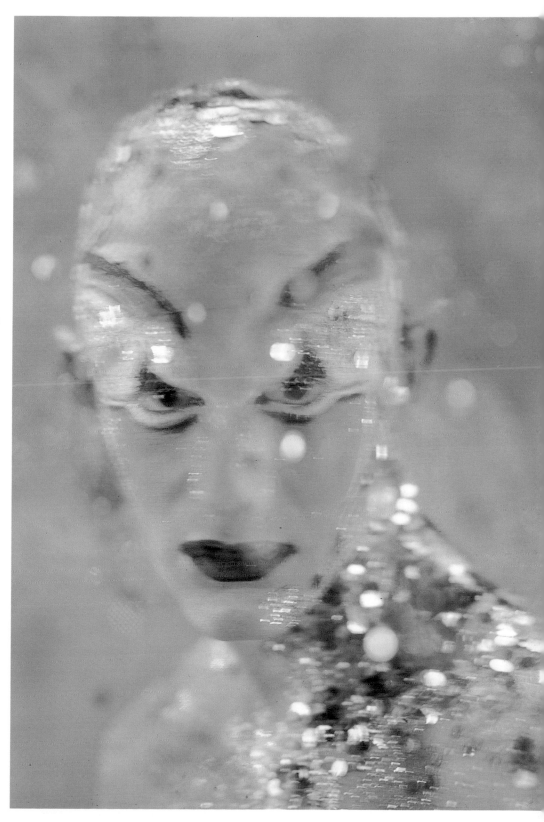

Londonderry
DONALD McCULLIN
December 31, 1971

"Every Saturday afternoon—around about
3, when the pubs turn out—that was the
signal for fun and games to begin," says Don
McCullin about the troubles in Londonderry,
Northern Ireland.

"I had press credentials from the British, but
they hadn't any value when I crossed through to
the Catholic side. Two heavies I took to be
Provisional I.R.A. searched me. I told them I
worked for the *Sunday Times* in London, which
had a reputation then of being fair. Later the
night porter at the hotel gave me a cryptic O.K.:
'Oh, by the way,' he said, 'it was *our man* [that's
a code phrase they use] stopped you in the street.
It's all been sorted out.'

"On that particular Saturday, a charge was
made by the Royal Anglian Regiment from East
Anglia, where Constable painted.

"Of course, I saw the women in the doorways,
but I didn't know one of them would reward me
with the ultimate expression. I was too busy
watching out for bricks from one side, rubber bul-
lets from the other."

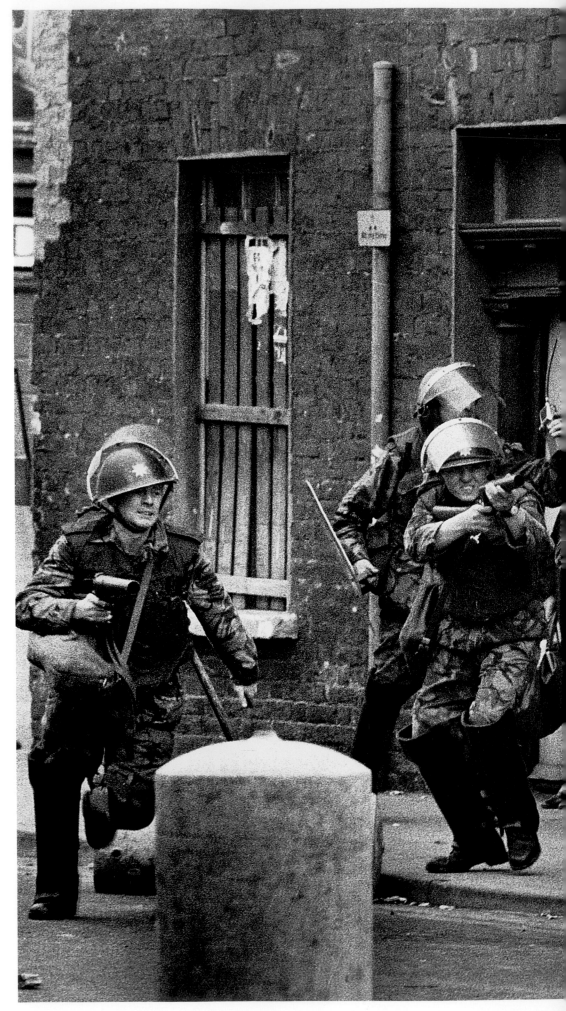

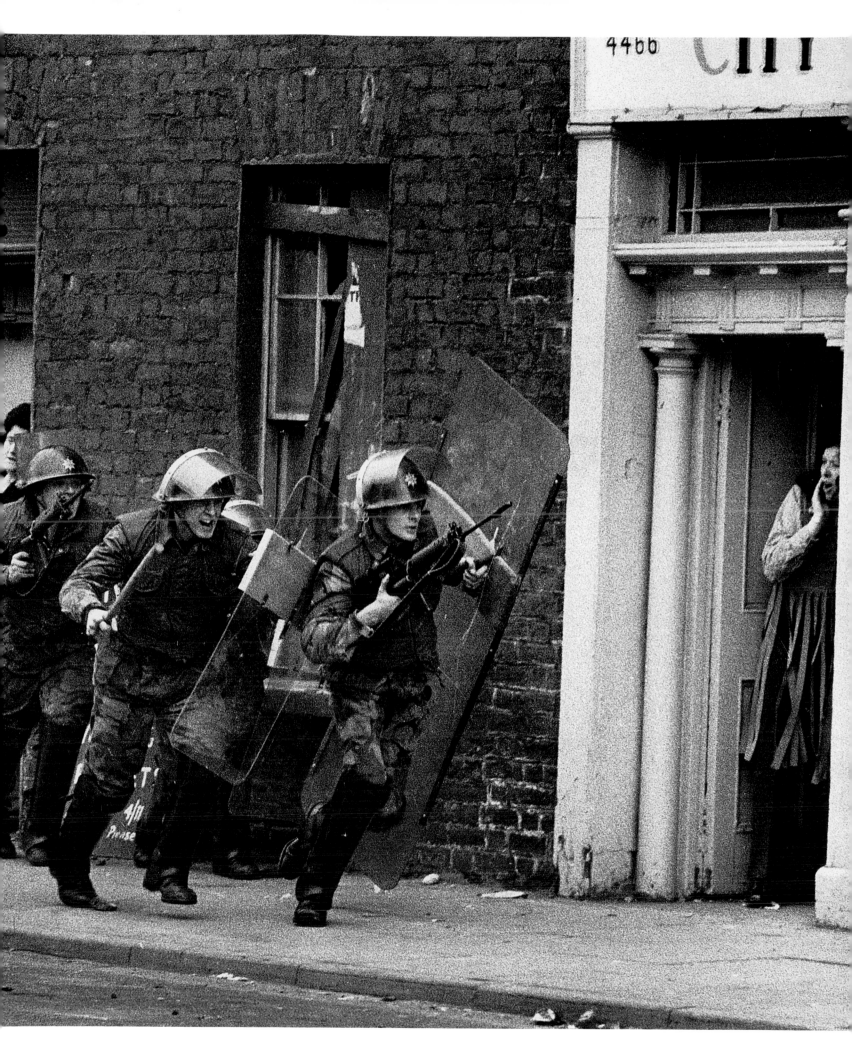

Lega Warrior
ELIOT ELISOFON
October 13, 1961

The 1935 exhibit "African Negro Art" at Manhattan's Museum of Modern Art opened Eliot Elisofon's eyes to the beauty of African culture, but according to a daughter, it was his friend Gypsy Rose Lee's gift of a small Pende ivory figure that turned him into a collector.

Elisofon first traveled to Africa for *Life* in 1942 to cover the American troops who were fighting in Tunisia. The U.S. commander, General George Patton, dubbed him "Hellzapoppin," an apparent play on the pronunciation of Elisofon's name.

In 1947 he visited again, photographing the King of the Kuba peoples in what is now Zaïre, and in 1950 he recorded the passage of the Nile from its source to the sea.

Three years later, on a honeymoon with his second wife, Elisofon led an expedition through mud, avalanches, and elephant charges toward the summit of the Mountains of the Moon and up the volcanic slopes of the Virunga Mountains. (Despite all that, the marriage lasted 13 years.) In 1959, for a story called "Literary Africa," he found this battle-painted Lega warrior in Zaïre.

On his death in New York City in 1973, just days before his 62nd birthday, Elisofon's bequest of more than 80,000 photographs and 609 pieces of sculpture became a milestone in the creation of the Smithsonian's National Museum of African Art.

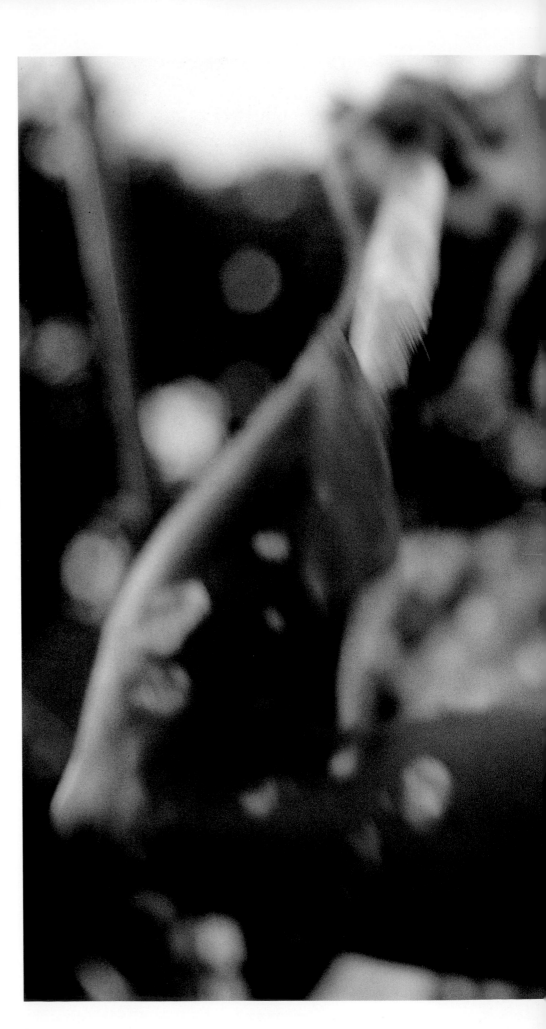

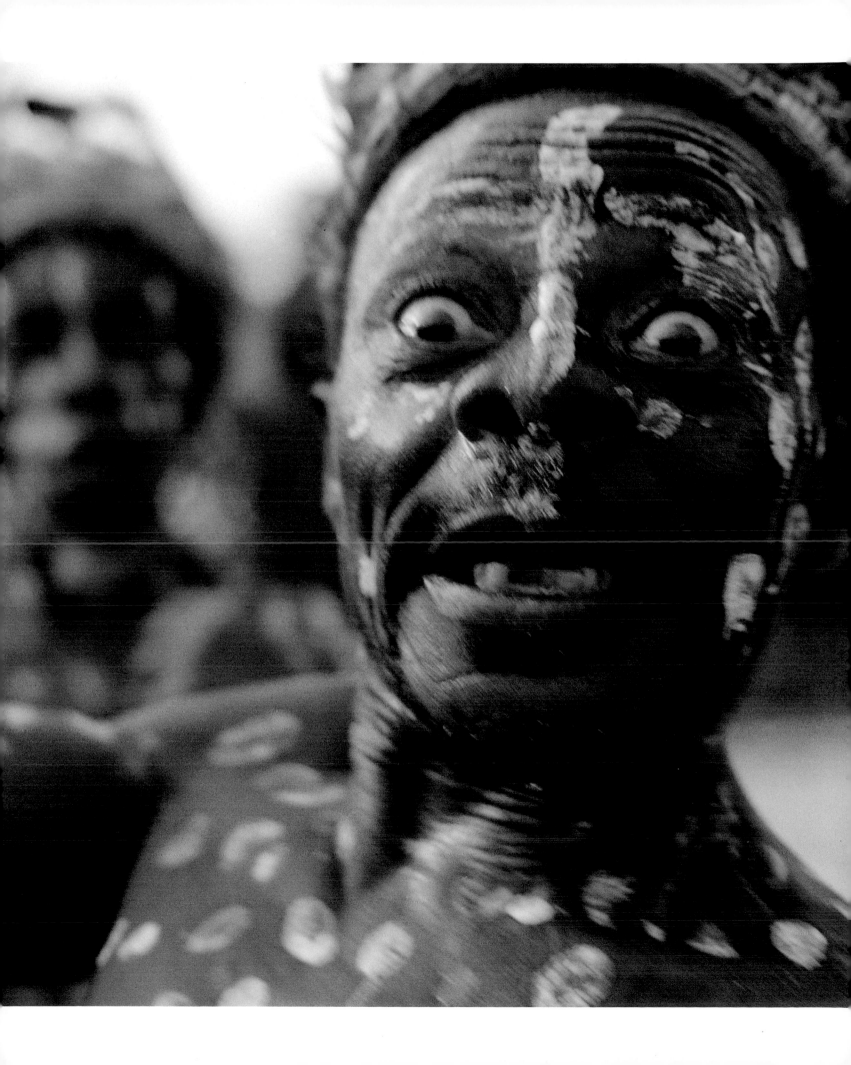

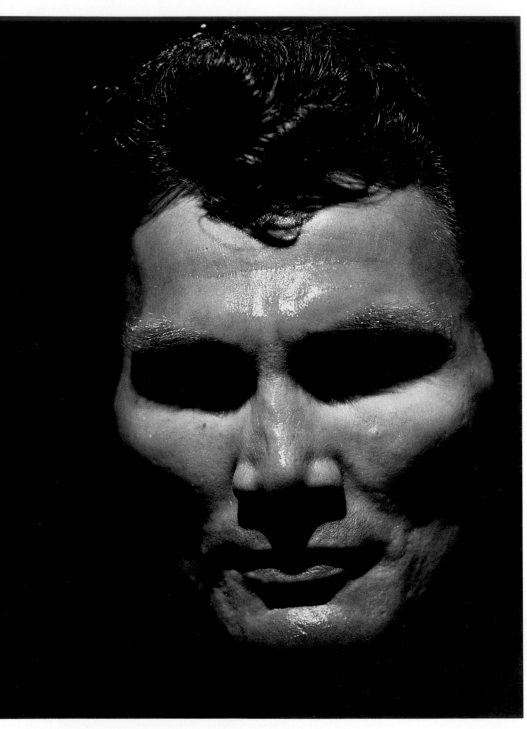

Jack Palance
LOOMIS DEAN
September 1, 1952

"**O**ne movie reviewer described Jack Palance's face as looking like a jack-o'-lantern, so I decided to photograph him looking like one," says Loomis Dean. Palance, an ex-prizefighter and frightening screen presence, was playing Joan Crawford's husband in *Sudden Fear.* "Crawford screeches, shivers and writhes through the leading role," wrote *Life.* "She is helped no end by the peculiarly hideous looks of her leading man."

Dai Llewellyn
ROB KINNEAR
March 14, 1969

Dai Llewellyn, age 73 in 1969, was a Welshman who practiced making funny faces ("gurning") and claimed to be runner-up in the World Gurning Championship. "He seems," *Life* wrote, "not to have listened to his mother's admonition, 'If you don't watch out, your face will stay that way.'"

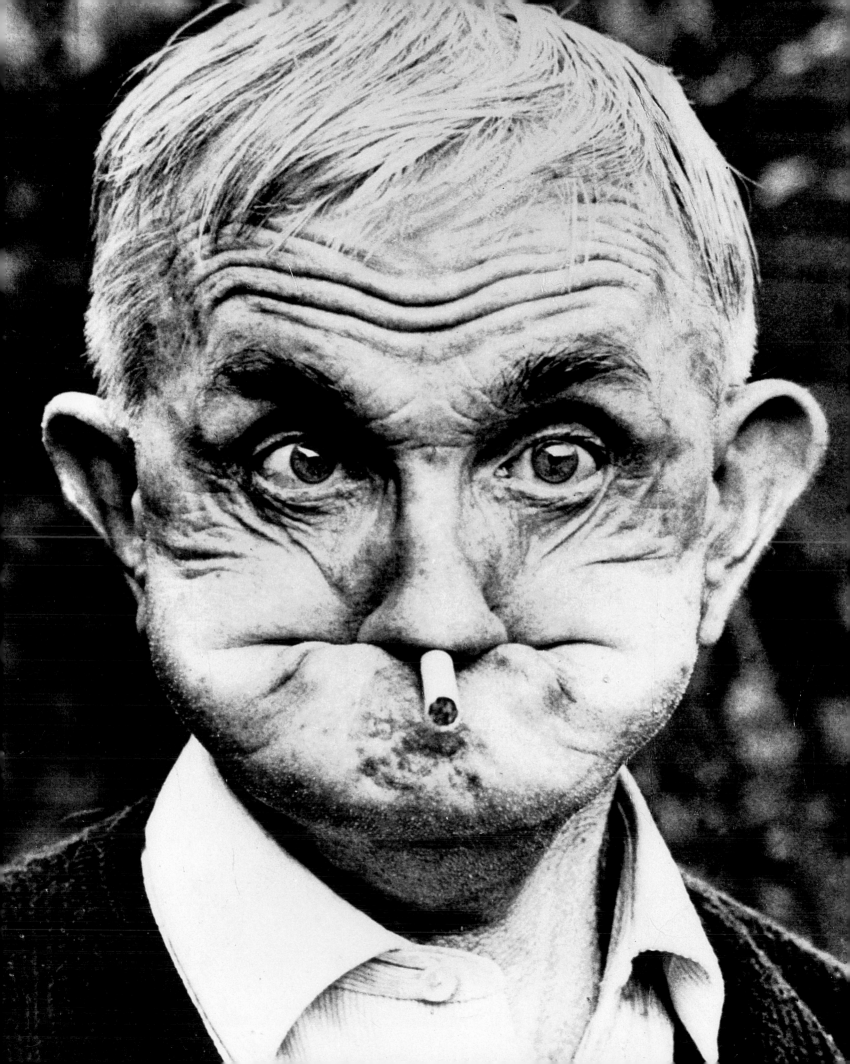

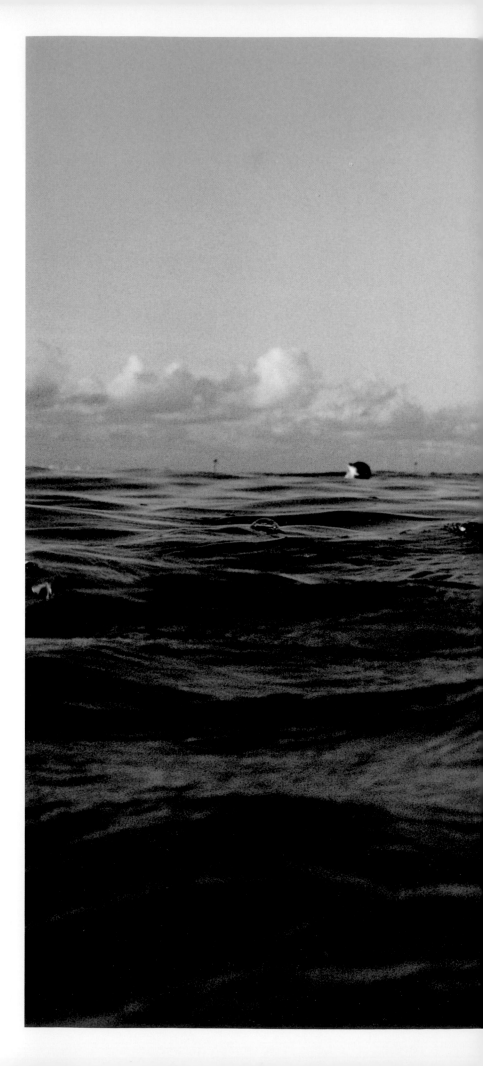

George Bush
JOE MARQUETTE
January 1991

"Even before I left Washington, I thought he might do it," says Joe Marquette, who covers the White House for United Press International. "I told my wife, 'If Bush goes swimming, I'm going swimming.' Then I asked if I could borrow her camera. It's one of the amateur point-and-shoot kind, but it's waterproof.

"At breakfast the morning after Bush arrived in Honolulu, I saw him walking down to the water. I ran out, pulled my wallet out of my shorts, handed it to a White House photographer, and dove in after the President. The Secret Service knows me, so they left me alone.

" 'What are you doing here?' Bush asked. I told him. We swam along for half an hour, making small talk. I took this picture as he treaded water.

"Swimming is sort of a hobby of mine. The next morning when Bush came down, he spotted me and asked, 'Are you ready?' In we went again. You know how it is: some of the press gets to jog with the President. I got to swim."

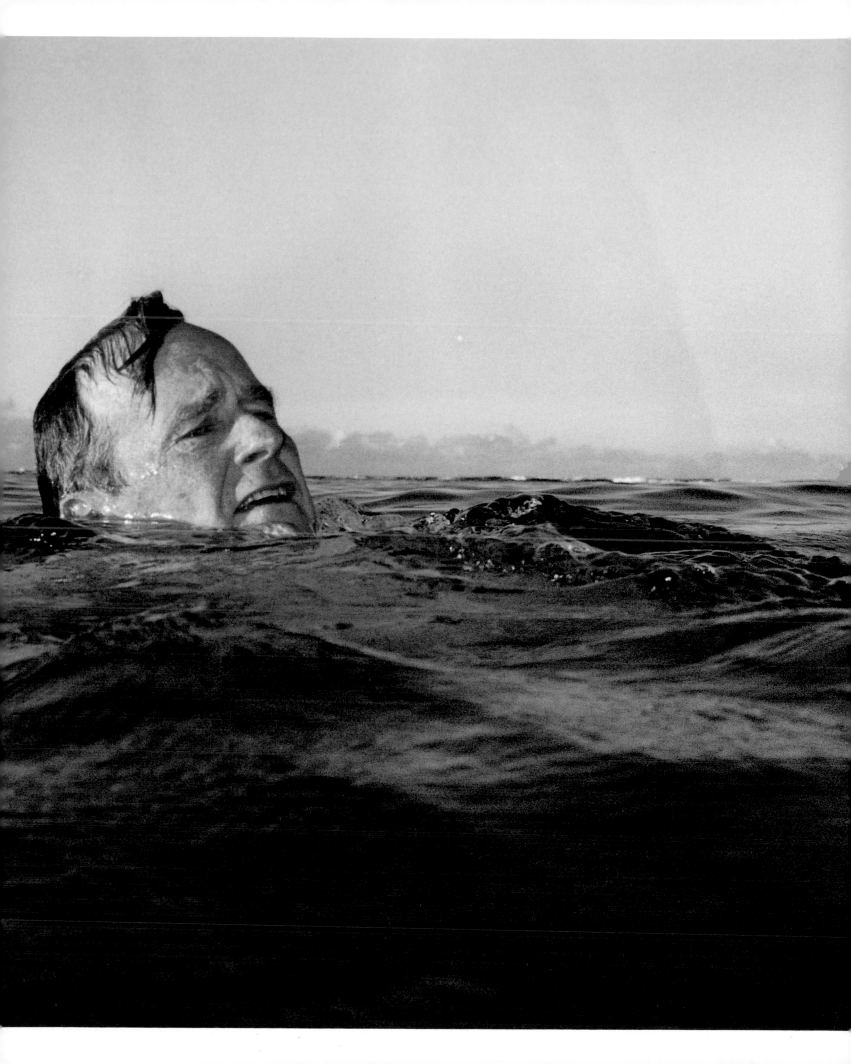

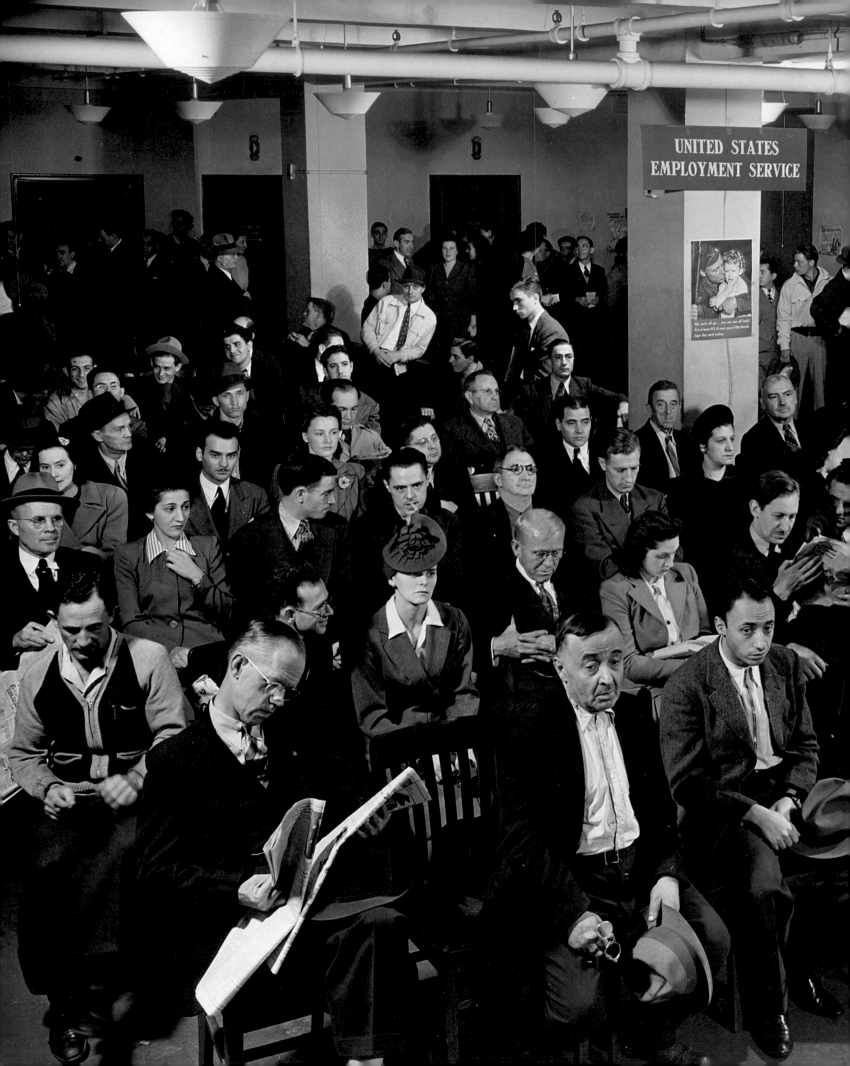

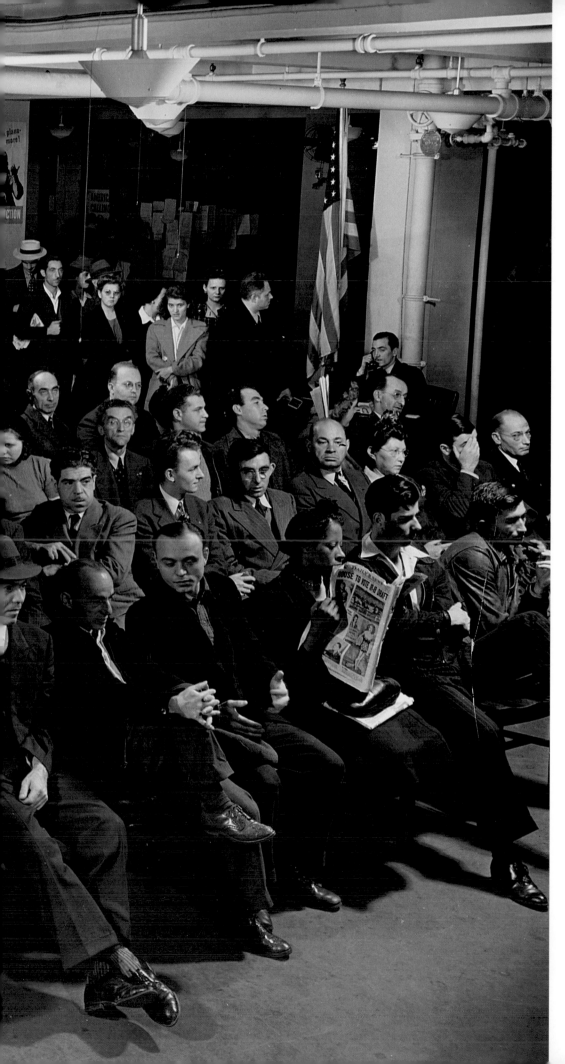

Employment Office
HERBERT GEHR
October 26, 1942

In New York City the Industrial, Food, Transportation and Amusement branch of the U.S. Employment Service was open for business. One of 4,500 federal offices nationwide, it provided prospective employees with job contacts and interviews. A year after Pearl Harbor, aided by the mobilization for World War II, the economy at last was shaking off the Great Depression.

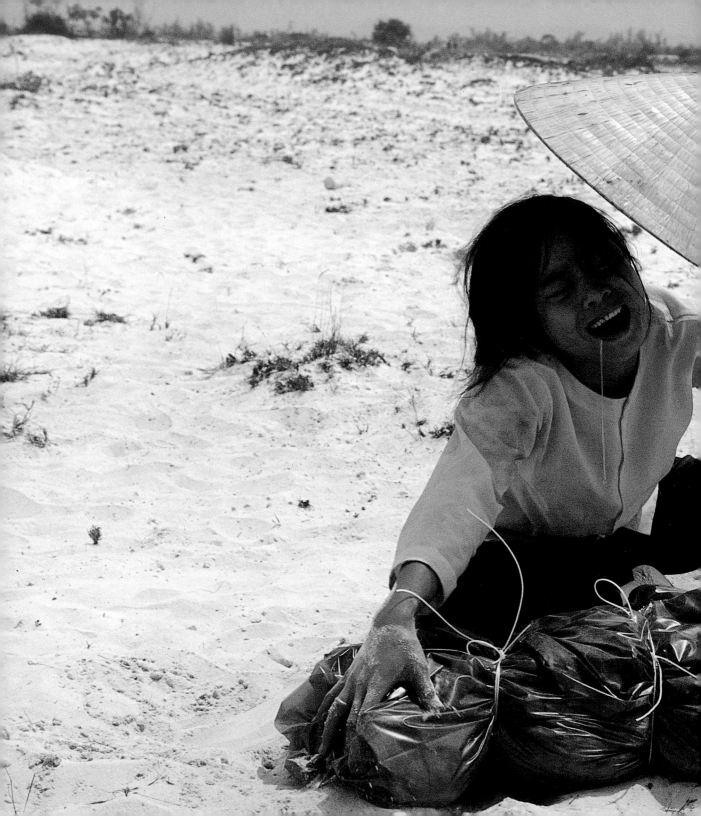

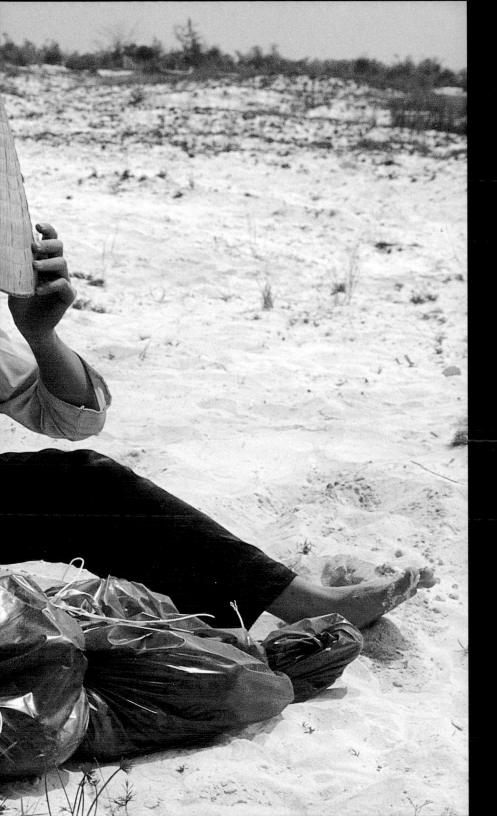

Grieving Widow
LARRY BURROWS
September 19, 1969

"I arrived in Hué in late April, just after they found the first mass graves, some 800 people buried under four feet of sand," wrote Larry Burrows, an Englishman who joined *Life's* staff in 1961 and moved from London to Hong Kong.

Because of the move and quite by chance, Burrows became involved in covering Vietnam, a story that would bring him fame and engage him for the rest of his life until his death in a helicopter crash in Laos in 1971.

"The killings had happened during Tet—February 1968—when the enemy occupied Hué," Burrows wrote. "Hundreds were rounded up—some officials, some military, some women, some children—and under cover of darkness were taken into the countryside. Eventually, under the pretext of being moved to a 're-education center,' they were tied with bamboo strips or communications wire, marched to open graves, and shot or clubbed to death. The people of Hué knew only that they had disappeared.

"When the graves were discovered and opened more than a year later, after the area had been pacified, the bodies were no more than collections of bones held together by rotting cloth. The bodies were then wrapped in plastic sheets and laid out in rows. The people of Hué came in tears to seek their missing relatives. Jewelry and clothing made identification possible in a few cases; the rest were put in wooden coffins and buried again in a mass ceremony. When it was over, the people walked back to their homes in stunned silence."

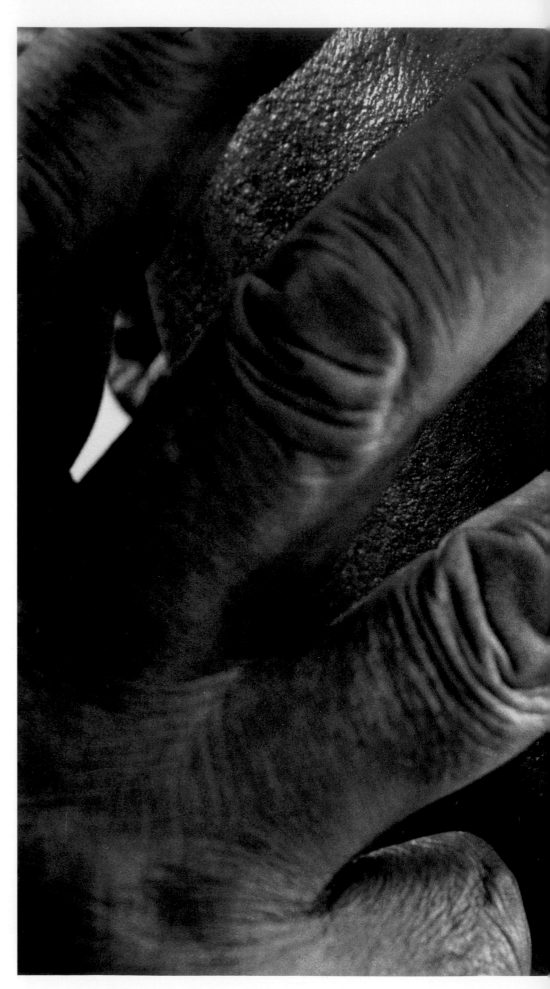

Louis Armstrong
JOHN LOENGARD
April 15, 1966

Photographs that are taken to convey necessary points of information in a narrative but lack pictorial power are known to editors as "point pictures." Normally they appear as small pictures in a layout, used to advance the story without harming its visual impact.

In 1965 writer Richard Meryman spent several months interviewing the 65-year-old Louis Armstrong, taking down his life story in the musician's own words. At the time the question in the air was "Has Armstrong lost his lip?"—meaning, Could he still play the trumpet with the authority and control he had possessed in his youth? Naturally there was nothing to *see* regarding this question except possibly the care Armstrong took to massage his lips with balm after every performance. But you never know. A visually undramatic situation, expected to produce only a point picture, here led to a startling examination of Armstrong's face.

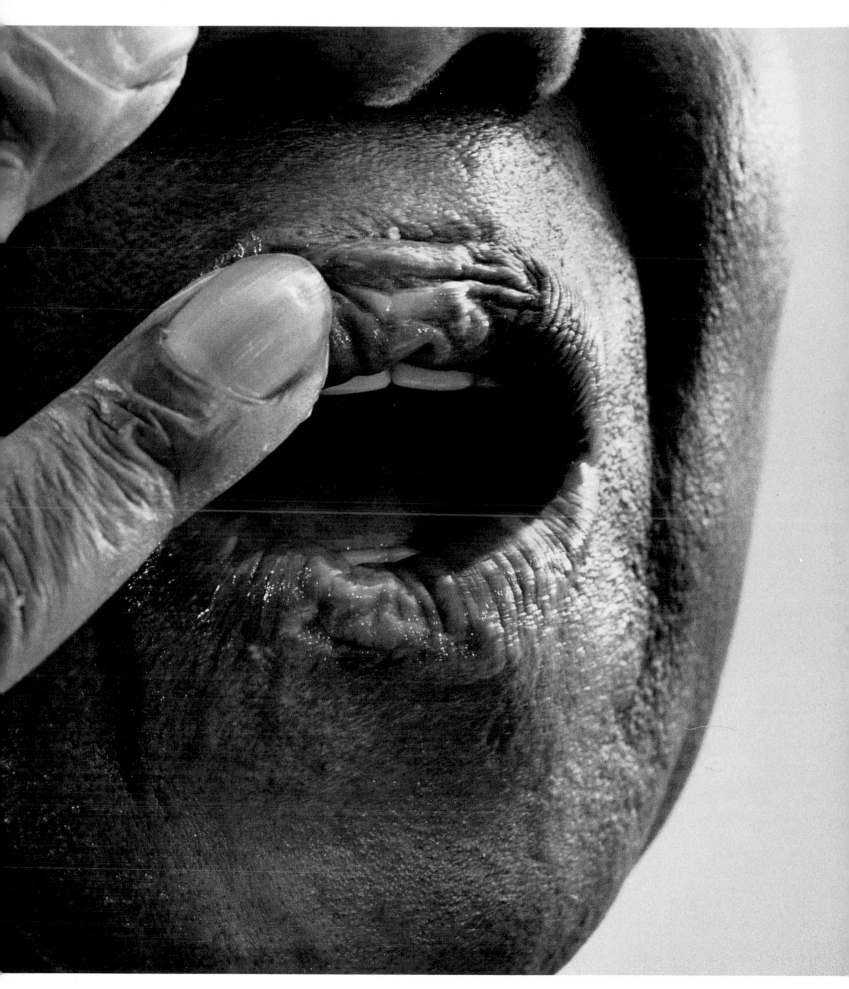

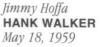

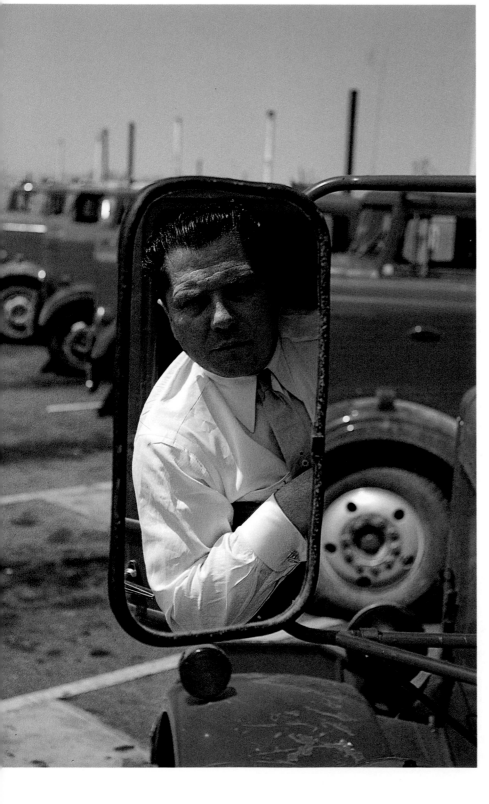

Jimmy Hoffa
HANK WALKER
May 18, 1959

From Washington, Hank Walker suggested a story on James Hoffa, then president of the International Brotherhood of Teamsters and the recent target of a Senate investigation into corruption in the Teamsters union. *Life* editors in New York gave an O.K. if the magazine had complete access to Hoffa.

Hoffa said sure. "He's the most completely realistic guy I've ever been around," says Walker. With *Life* editor Roy Rowan, Walker spent two months going to all Hoffa's meetings, listening in on his phone conversations, eating breakfast, lunch and dinner with him.

"For a cover I wanted to photograph Hoffa in the driver's cab of a red truck," says Walker. "I kept looking for the right spot as we visited Teamsters around the country. We were driving down a freeway in Southern California when I finally saw the perfect place. Hoffa pulled off the road and went into the truck terminal I'd spotted. He started telling the drivers what I wanted, and they began to put their rigs where I needed them. Of course, the owners came out fit to be tied, shouting, 'What the hell's going on here!' But when they saw who I was with, it all changed. 'Oh, hi, Jimmy! Great to see you! What can we do for you, Jimmy?' was all they wanted to say."

Mr. Singh and Shyanna
MARY ELLEN MARK
February 1991

"I must have lived in India in an earlier life," says Mary Ellen Mark, who grew up in Philadelphia. "When I'm in India I'm transformed; I feel my true self.

"Everything there is tinged in irony. It is humorous and sad at the same time. It is heartwrenching and beautiful. It's where I have had the happiest moments of my working life."

Mark spent two years photographing India's 18 circuses (the first was brought to India by an Italian named Chirini in 1878). "It was hard to find out where they'd be because they're very competitive," says Mark. "They wouldn't let me know where they were going next until the last moment.

"I loved the performers' sense of perfection. In Ahmedabad at 6:30 in the morning, Ram Prakash Singh, the ringmaster of the Great Golden Circus, worked for an hour with me. At the end, when Shyanna put her trunk around his neck…I'm not sure; we'd been making her pose so long. I look at her expression in the picture and think she wanted to strangle him."

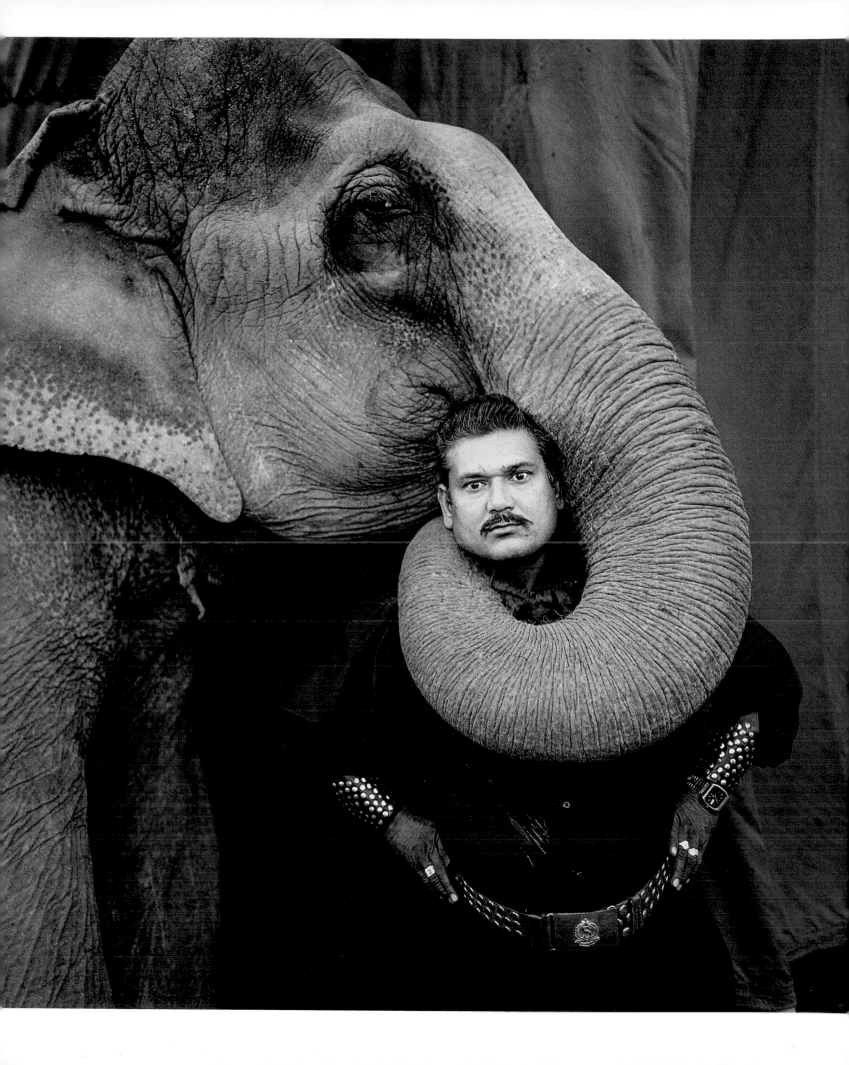

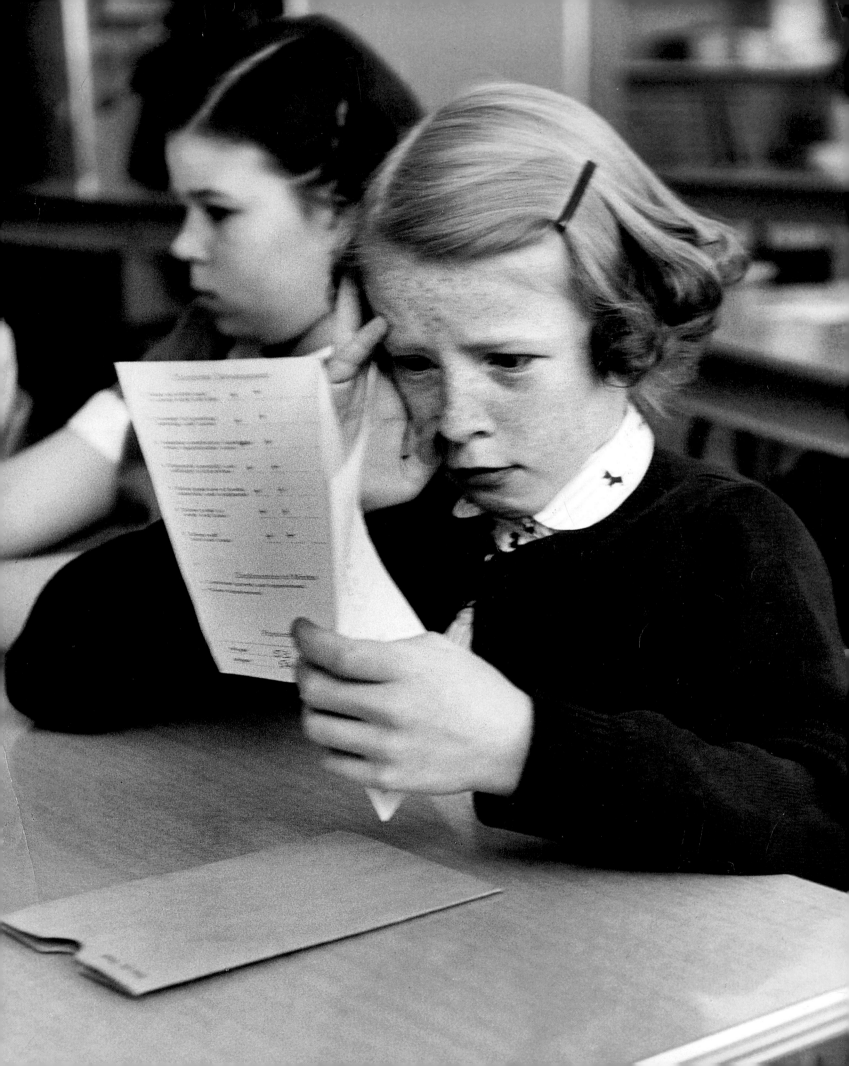

Cheryl Pond
EMMONS WILLIAMS
February 28, 1955

Life isn't fair. Getting a C in spelling is fair. You earned that grade yourself. It's also fair for a fifth-grade teacher to have a hobby of taking pictures. What's not fair (maybe) is when that teacher photographs his class the day he hands out report cards, as Emmons Williams did in Cheryl Pond's class at the Lakeridge School in Renton, Wash.

Kang Koo Ri
MICHAEL ROUGIER
July 23, 1951

American soldiers in Korea found Ri cringing in a corner of his home beside his mother, who had been dead for several days. Whether U.S. bombs or Chinese shells had killed her was not known.

Many weeks later, Michael Rougier met Ri at an orphanage, where he was known as "the little boy who wouldn't smile." After this picture was published, readers sent donations of packages and money. Five years later, an American widow who remembered the picture brought Ri to Los Angeles and adopted him.

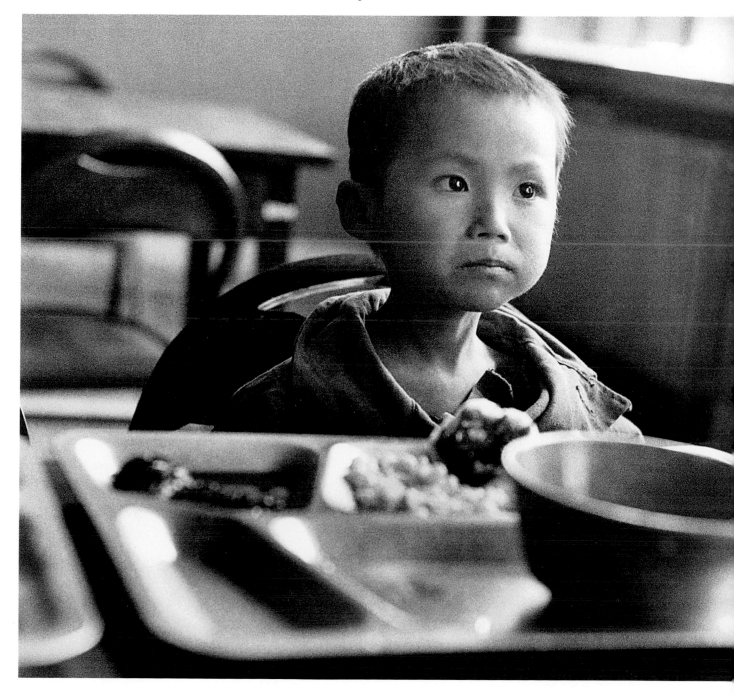

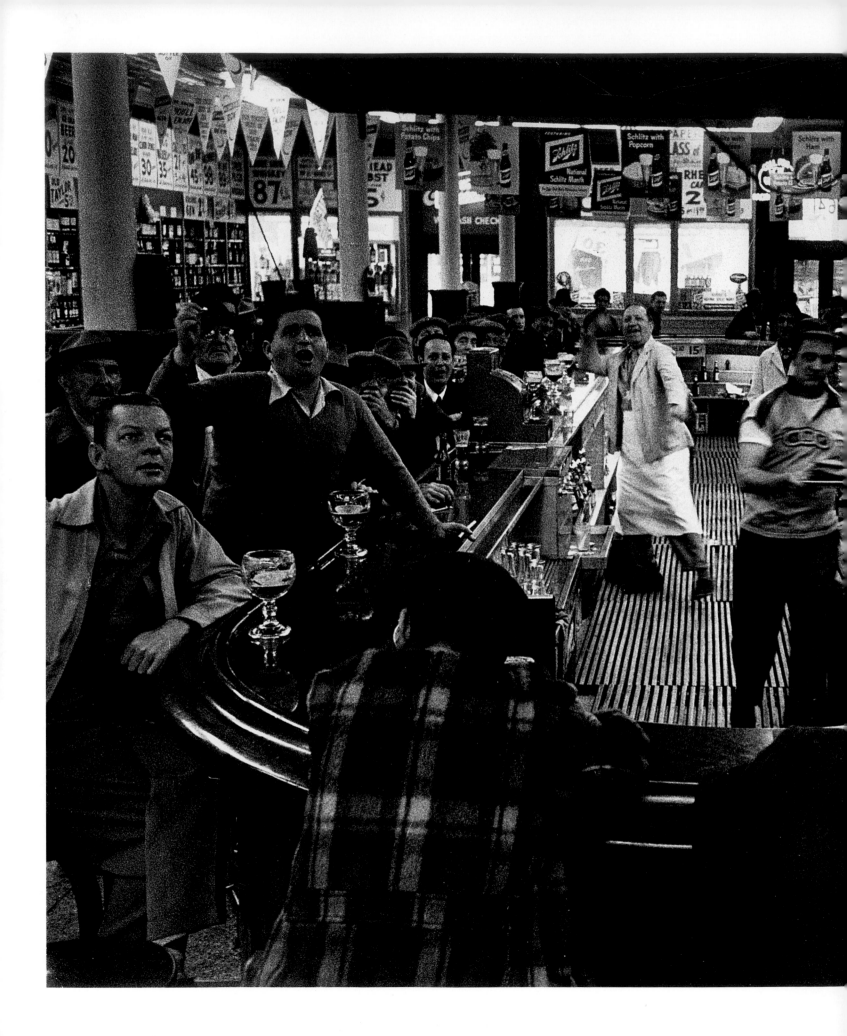

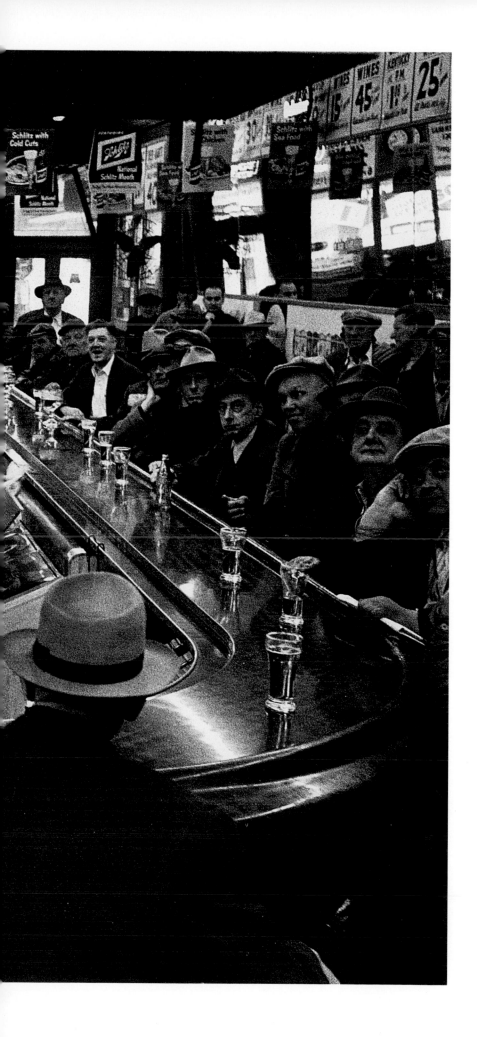

World Series
FRANCIS MILLER
March 1989

The 1952 World Series, between the New York Yankees and the Brooklyn Dodgers, was one of the first to be broadcast widely by network TV. "For seven days," *Life* wrote, "the midday life of some 70 million Americans was disrupted."

Looking for a TV crowd in Chicago, Francis Miller reported apathy ("It's not our Cubs or White Sox"). But during the seventh game, he found some action inside a bar called the House of Rothschild, on East Madison.

"The gentlemen lining the two sides of the big circular bar," wrote Miller in captions he sent with his film, "are neither bankers nor stock-exchange members. With half-empty glasses of beer before them (the largest schooner costs only 15¢, and the best whiskey only 35¢), they are coasting through the game on one or two beers and staying warm at the same time. Interest was about evenly divided, no more Yankee fans than Dodger fans."

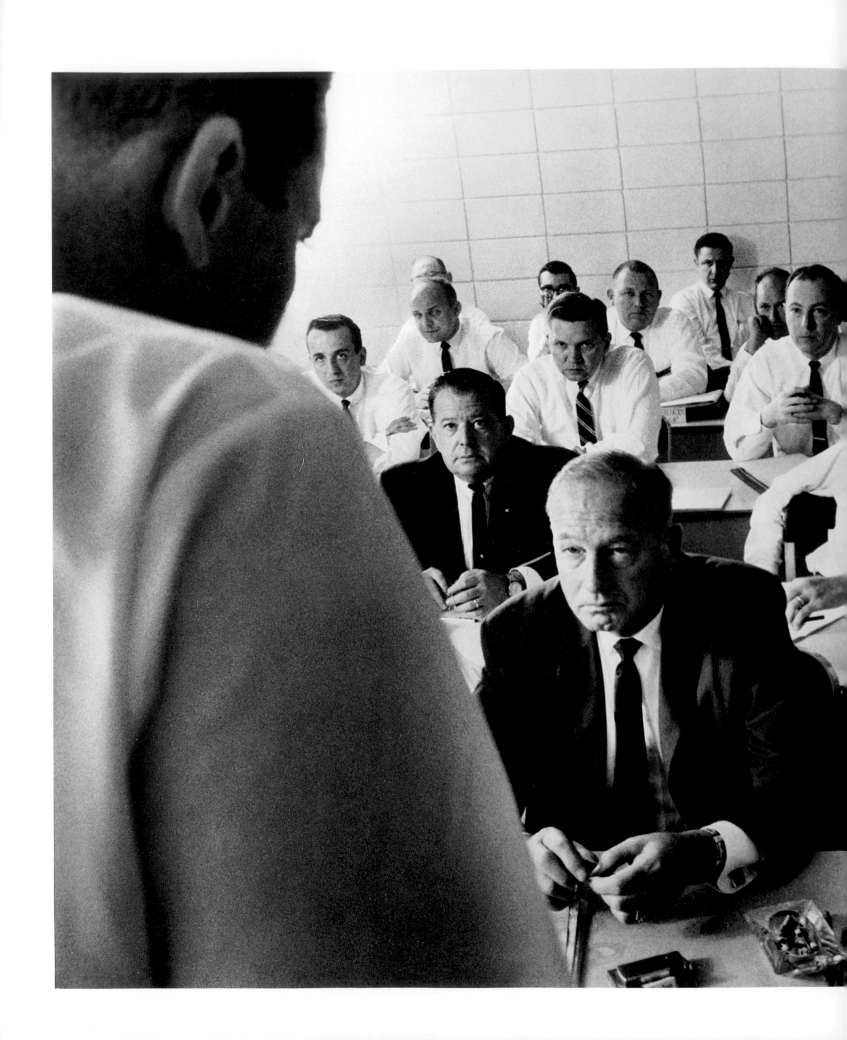

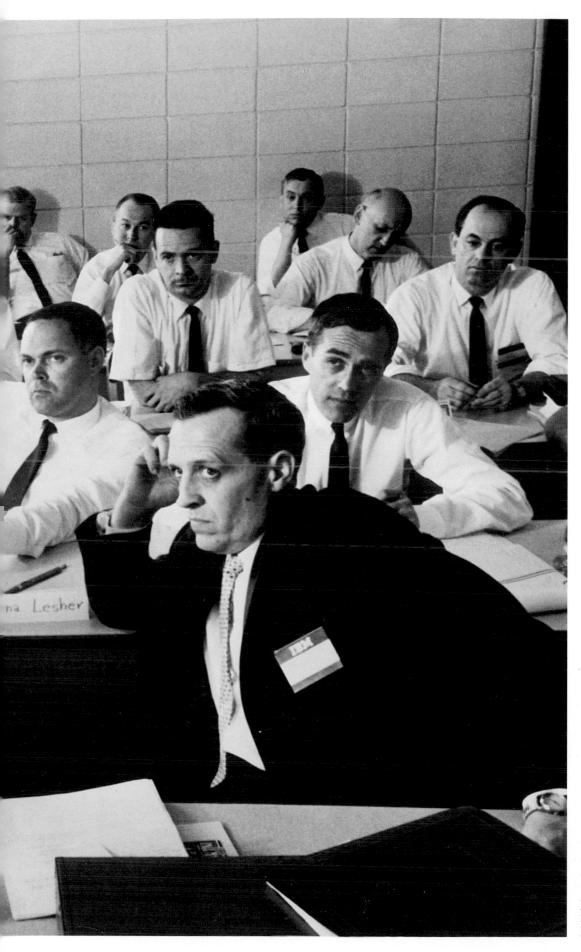

John Dammeyer
HOWARD SOCHUREK
May 5, 1967

"It was so nonpictorial it was a hell of a difficult story to bring off," says Howard Sochurek. "I wanted to show the pressure on a manager at the middle level of a large corporation—a manager who's selling the wonders of technology in a highly charged atmosphere."

The man was John Dammeyer, a 36-year-old systems manager at IBM. As Dammeyer tried to persuade IBM computer-plant managers from around the country to use an innovation he proposed, Sochurek says, "I watched from the sidelines. I was trying to work as inconspicuously as I could. I waited until late in the meeting. Then I moved in and out behind Dammeyer quickly."

That day Dammeyer didn't get everything he wanted—but he got enough. IBM, which voiced displeasure with the image of corporate life depicted in the *Life* article, gave him a promotion and stock options. But Dammeyer felt his new position actually gave him less to do. Within months an offer of a better job came from Control Data Corp., and he took it.

Sitting
HENK JONKER
September 14, 1953

Touch dancing disappeared in America in the
'60s, but if Hendrik and Jansje Kuiper are celebrating their 50th wedding anniversary this year,
it's probably alive and well—and being over-
done—in Holland.

Married in 1941 during the German occupation, the Kuipers thought it a poor time for festiv-
ities, so they decided to wait to celebrate their
union. Finally, in 1953, with 50 of their friends—
and their own children—they threw a party. As
the evening progressed, so did the gaiety, and
when a whistle blew during this dance, one part-
ner made a lap for the other to sit.

Priest
JAN SVAB
November 1982

Is it any wonder that elsewhere than
Czestochowa, Poland, the Roman Catholic
Church builds confessionals that are opaque?

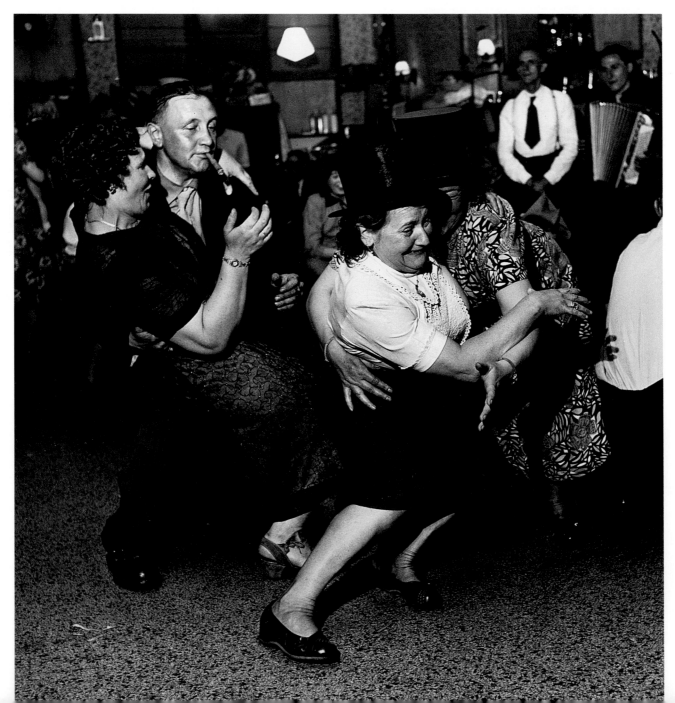

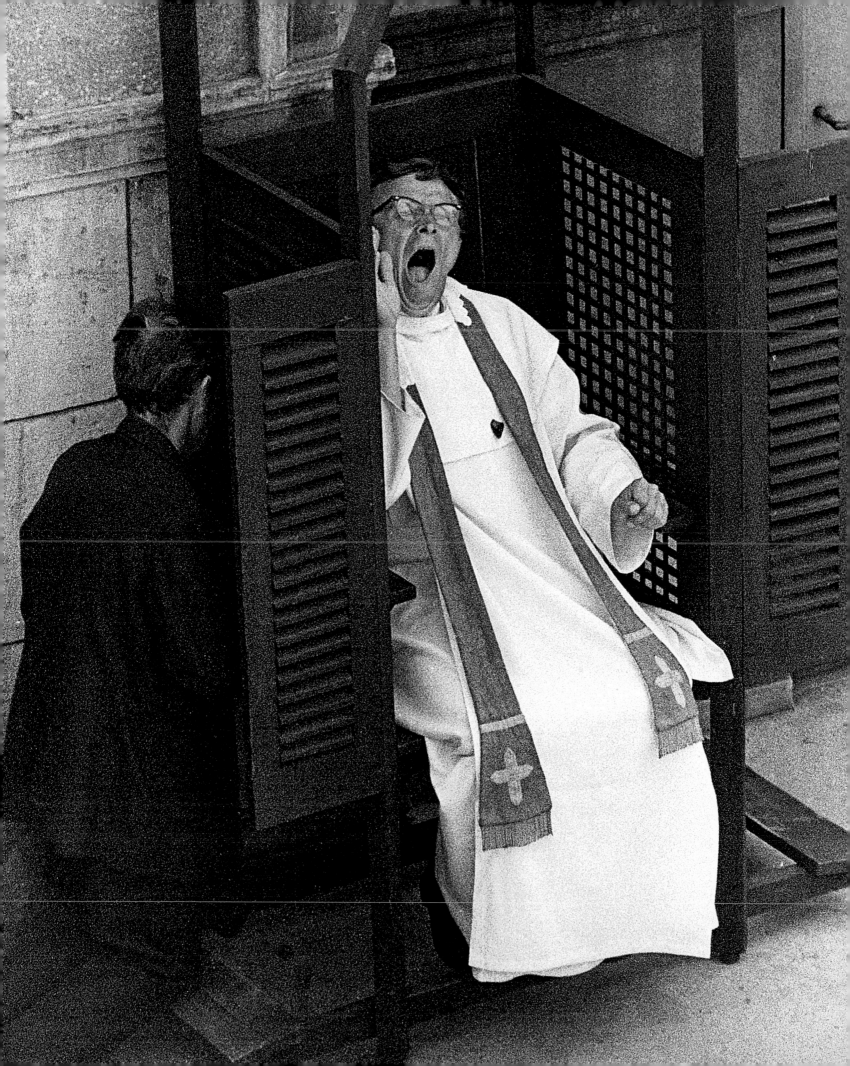

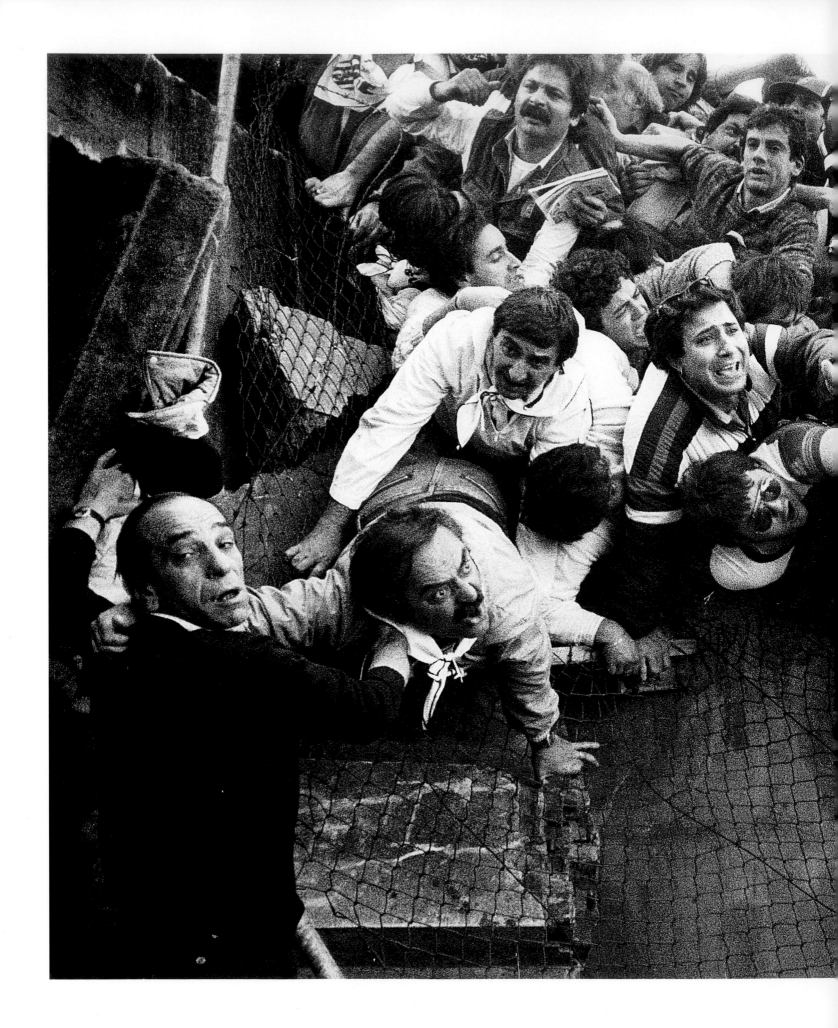

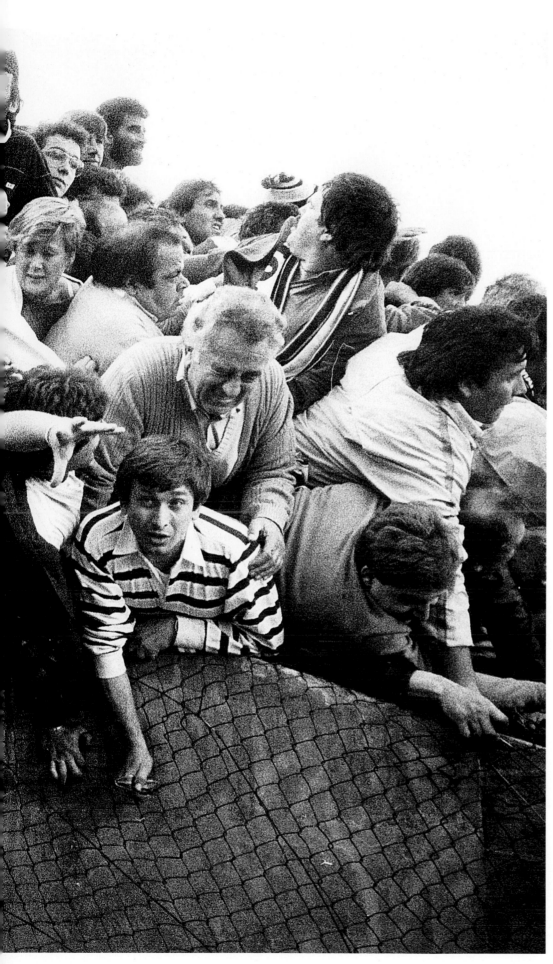

Soccer Disaster
EAMONN McCABE
July 1985

"**A**s at your Super Bowl, the spectators are on a high even before the soccer game starts," says Eamonn McCabe describing the atmosphere surrounding the European Cup. In Brussels in 1985, English fans supporting Liverpool began to mix it up with Italian fans backing Turin well before the opening kick.

As they did, from the far end of the 60,000-seat stadium, McCabe noticed an odd movement in the crowd. He ran forward expecting to photograph a fight, but as he approached, he heard a loud crack and saw a portion of the stadium give way.

"It felt as if it was going to fall on top of me," McCabe recalls. Most of the 38 spectators who died and the more than 200 who were injured were crushed under the falling rubble.

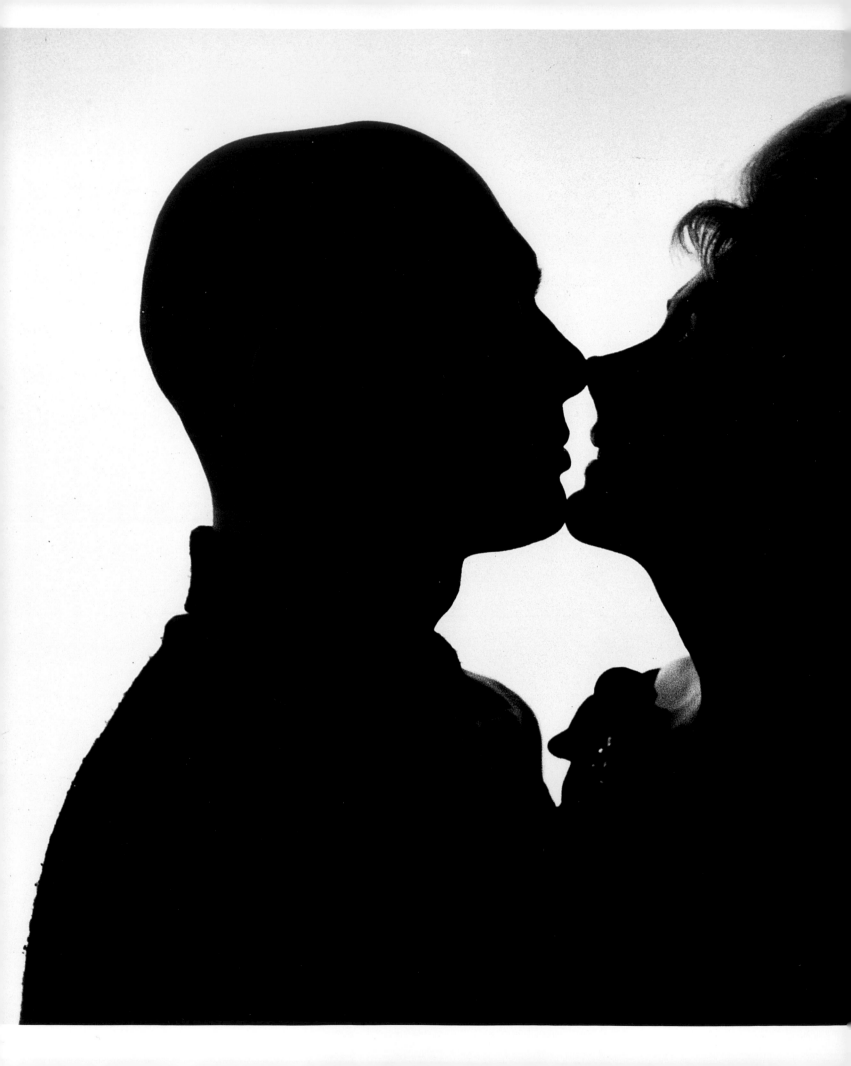

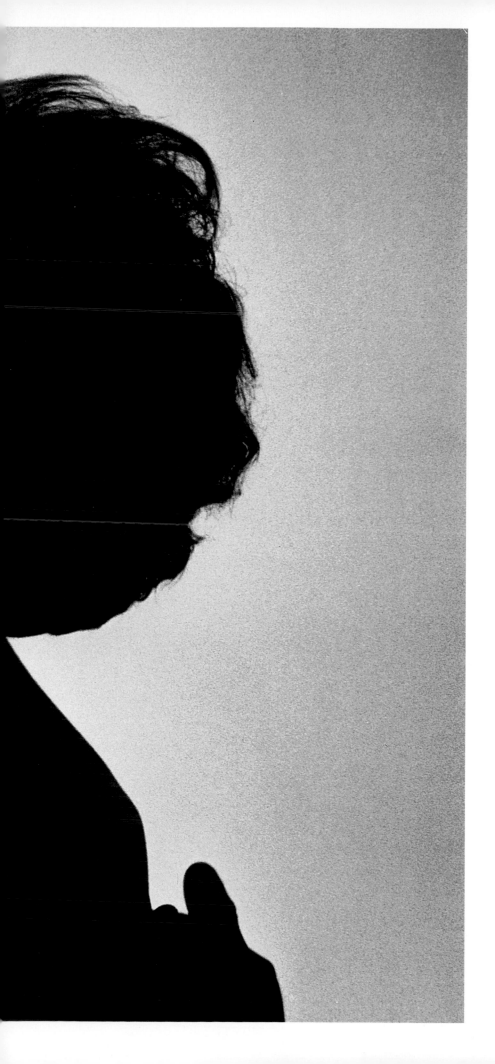

Kay Kendall and Yul Brynner
BOB LANDRY
July 20, 1959

Bob Landry discovered the answer while taking pictures in Paris on the set of *Once More with Feeling*. "As you can see," he wrote, "I did find out what happens to noses when people kiss head on: it's exactly the same thing that happens to chins."

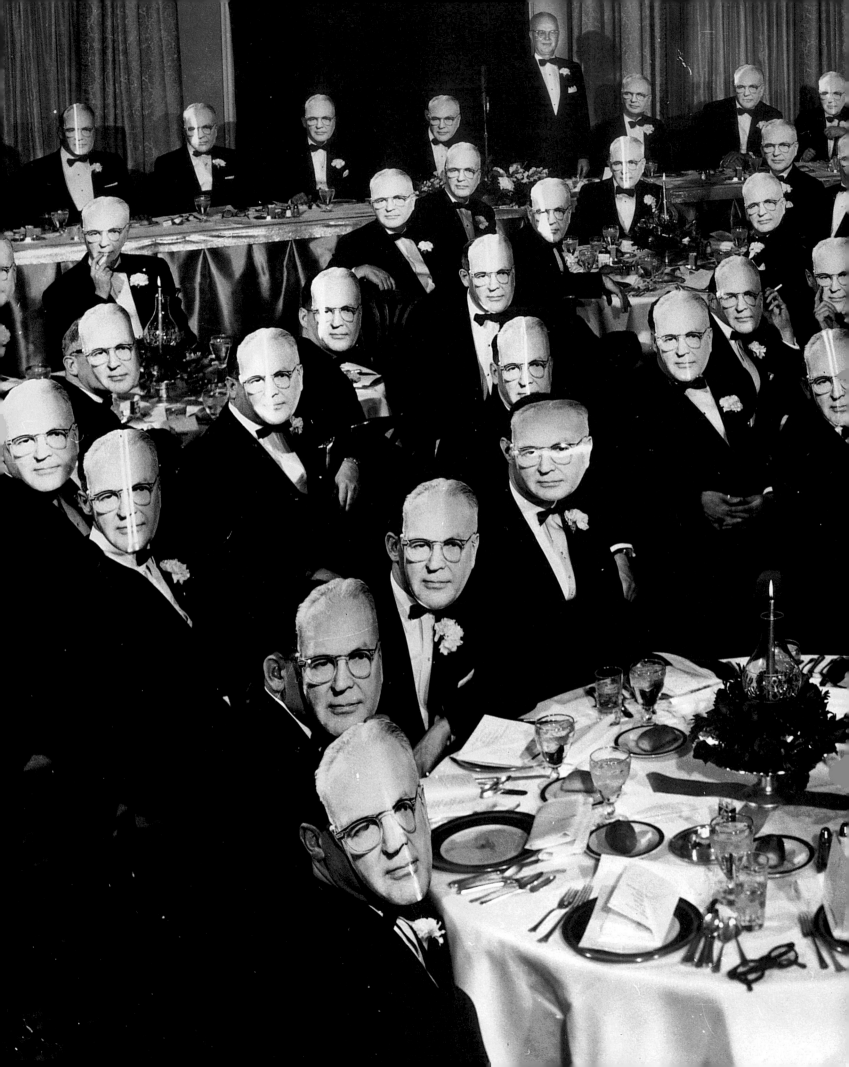

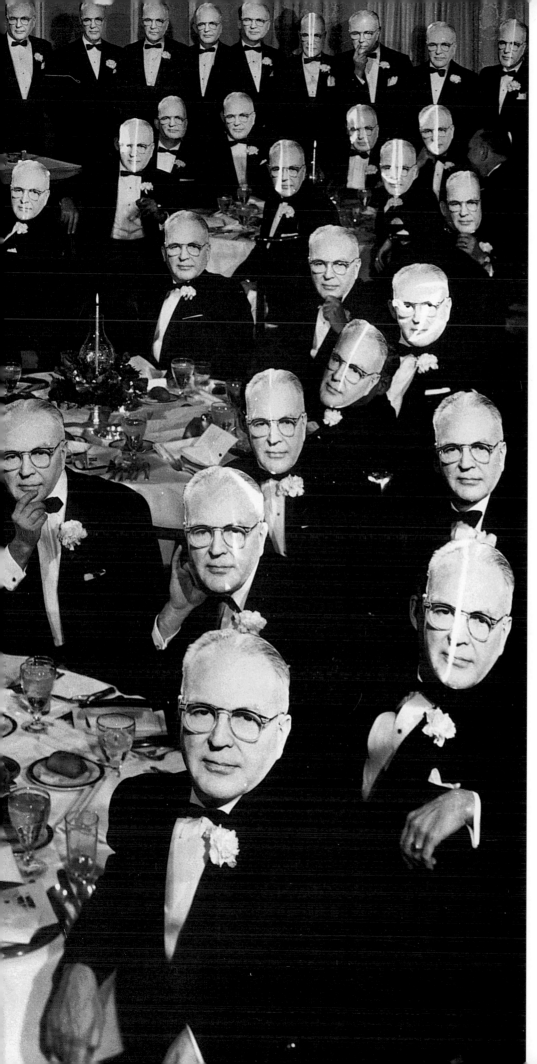

Just Us Corbits
KEN SPENCER
March 7, 1960

"The sight was enough to keep a photographer under the cloth of an old-fashioned camera," *Life* wrote. Ross Corbit, president of Hiram Walker Inc., was being honored for his 25 years of service to the company with a dinner at the Detroit Athletic Club.

Ken Spencer's picture of the celebrating business executives wearing masks (fastened by rubber bands around their heads) may seem to be a nightmare of corporate conformity, but it has an odd twist. Having risen to the top, Corbit (back row, fifth from the left) is the only man in the room who doesn't look like himself.

Toulouse-Lautrecs
HENRI de TOULOUSE-LAUTREC
May 15, 1950

It is a simple trick to expose one part of a piece of film now and another later, blending the exposures seamlessly. Realizing the possibilities, painter Henri de Toulouse-Lautrec was clearly beside himself.

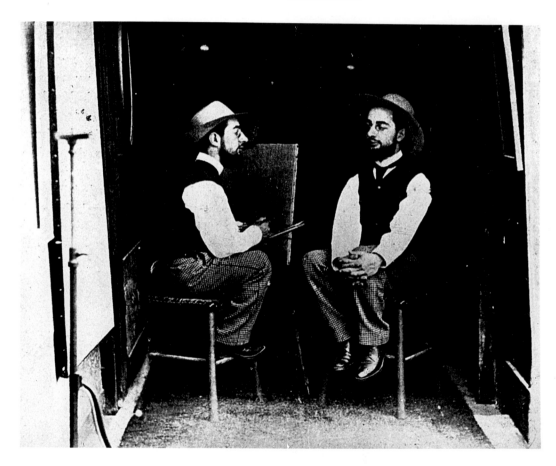

Debutantes
LOOMIS DEAN
August 12, 1946

In 1946 *Life* estimated that there were 2,000 debutantes in the U.S. In St. Louis, Mary and Debbie Love made their debut into society on July 4 at Whitestone, their parents' home. Wearing identical gowns, the sisters sat for their photograph under a portrait painted when they were three and two.

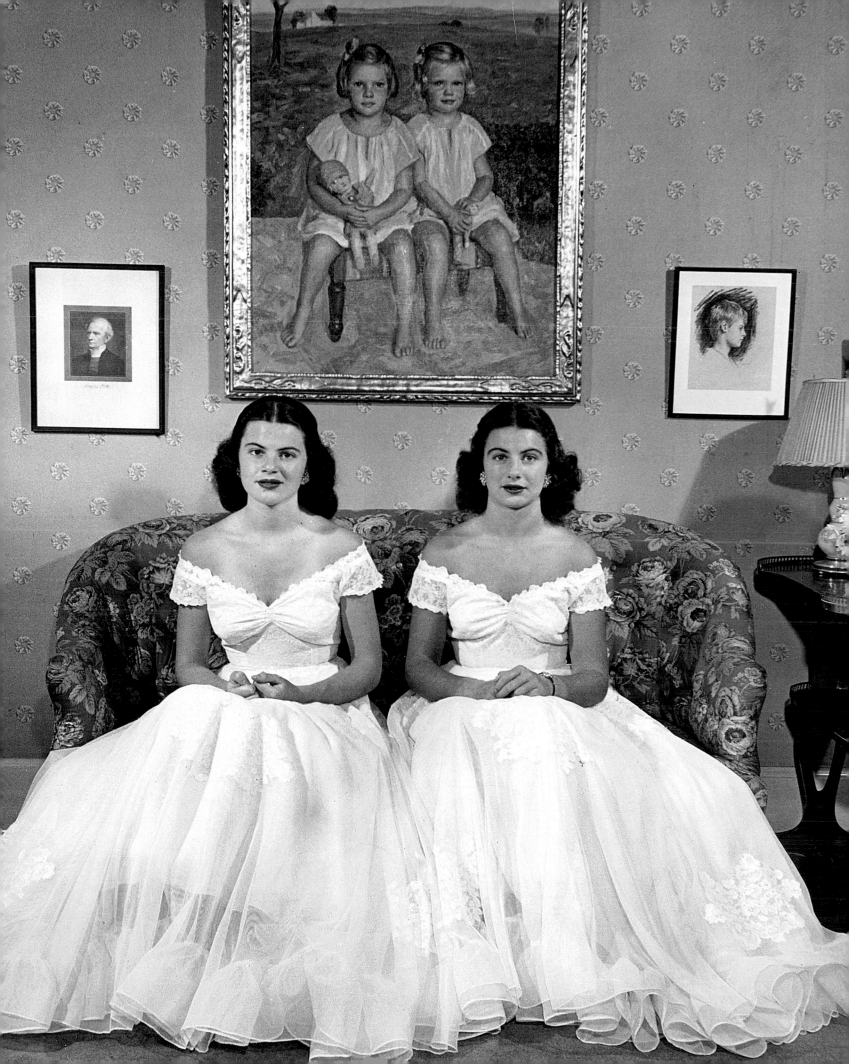

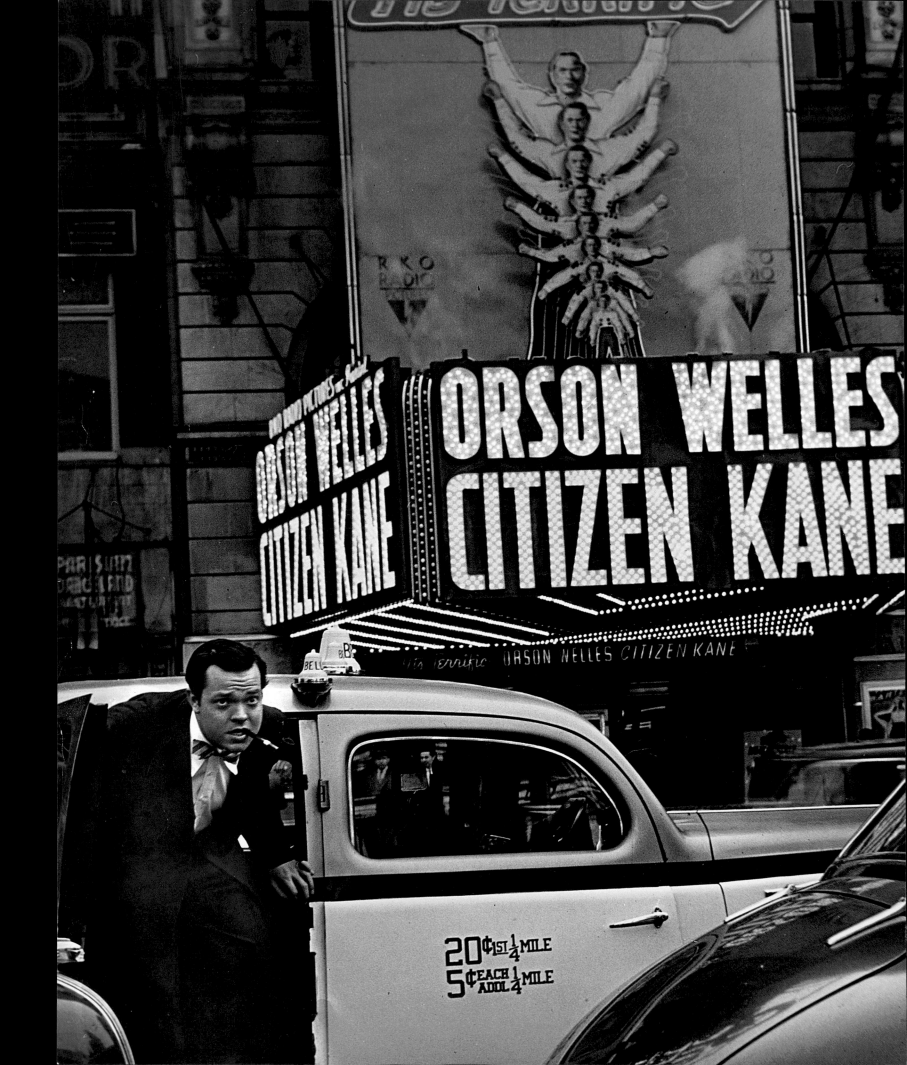

Orson Welles
W. EUGENE SMITH
May 26, 1941

The American movie masterpiece had opened in seven cities. In New York it was grossing $28,000 a week at the Palace Theater at 47th Street.

Orson Welles, the movie's director, co-writer and star, was 26 years old, 6 ft. $3\frac{1}{2}$ in. tall, and 221 lbs. *Life* reported that he "never walks fast but lumbers along ungainfully to conserve his energy. He never exercises but is exceptionally strong."

Weeks before W. Eugene Smith photographed him in Times Square, Welles had feared that publisher William Randolph Hearst (on whose life the movie was based) would sue RKO to stop the film's release. Welles, an amateur magician, talked of buying the movie back from the studio and touring the country, performing magic tricks, if necessary, to draw customers in to see it.

In fact, Hearst did not sue, but he wasn't unconcerned. His newspapers refused to print any advertisements for *Citizen Kane*.

Vivien Leigh and Laurence Olivier
PHILIPPE HALSMAN
December 17, 1951

"When Philippe made a cover picture, he planned carefully," recalls Yvonne Halsman, his widow. "He even sketched this one out. He wanted to put his camera very, very close to Vivien Leigh's and Sir Laurence's faces. Both would look straight out at the viewer. The picture would be very solid, very strong."

In a London theater, Olivier and his wife were playing (on alternate evenings) the title roles in Shaw's *Caesar and Cleopatra* and Shakespeare's *Antony and Cleopatra*. The sets for both plays were the same. Advance sales for the New York productions had already topped $1 million.

In the apartment they used for the picture session, Halsman explained his idea. The actors put their heads together. Suddenly Leigh glanced at her husband, and Halsman's idea was graced with spontaneity.

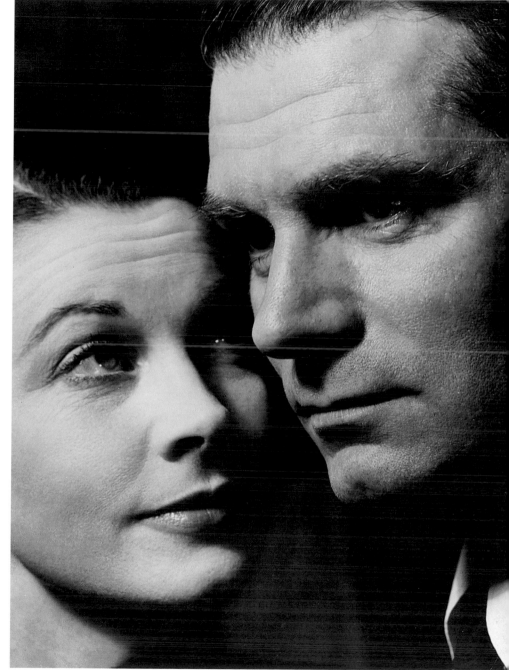

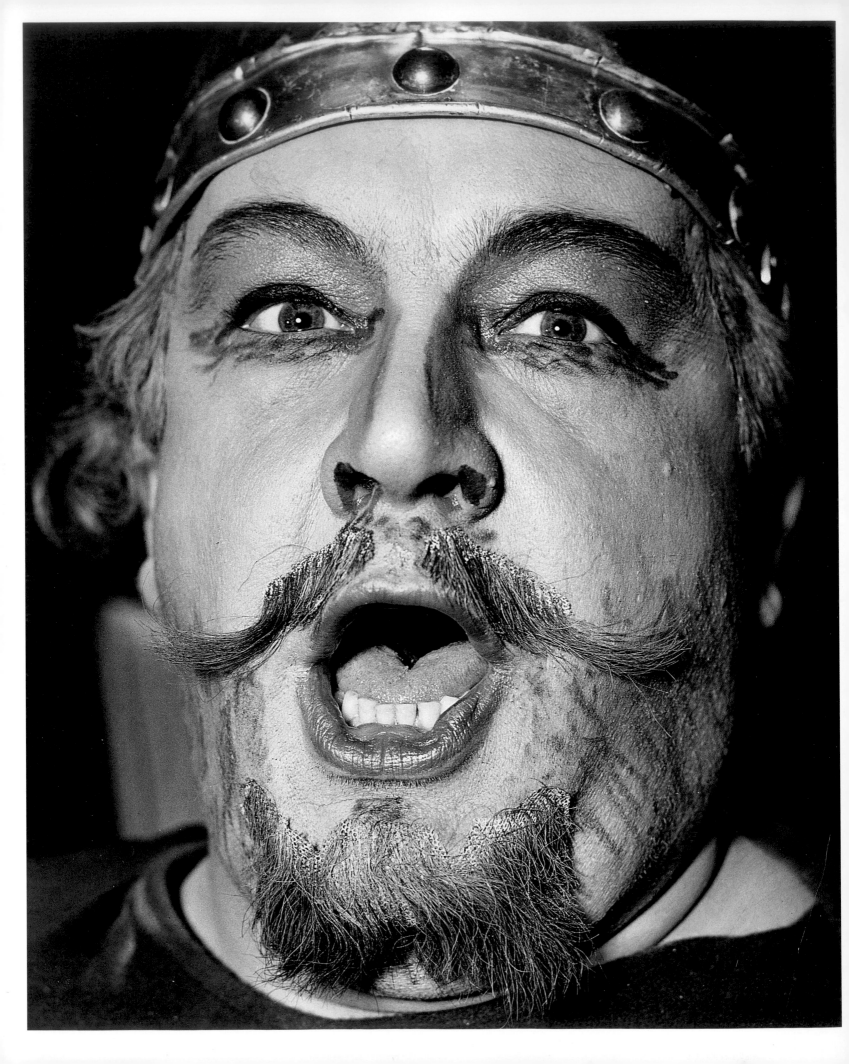

Lauritz Melchior
UNKNOWN
December 13, 1937

Certain arts are more favored by the picture press than others. Performers of the stage and screen are photographed more often than poets and sculptors. Why? Well, what sculptor or poet would put on a false beard and help a newspaper photographer take a picture of his tonsils? O.K., maybe Lauritz Melchior's glands *are* in shadow, but the Danish tenor was clearly doing his best before doing the same in *Tristan and Isolde* on opening night of the Metropolitan Opera's 1937 season.

Marseille
UNKNOWN
March 3, 1941

At the harbor in Marseille, France, a Movietone newsreel cameraman filmed spectators watching as regimental flags—not needed since France had been crushed by Hitler the summer before—were carried aboard a ship for safekeeping in North Africa. A frame from the film was enlarged and printed as this still picture.

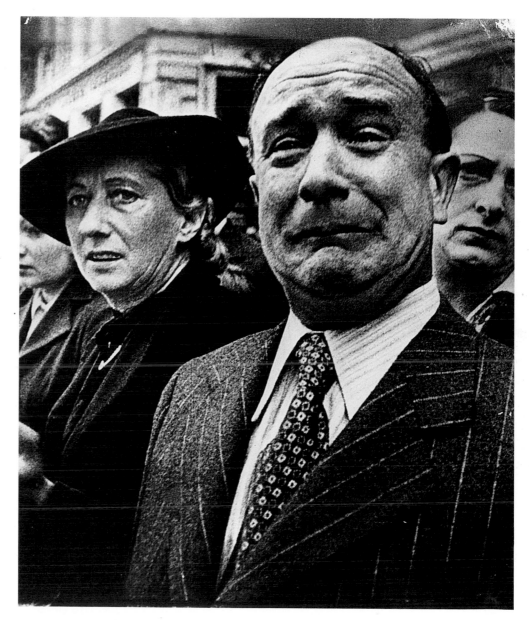

85

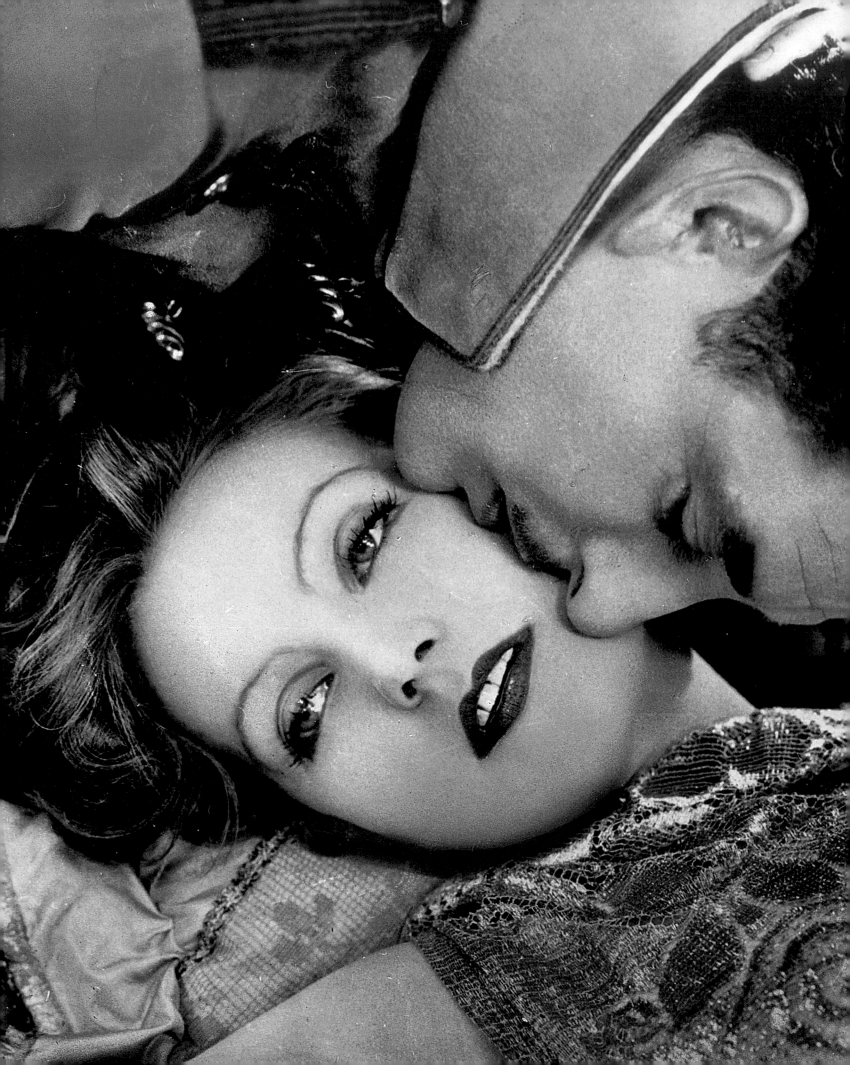

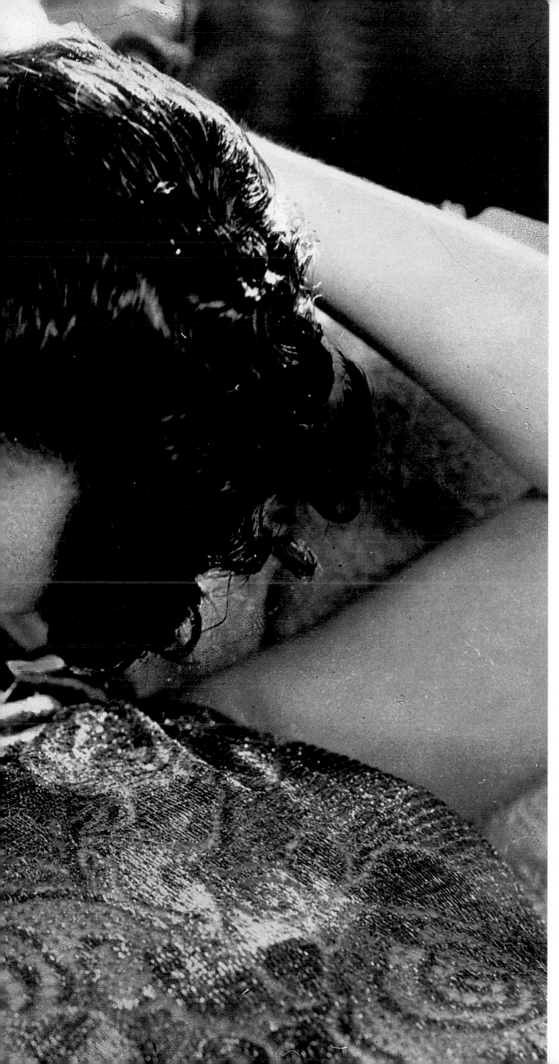

Garbo and Gilbert
RUTH HARRIET LOUISE
January 10, 1955

Garbo was 20. Gilbert was 29. Clarence Brown, the movie's director, claimed, "I am working with raw material. They are in that blissful state of love that is so like a rosy cloud that they imagine themselves hidden behind it, as well as lost in it."

He wasn't just hyping Greta Garbo's third Hollywood film, *Flesh and the Devil.* John Gilbert, the twice-married, twice-divorced matinee idol, was Garbo's main squeeze. He called her "Fleka," derived from *flicka,* which means girl in Swedish.

In time, however, Garbo balked at marriage, locking herself into a hotel ladies' room rather than go through with a spur-of-the-moment wedding ceremony.

After seeing Gilbert on the street a few years later, Garbo turned to a friend and said, "*Gott,* I wonder what I ever saw in him. Oh, well, I guess he *was* pretty."

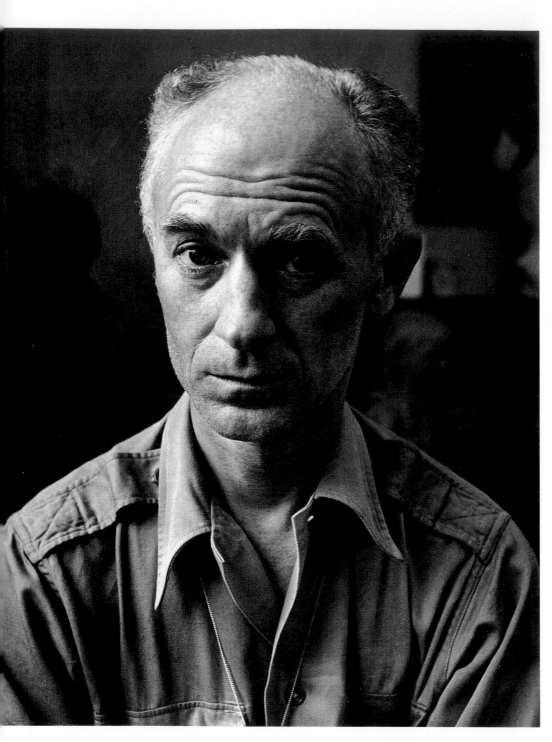

Ernie Pyle
ALFRED EISENSTAEDT
October 2, 1944

Ernest Taylor Pyle, a newspaper reporter, spent 24 months on the front lines during World War II interviewing American troops, writing down their names and hometowns, and telling their stories. In September 1944, Alfred Eisenstaedt dropped by as sculptor Jo Davidson began a bust of Pyle in New York. "I was there less than half an hour," says Eisenstaedt.

Leaving France weeks before, Pyle had written, "My spirit is wobbly, and my mind is confused. The hurt has finally become too great. All of a sudden it seemed to me that if I heard one more shot or saw one more dead man I would go off my nut."

After a brief rest, Pyle went on to write about the fighting in the Pacific. Japanese machine-gun fire killed him the following spring on the island of Ie Shima. "Of course, I haven't seen the pictures yet," wrote Pyle in Eisenstaedt's autograph book, "you've just now taken them but if they're as understanding as your presence while taking them (which of course they will be), then they will please us all."

In 1971, the portrait Eisenstaedt took was reproduced on a postage stamp commemorating the journalist's career.

Last Soldier
THOMAS McAVOY
May 11, 1959

No matter how it seemed in 1865, the last soldier alive after the Civil War ended was a Confederate. It just took 94 years for this to be clear.

Walter Williams joined Texas General John B. Hood's army in 1864. His duties included foraging for food and horses. At war's end, he said, "I wasn't discharged. We just broke up."

Blind, weak and 116 years old when Thomas McAvoy took his picture in 1959, Williams had fathered 19 children and still liked a good cigar. Living in Houston with a daughter born when he was 64, his favorite song was *Cotton-Eyed Joe,* which has lines like "O Lawd, O Lawd, come pity my case,/ For I'm gettin' old and wrinkled in the face."

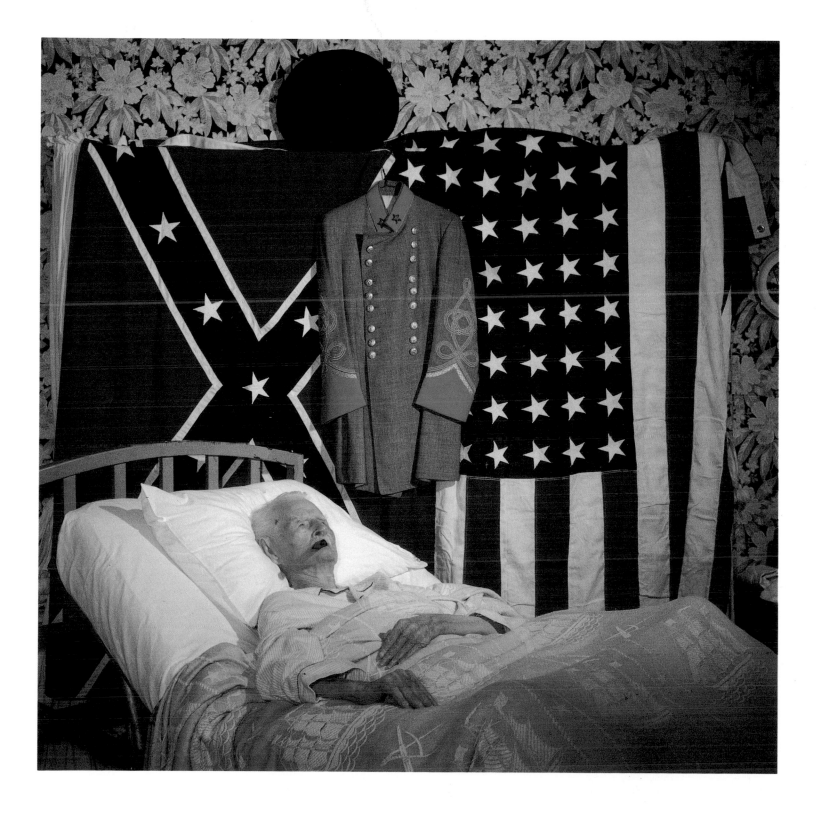

Joseph Stalin
MARGARET BOURKE-WHITE
January 20, 1947

In 1941 Harry Hopkins, adviser to President Franklin Roosevelt, went to Moscow to gauge the Soviets' ability to repel Germany's sudden invasion and to offer aid. At the end of his second meeting with Joseph Stalin, on August 1, Margaret Bourke-White took pictures at Stalin's office in the Kremlin.

"Suddenly I was in a long, bare room with Mr. Hopkins and Stalin standing very stiff and straight in the center of the carpet," Bourke-White later wrote. "As I sank to my knees to get some low viewpoints, I spilled out a pocketful of peanut flashbulbs, which went bouncing all over the floor.

"I guess Stalin had never seen an American girl on her knees before. He thought it was funny and started to laugh. The change was miraculous. It was as though a second personality had come to the front—genial and almost merry. The smile lasted long enough for me to make two exposures.

"I wanted badly to get him sitting down, or talking," she wrote at the time, "but I don't know what you can do with a dictator when he thinks he wants to stand in the middle of the rug."

Joe DiMaggio
HY PESKIN
August 1, 1949

"He looks, affable, smiling, cooperative—just the opposite of the way he was that day," Hy Peskin remembers. "That was because DiMaggio was very, very shy. He knew me for years, but still I wouldn't expect him to say hello."

A bone spur in DiMaggio's right heel had begun to hurt him the previous summer, and he had finished the season in constant and intense pain. Despite an operation on the heel that fall, DiMaggio was unable to play when the '49 season opened.

"Sooner or later as you get into your 30s," DiMaggio wrote, "your legs are going to go back on you—then you're through and there's nothing anybody can do about it. But when it's just your heel, something you never thought about in your life, then it's hard to take."

By June, however, the heel had healed. DiMaggio "got back in uniform and—in perfect fairy tale fashion" wrote *Life,* "began breaking up game after game by hitting the ball out of the park."

In the dugout just before the All-Star Game at Ebbets Field, Peskin photographed the center-fielder for his second *Life* cover. Statistics being what they are in baseball, it may be important to note that the time between DiMaggio's two covers was exactly 10 years, three months, and no days.

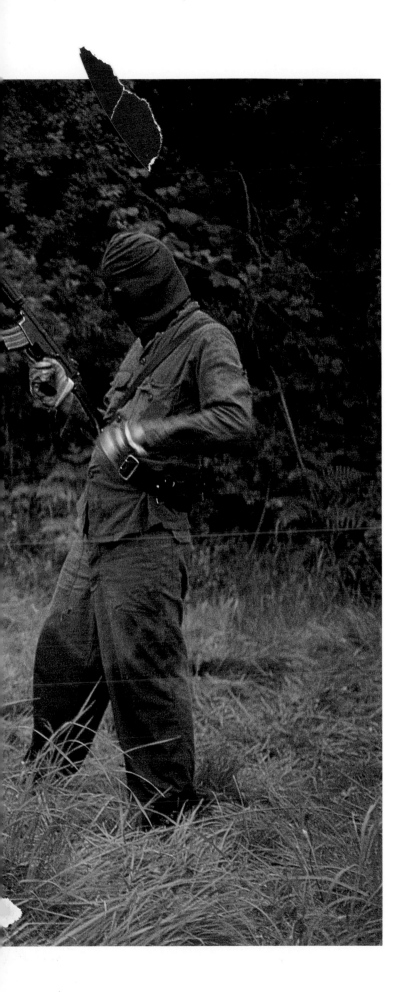

I.R.A.
HARRY BENSON
October 1985

"Invariably when you're doing a story, your two most important pictures are your first and your last," says Harry Benson. "The first sets the tone for your work—'Ah, that wasn't bad!' With the last picture you take a chance. You don't know exactly how the subject might react. You're going for a knockout. I hate to say it's a high, but you're onto something marvelous.

"I spent three nights at a safe house somewhere in Northern Ireland. On the fourth day, as we drove along, out of a hole in a hedge came this man wearing a Prince Charles mask. My heart lifted up. My God, what a wonderful picture! It had big ears and everything. He and his I.R.A. buddies were having fun. But it was not nice fun. Not like some tableau at the Abbey Theatre or off-Broadway. These were real I.R.A. killers.

"The man in the mask drove us to another place where more troops were hiding. The light was going, so I quickly asked the men with the rifles, 'If this *were* Prince Charles, what would you do?' "

Accident
LOU LIOTTA
June 1979

"I got a call to go over to this building where a woman was doing a promotional stunt," says Lou Liotta, of the New York *Post,* who's been taking news pictures for 54 years.

"I got there late, as she was being raised up to the top of the building, holding on to a cable with her teeth. I put a long lens on my camera, and I could see there was a strained look on her face. Her body was spinning around. I saw her lose her grip and followed her down—like you do covering a horse race or some other action. I took one picture. When I called the office later, I said I didn't know what I'd got."

A year later, Diane Terdik, who had fallen 35 feet onto wooden planks, broken both wrists and ankles, and injured her spine, paid a visit to the *Post.* She and Liotta stood together in front of a large print of his award-winning photograph and had their picture taken.

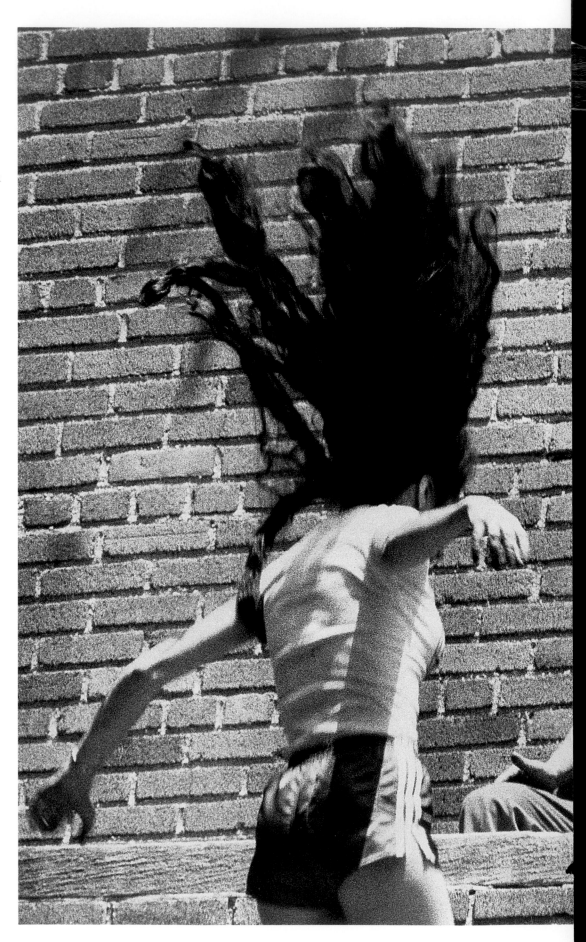

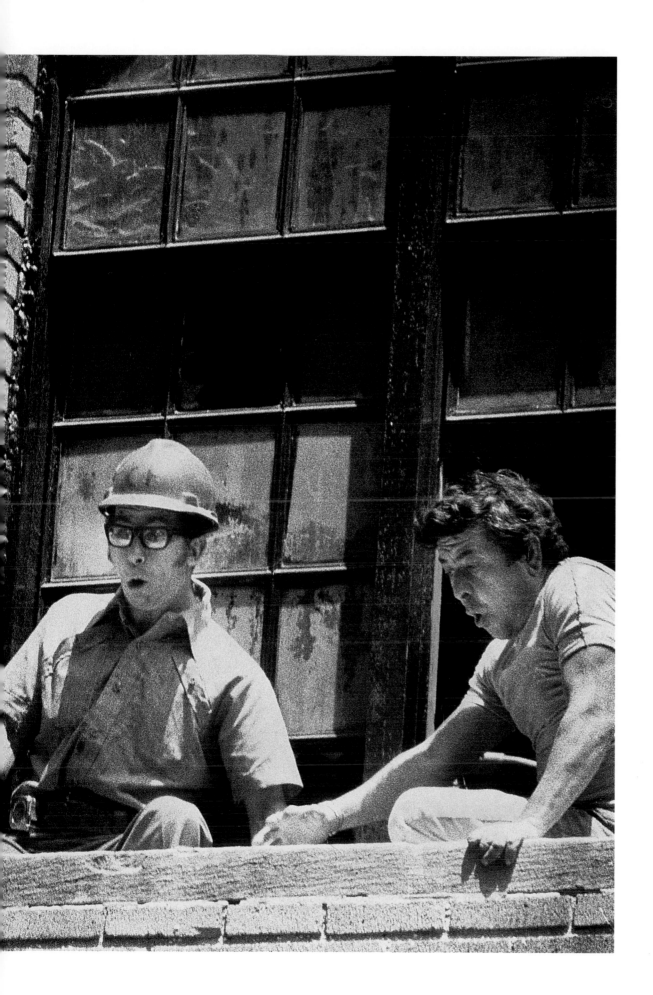

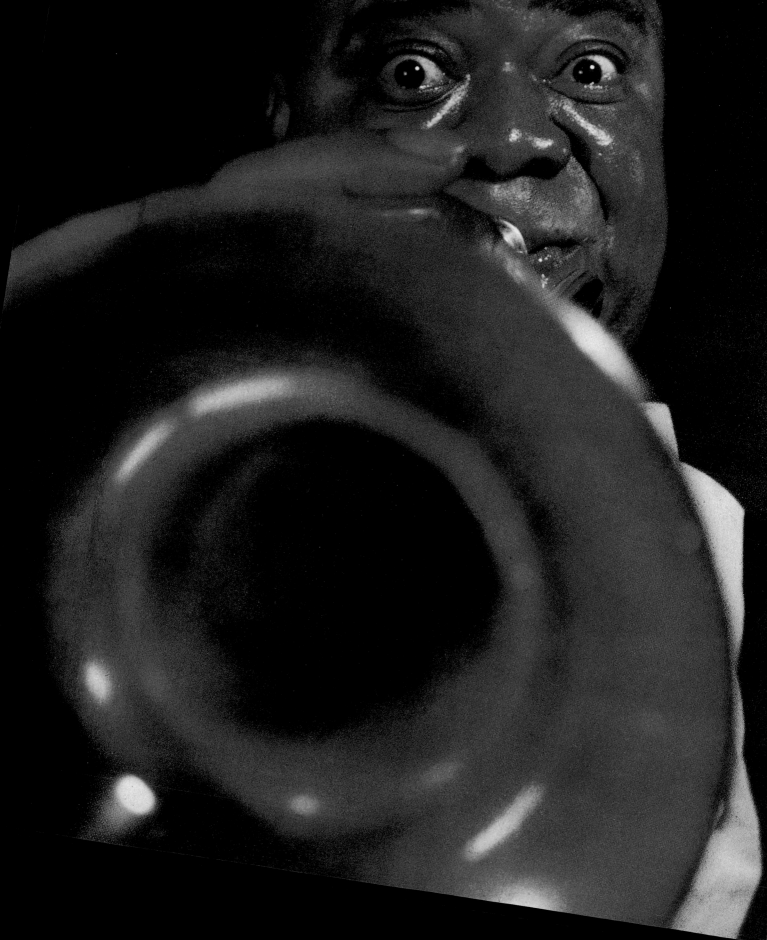

Louis Armstrong
ELIOT ELISOFON
January 17, 1955

"To me Louis Armstrong symbolizes the simple, direct, passionate approach to jazz, full of vigor, spirit, and even violence," wrote Eliot Elisofon, who sketched out the elements of this picture in advance. Elisofon wanted to show only part of Armstrong's head above his trumpet and—as a visual accent to emphasize the edge of the horn—just a bit of the white handkerchief Armstrong kept in his hand while performing.

When the photographer and the touring jazz musician met in a hotel room in Tulsa, Okla., Elisofon hadn't anticipated Armstrong's white shirt cuffs and thought they would ruin the picture. No problem: "When I asked Louis to push them back," recalls Elisofon, "he removed his jacket and tore off both sleeves before I could stop him."

William Randolph Hearst
BOB LANDRY
August 27, 1951

In 1938 William Randolph Hearst dressed up as President James Madison and rode a carousel at his 75th birthday party. The party was given by his mistress, actress Marion Davies, at her beach house in Santa Monica.

Thirteen years later, at Hearst's home in Beverly Hills, Davies sat through the night with the gravely ill publisher. Going to sleep in her own bedroom near dawn, *Life* reported, she was not awakened until 10 of 10, an hour after Hearst's death. By then his sons had taken his body to a mortuary.

"I asked where he was, and the nurse said he was dead," Davies told *Life*. "His body was gone, *whoosh,* like that. Old W.R. was gone, and the boys were gone. I was alone. Do you realize what they did? They stole a possession of mine. He belonged to me. I loved him 32 years, and now he was gone. I couldn't even say goodbye."

Davies, who was not invited to the funeral in San Francisco, considered going but decided not to. "He knew how I felt about him, and I knew how he felt about me," she explained. "There's no need for dramatics."

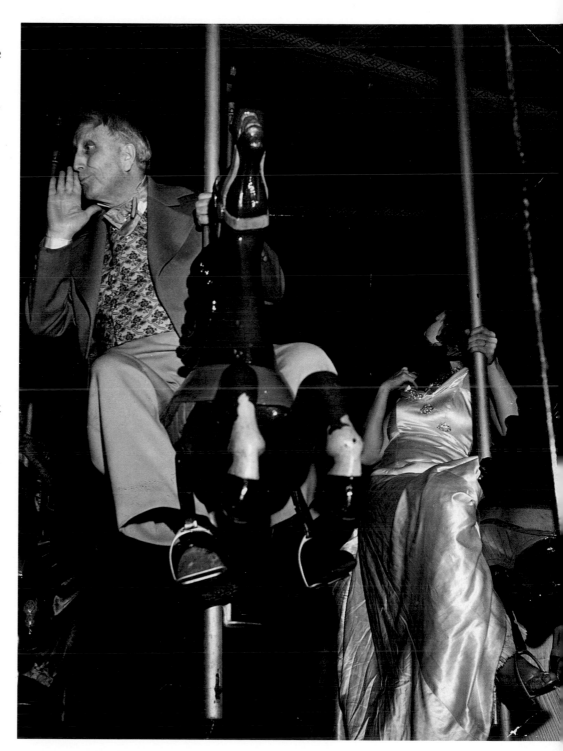

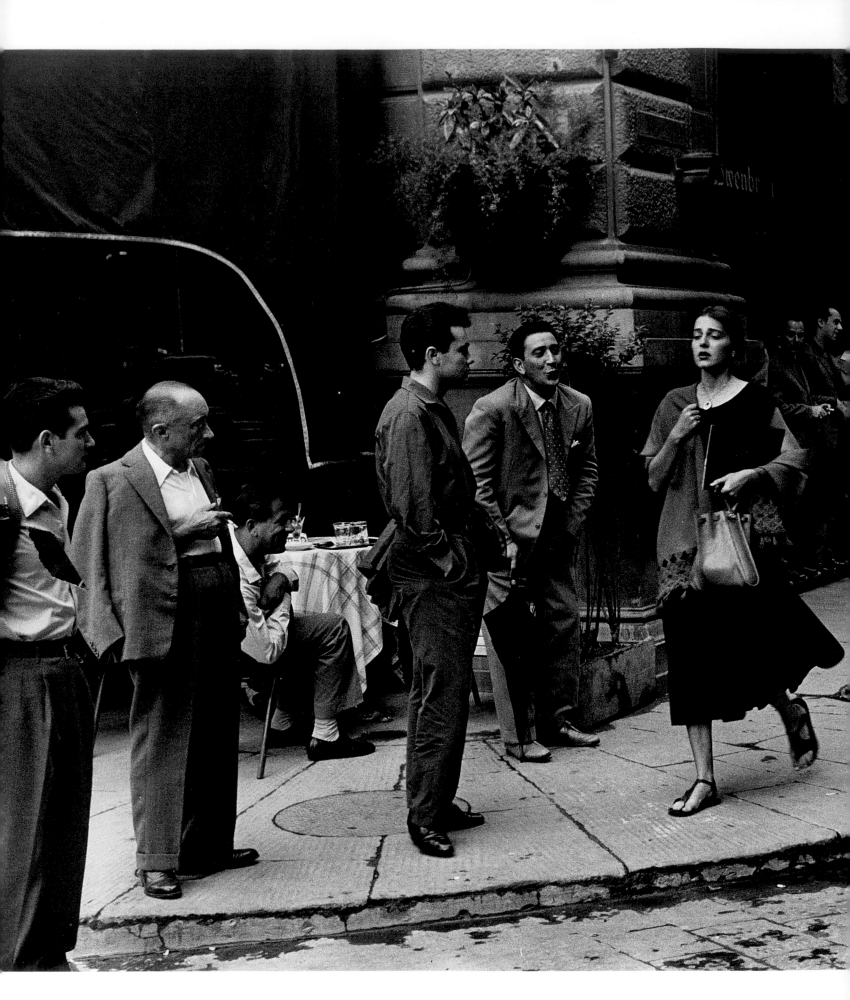

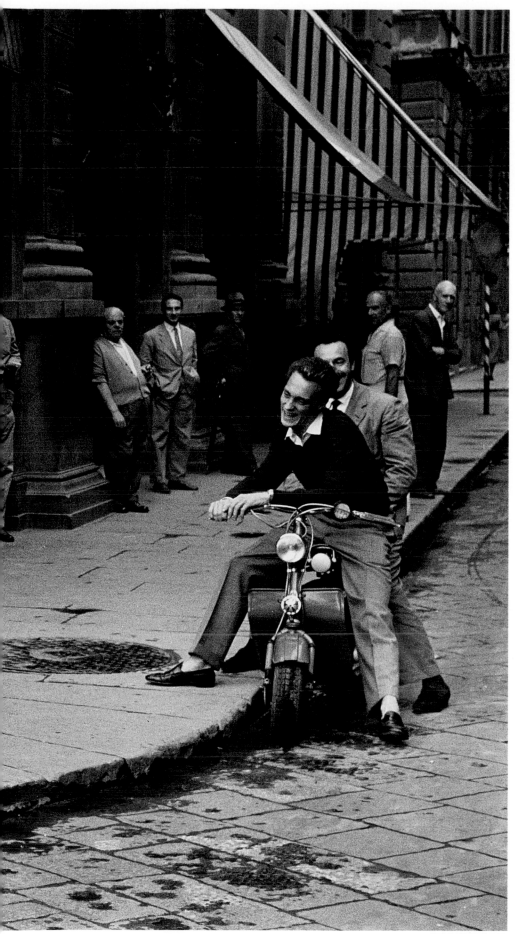

American Girl in Italy
RUTH ORKIN
Fall 1988

In the same year Ruth Orkin won third prize in *Life's* contest for young photographers, she made friends in Florence with a New York model named Jinx Allen. They decided, with tongues in cheek, to act out the hazards facing a single American woman traveling in Europe in 1951.

"I'd had this photograph in my mind for years," says Orkin, "ever since I had been old enough to go through the experience for myself." All the pieces fell into place in the Piazza della Repubblica, where Orkin asked one of the men on the scooter to help. He understood English and explained things to his countrymen. They quite gracefully displayed their native "charm."

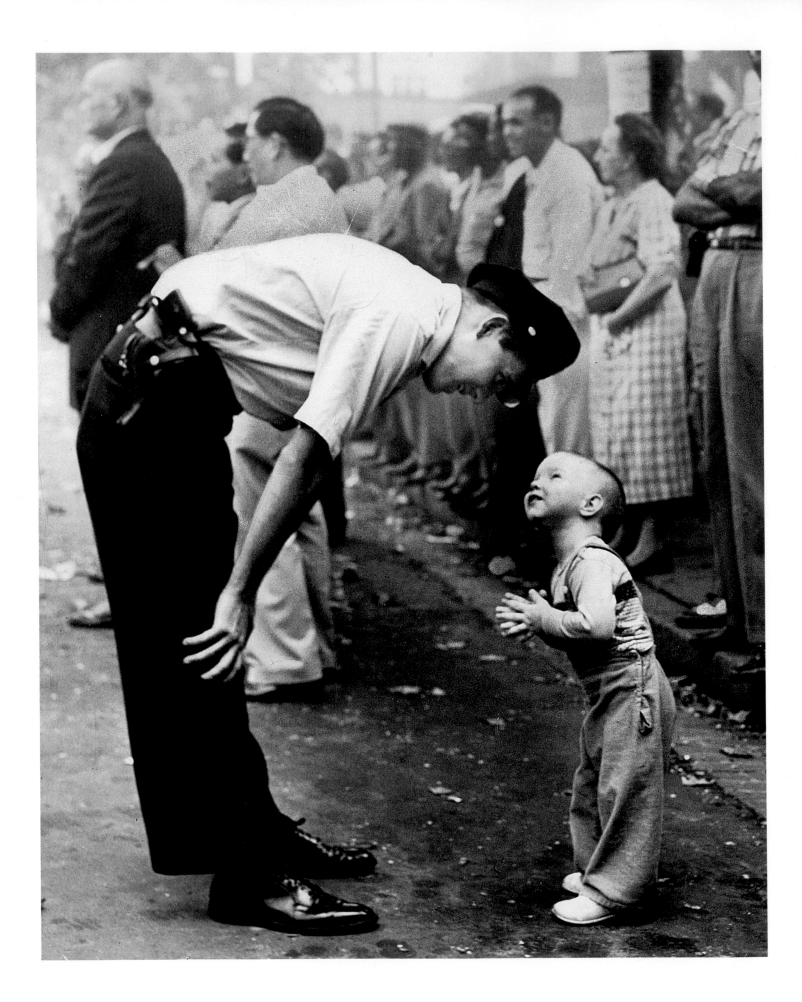

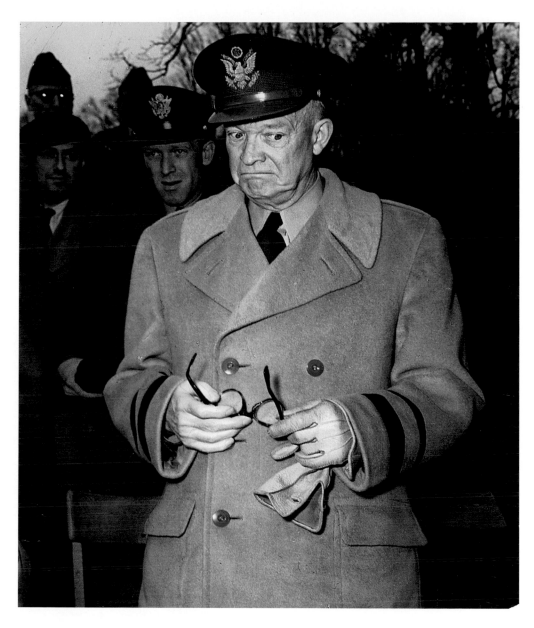

Good Cop
BILL BEALL
October 14, 1957

Two-year-old Allen Weaver stepped off the curb for a closer look at a paper lion during a Chinese festival in Washington, D.C., and policeman Maurice Cullinane went over to chat with him about the dangers caused by the firecrackers that were being tossed about in celebration. When the Washington *News* published this picture, a reader who worked at the National Security Council was impressed. She and 23 fellow workers got up a petition to have *Life* publish it too.

"It made such an impression," Mrs. Ella Ford wrote, "we feel it will arrest the thoughts of people throughout the United States." As a matter of fact, it did. J. Edgar Hoover, head of the FBI, thought the picture "worthy of a prize." He was correct: it won a Pulitzer.

Equally important, nice guys finish first: in 1974 patrolman Cullinane became Washington's chief of police.

Ike
FRANCIS J. GRANDY
April 23, 1951

In Koblenz, Germany, Francis J. Grandy of the armed services newspaper *Stars and Stripes* photographed the commander of NATO forces just as reporters told him that President Harry Truman had fired General Douglas MacArthur for insubordination. After collecting his thoughts, General Dwight David Eisenhower's official statement was "When you put on a uniform, you accept certain inhibitions." His unofficial statement had already been seen.

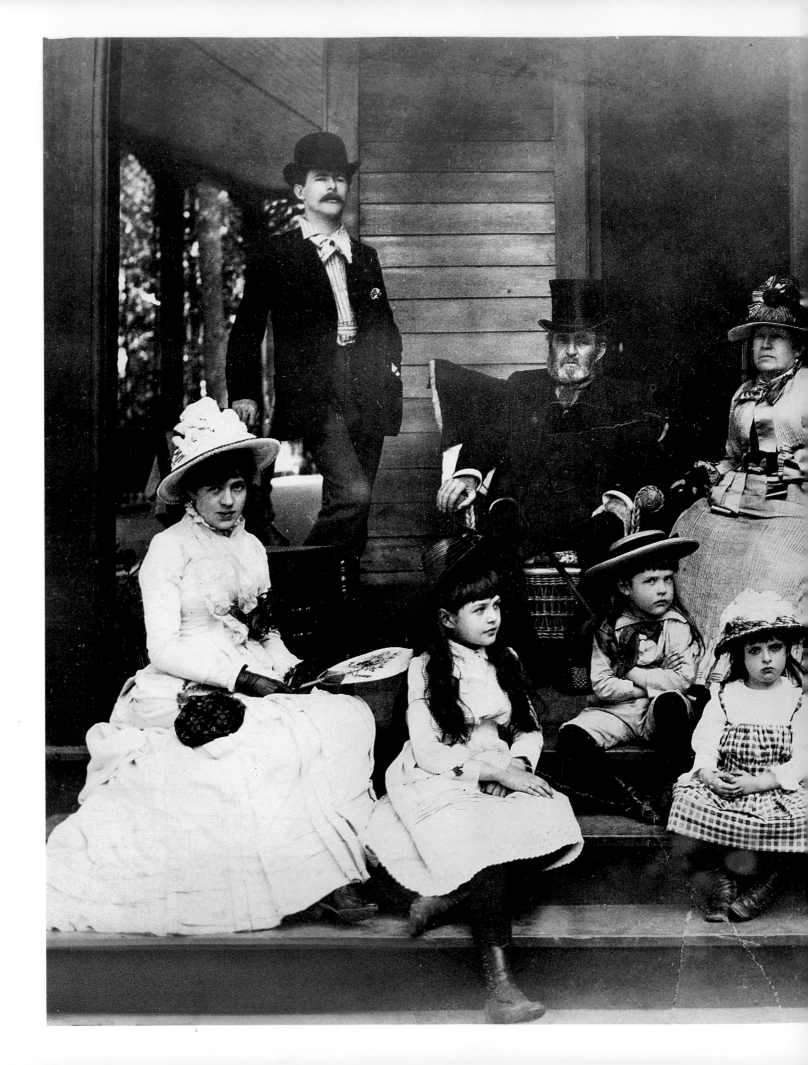

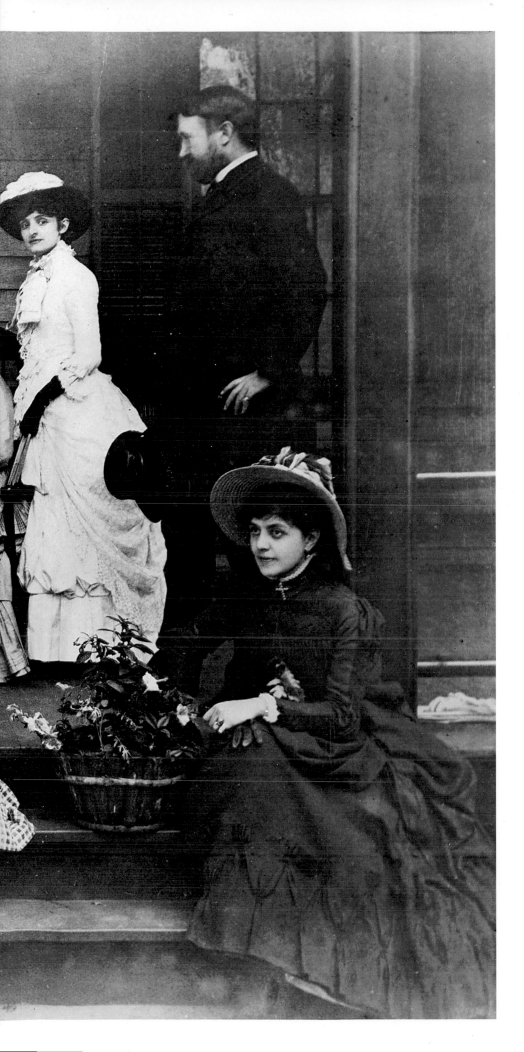

Ulysses S. Grant
F.L. HOWE
March 26, 1951

In the middle of June 1885, former President Ulysses S. Grant retired to Mount McGregor near Saratoga, N.Y., to finish his memoirs. His friend James W. Drexal, lent him the house. Surrounded by his family and in great pain from a cancer of the throat, Grant wrote the final pages only a week before dying on July 23.

Author Mark Twain was Grant's publisher. The book sold 300,000 copies in two years, earning $450,000 for Grant's impoverished heirs. In 1962, critic Edmund Wilson, who favorably compared Grant's writing to *Walden* and *Leaves of Grass* noted, "The thick pair of volumes of the *Personal Memoirs* used to stand, like a solid attestation of the victory of Union forces, on the shelves of every pro-Union home."

English critic Matthew Arnold (who once met Grant and had thought him dull) wrote, "I found the language straightforward, nervous, firm, possessing in general the high merit of saying clearly in the fewest possible words, what had to be said, and saying it, frequently with shrewd and unexpected turns of expression."

Oooh! Ah! Eek!
HANS LEURS
Winter 1978

These "five unartful dodgers are cringing so uniformly that they might be trying out for a road-show *Chorus Line*," *Life* reported. "This decidedly anxious and defensive group belongs to West Germany's Schalke 04 soccer team, and they're waiting for player No. 5—a member of the opposing Borussia Mönchengladbach team— to unleash a free kick on their goal. Their job: protect it. He missed, and they won. But, oooh, how it almost hurt!"

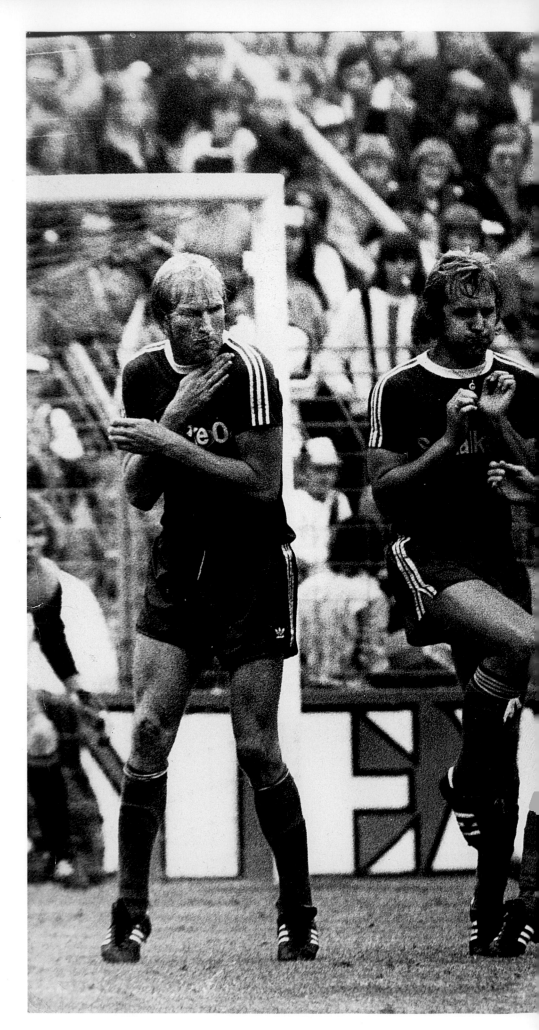

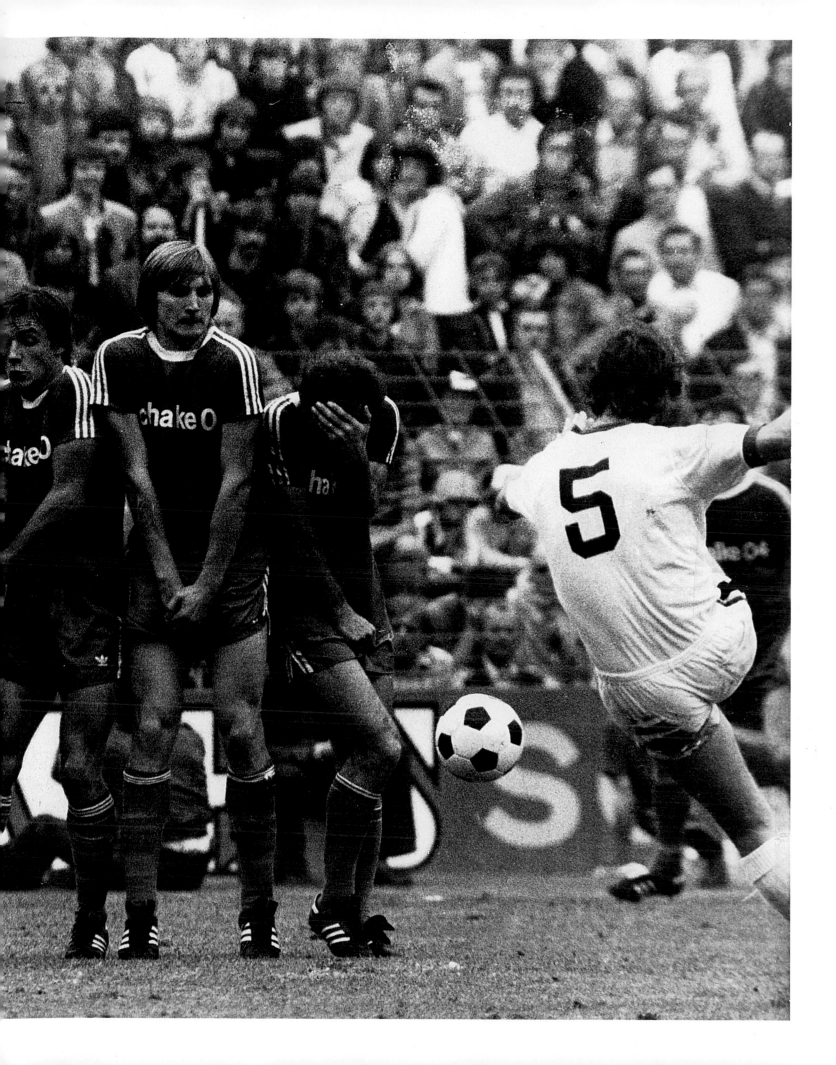

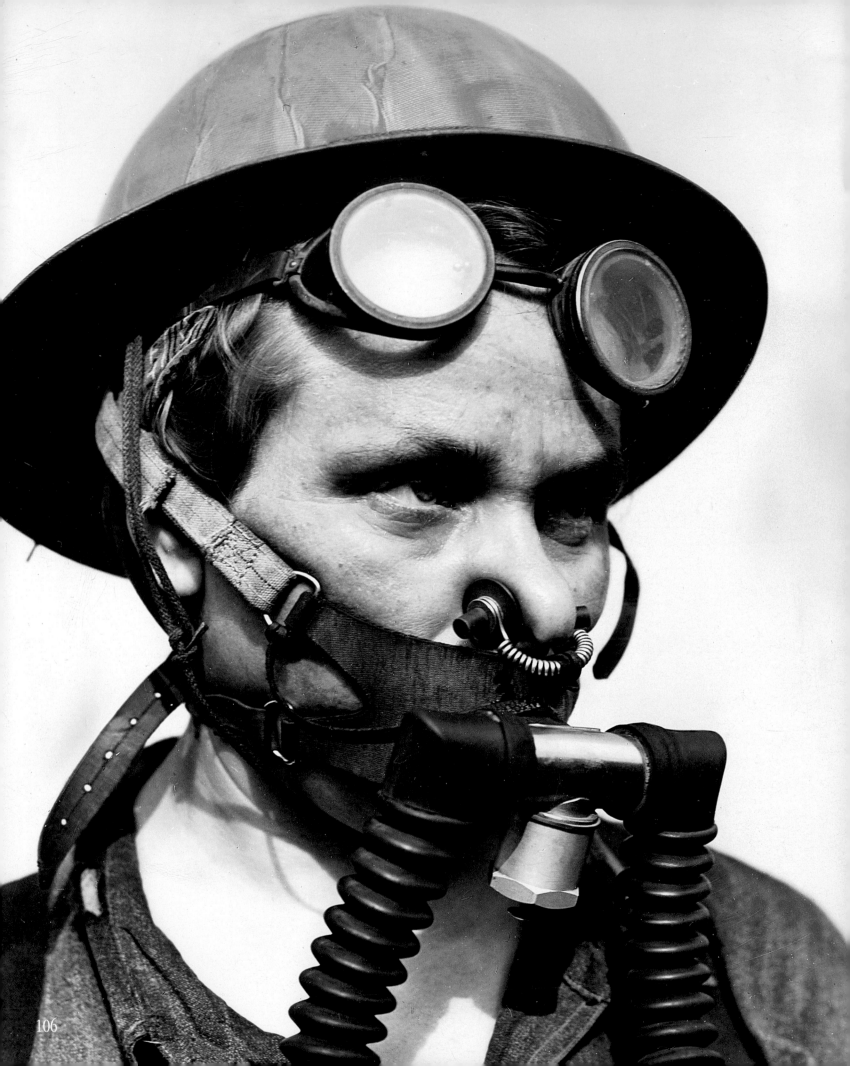

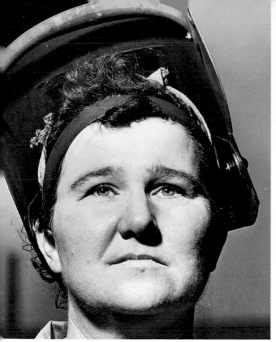

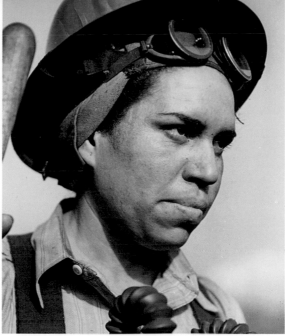

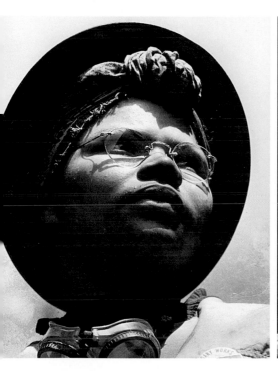

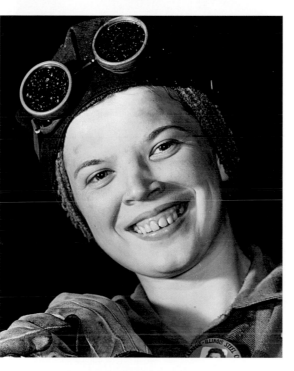

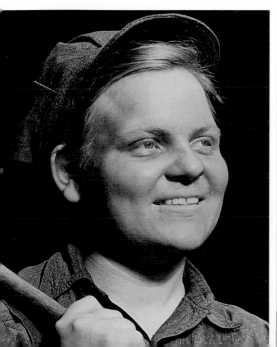

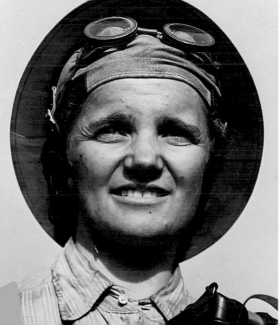

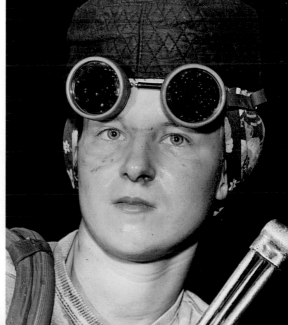

Steelworkers
MARGARET BOURKE-WHITE
August 9, 1943

"When Margaret Bourke-White started photographing steel mills in 1928, it was unprecedented for a woman to even enter a foundry," noted *Life.* Times change. In 1943 Bourke-White (who was just back from covering the air war in North Africa) went to Gary, Ind., to photograph a new phenomenon: women steelworkers. She found female welders, crane operators, tool machinists, laborers, electrical helpers, grinders, oilers, coil tapers, foundry helpers, checkers, loaders, metallurgical helpers, painters, cleaners, engine operators, furnace operators, packers, and shippers—including Bernice Daunora, 34 (far left), a member of the "top gang," who was wearing a "lightweight breathing apparatus" for protection against blast-furnace fumes. The women's wages were the same as men's (basic pay: $40.56 for a 48-hour week that included eight hours at time-and-a-half pay). In 1943, 4 million women were working in the defense industries. To no one's surprise, when war ended and the men came back home, the women went back home.

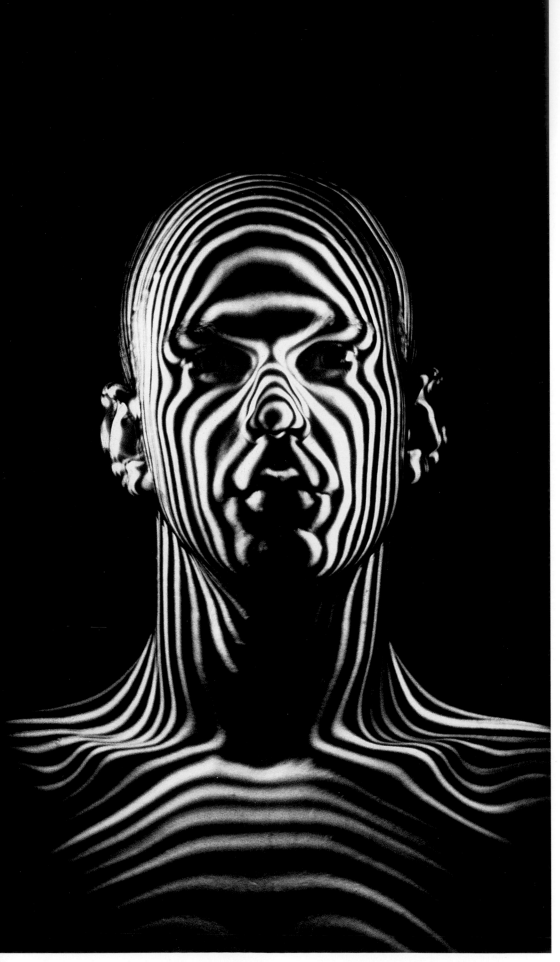

Jet Age Man
RALPH MORSE
December 6, 1954

"In 1954 the Air Force was studying how to make space helmets in three sizes: small, medium and large," says Ralph Morse. "They measured thousands of guys to see how big their heads were, taking measurements with a small strobe light that moved in an arc across the head from front to back. I sat a guy down in the dark, with an old-fashioned photographer's clamp holding his head steady. Then I left the shutter open and moved the light through its path a dozen times until its pattern recorded on the film." When NASA was created in 1958, however, its budget was large enough to allow each astronaut's helmet to be custom crafted.

Marilyn Monroe
PHILIPPE HALSMAN
October 10, 1949

Philippe Halsman thought it would be a good idea—and great fun—if eight Hollywood starlets emoted in the manner of the silent screen. He photographed each woman "tasting a drink," "embracing a lover," "hearing a joke," and "seeing a monster." The last is what Marilyn Monroe is doing here. Whatever one might think of her performance, Halsman told *Life,* "Monroe is a girl I'd love to photograph again. I think she has a lot of potential."

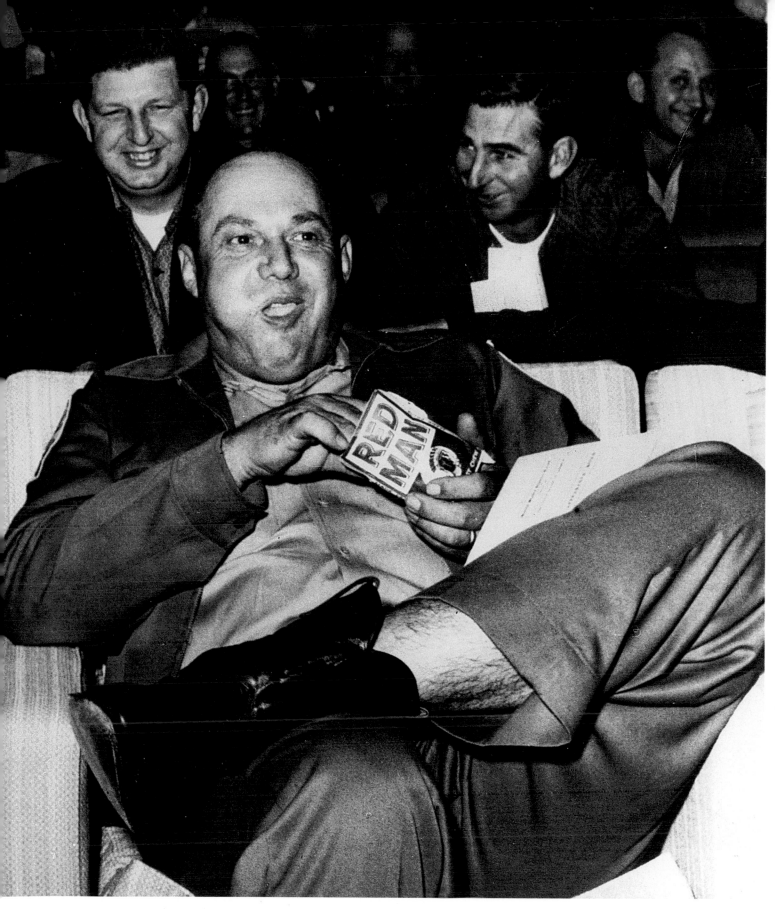

he asked Lawrence Rainey, "how about a picture?"

"Sure. Want some Red Man in it?" answered Rainey, sitting with his deputy, Cecil Price.

"I didn't know what he was talking about," says Reed. "I didn't know it was a chewing tobacco, but that's why everyone in the background is laughing." Charges against all 21 were dismissed on a technicality that afternoon. (Although the case went forward, Rainey himself would be acquitted.)

Reflecting the sentiment of the white community the next day, Price would boast, "It took me an hour to get to work this morning. I had to spend so much time shaking hands."

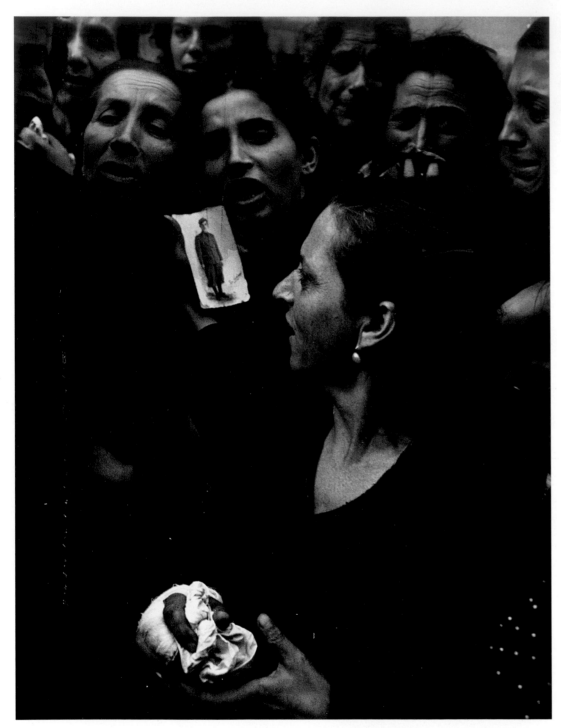

Naples
ROBERT CAPA
November 8, 1943

Robert Capa photographed grieving mothers at the funeral of 20 schoolmates in Naples who were killed during four days of guerrilla fighting with the Germans.

"I entered the school and was met by the sweet, sickly smell of flowers and the dead," wrote Capa. "In the room were 20 primitive coffins, not well enough covered with flowers and too small to hide the dirty feet of children—children old enough to fight the Germans and be killed, but just a little too old to fit in children's coffins."

James Leavelle
BOB ADELMAN
November 1983

Dallas detective James Leavelle was handcuffed to Lee Harvey Oswald as Jack Ruby approached and shot his prisoner dead.

Twenty years later, Bob Adelman photographed Leavelle and six others who had been caught in the events around the assassination of President John Kennedy. "I wanted them to remember it freely and show me how it felt," says Adelman.

Standing in the spot where the shooting took place, Adelman asked Leavelle to run through what he'd done that Sunday. Then, as the retired detective held a photograph of the crime taken by Bob Jackson of the Dallas *Times Herald,* Adelman kept peppering him with questions: "How tall was Oswald? What did he say? Did he walk right along with you?"

"There's a level of concentration and concern you can bring to a portrait session that lends it gravity. This was the most important event in Leavelle's professional life.

"But I don't remember what he answered," Adelman confesses. "My hands were full trying to find an instant in the present that would let us see into a moment in the past."

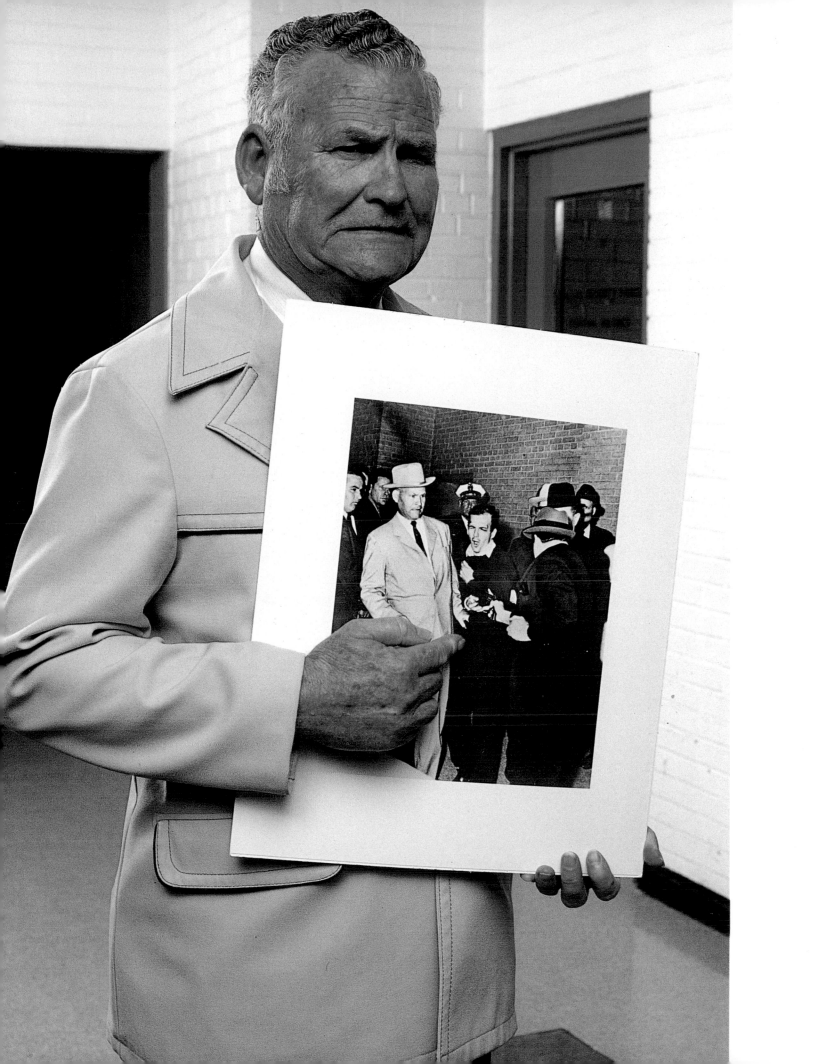

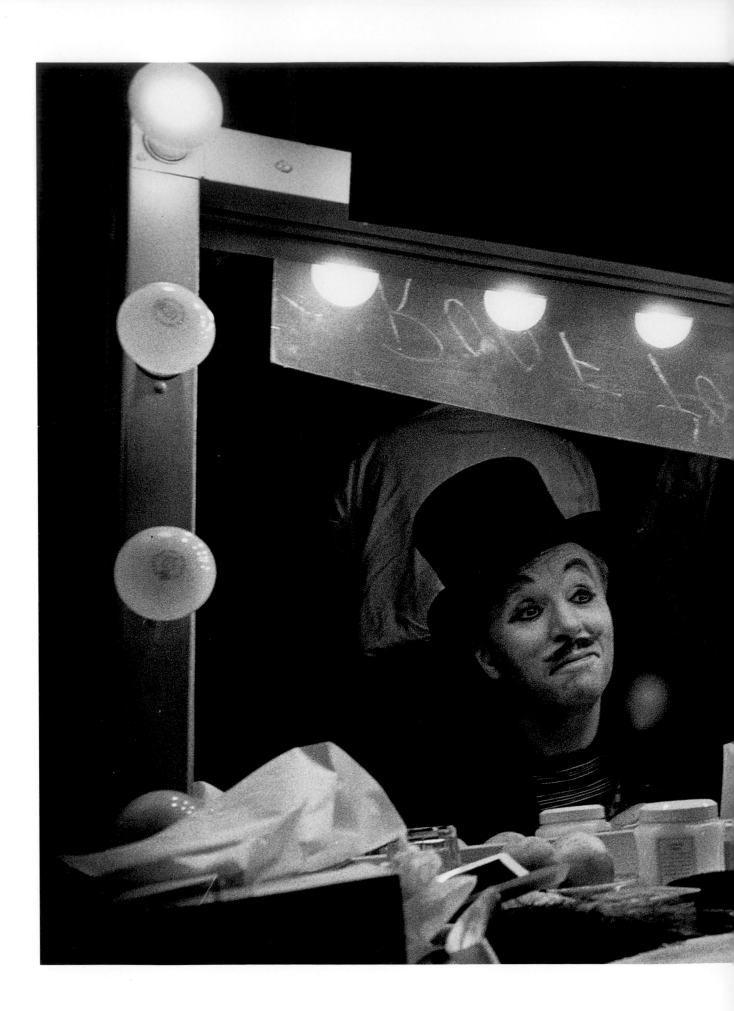

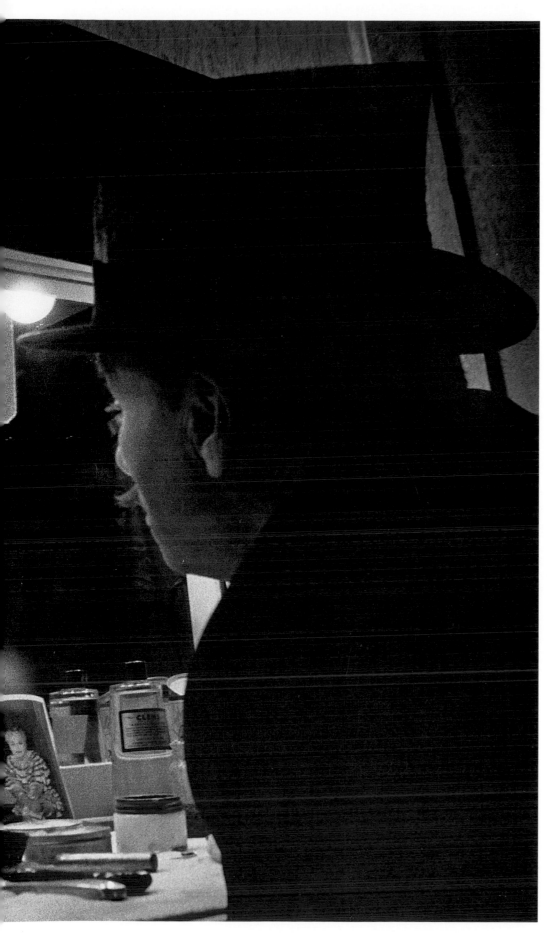

Charlie Chaplin
W. EUGENE SMITH
March 17, 1952

"For more than 30 years," wrote *Life,* "wherever movies have been shown, Charlie Chaplin has been top ringmaster of the best loved human sound—laughter. Not a single film Chaplin has made has lost money." W. Eugene Smith photographed Chaplin making his 81st picture. *Limelight's* hero, a gone-to-seed comedian, nurses a young ballerina back to health. In return she enables him to perform his last, greatest show in which he plays a variety of parts. As Chaplin put on makeup for these scenes, Smith photographed him becoming a clown, a comic violinist and, here, an animal trainer.

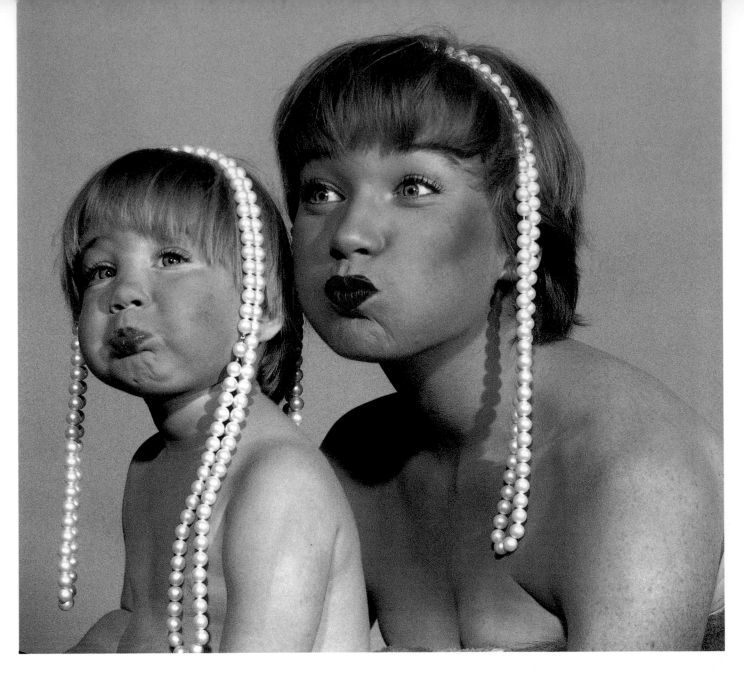

Shirley MacLaine and Sachi
ALLEN GRANT
February 9, 1959

"It was not how I planned it at all," says Allen Grant. His subject, actress Shirley MacLaine, was married to producer Steve Parker. Their daughter Sachi, a startling 2½-year-old look-alike of her 24-year-old mother, loved to upstage Mom by mimicking MacLaine's expressions. Knowing a good act when he saw one, Grant booked Parker & MacLaine for a cover.

On the designated date, the star was at home, but the second banana was four hours late, held up shooting a movie on another set. Like any other star-kept-waiting, Sachi, tired and ready for bed, pouted and refused to do her act when MacLaine finally arrived. Mom, however, came up with a plan. Using a mirror held beside the camera, Shirley began to imitate whatever her daughter did. From everyone's point of view, most of all Sachi's I suspect, this worked just fine.

"Sachi," said Shirley, "is a ham."

Madonna
JURGEN VOLLMER
April 1987

When expressions cross the President's face at a news conference, television viewers hear *zlonk-zwing, zlonk-zwing, zlonk-zwing* in the background. This sound comes from motorized still cameras recording the scene. If photographers taking pictures on a Hollywood set produced that kind of racket, the director would shoot them dead.

Therefore when Madonna stepped from a Checker cab onto a New York street during the filming of *Who's That Girl,* Jurgen Vollmer had his camera in a "blimp"—a specially made box with an electric shutter button on the outside and a glass window for the lens. No sound escapes.

"Shooting stills on a movie is very frustrating," explains Vollmer. "At best you're tolerated. But you have nothing to contribute. You're not involved in the *creation* of the film."

Vollmer has a reputation at Warner Brothers for finding "what hasn't been seen before." Such a talent may have been helpful to Madonna, who had noted, "The fact that I have something to offer has been accepted, but I don't think Hollywood is sure of what it is."

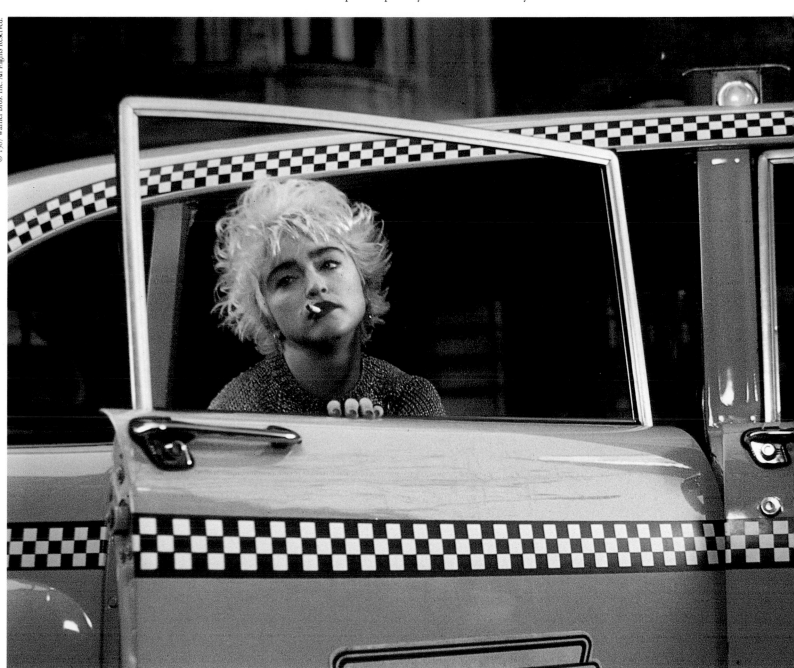

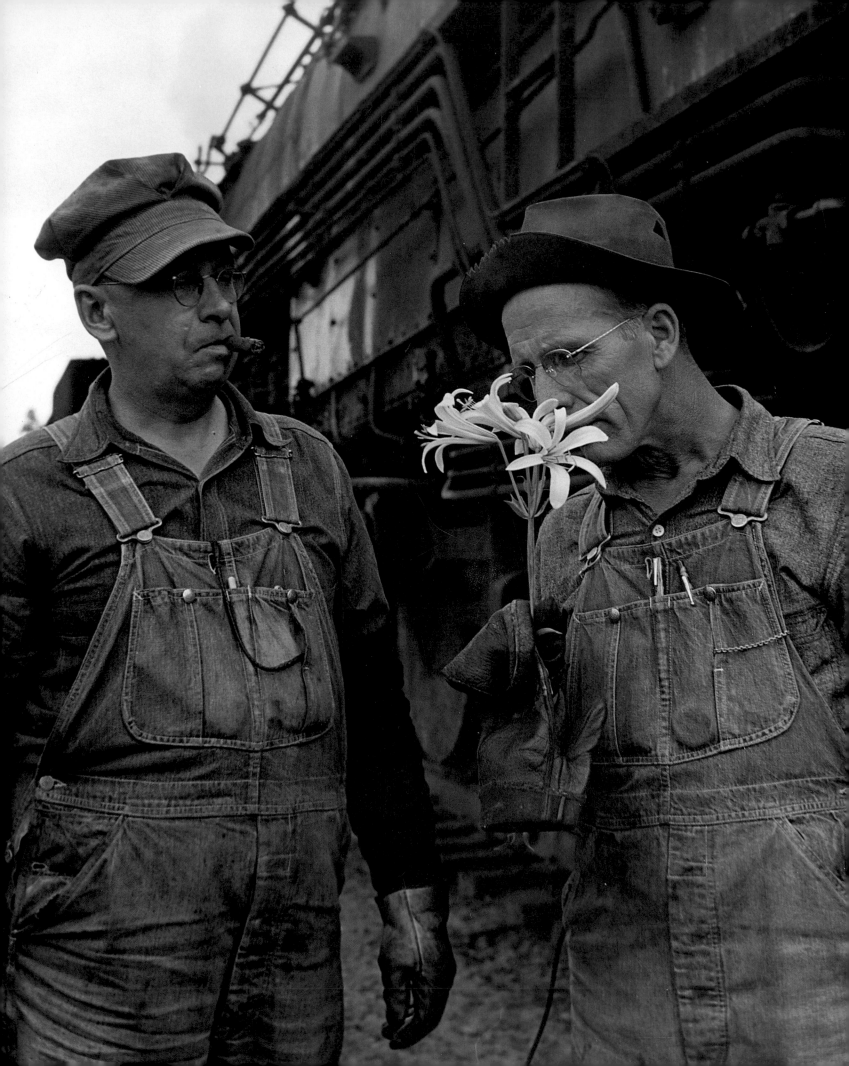

Railroad Men
PETER STACKPOLE
September 21, 1942

Photographing the nation's railroads as they adjusted to the work of war, Peter Stackpole was riding a Southern Pacific freight train from Sacramento to Reno. When the train stopped on a steep downgrade for the regulation cooling-off period, brakeman Harry Martin spied a tiger lily beside the track, and engineer Jimmy Belote waited his turn to get a sniff, neither of which they were trained to do.

Ouch!
SVEN-GÖSTA JOHANSSON
November 29, 1954

"Sent out to photograph the hazards of boxing," said *Life*, "Sven-Gösta Johansson of Stockholm came by chance on a remarkably pliable model. He was Stig Forsberg, who was pitted against another Swedish amateur, Bjoern Lindquist. Right in the first round, as Johansson started his picture taking, Stig forgot to duck and was caught looking cross-eyed at a solid punch in the nose. Later, when he saw the picture and got a more detached look at the punch, Stig remarked, *'Det var som tusan,'* or, 'Well, ain't that the devil.'"

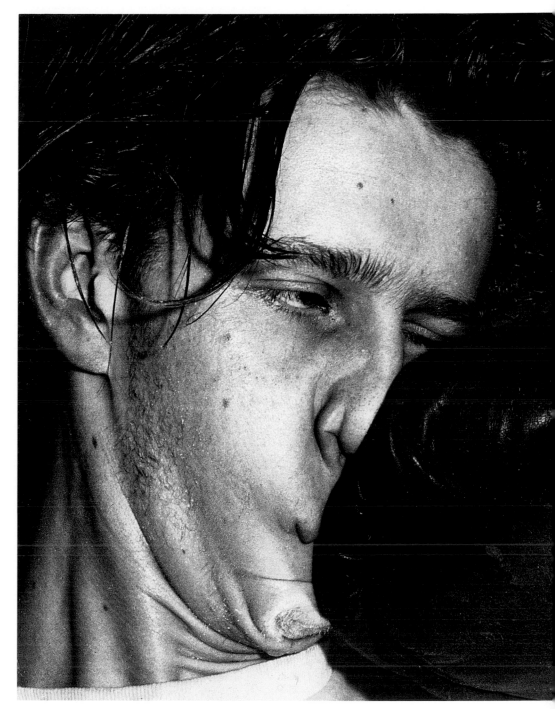

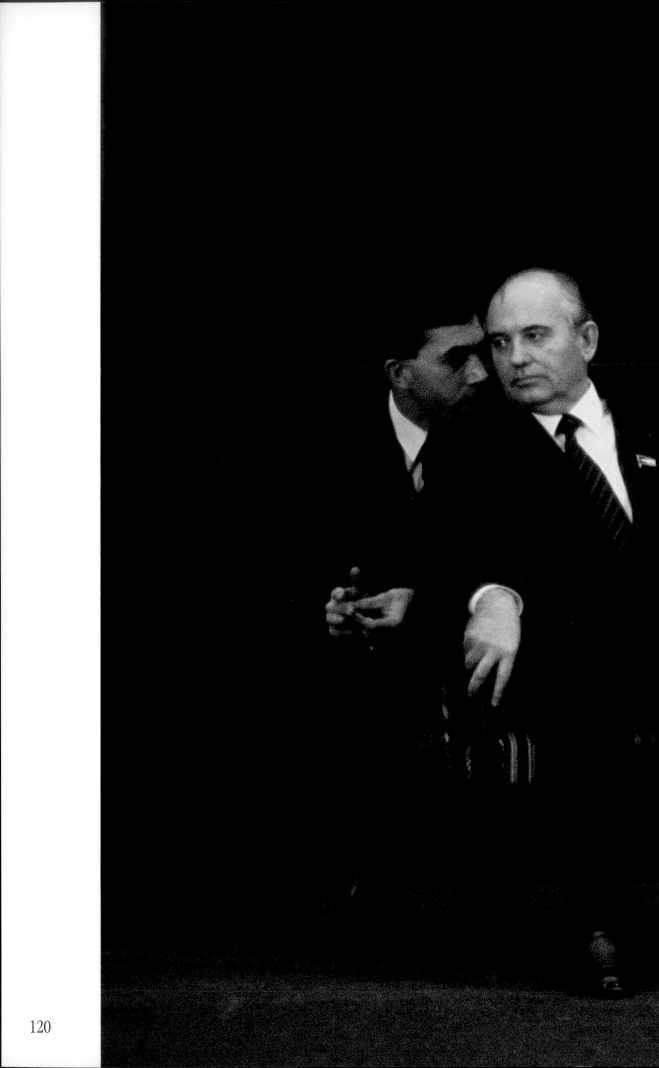

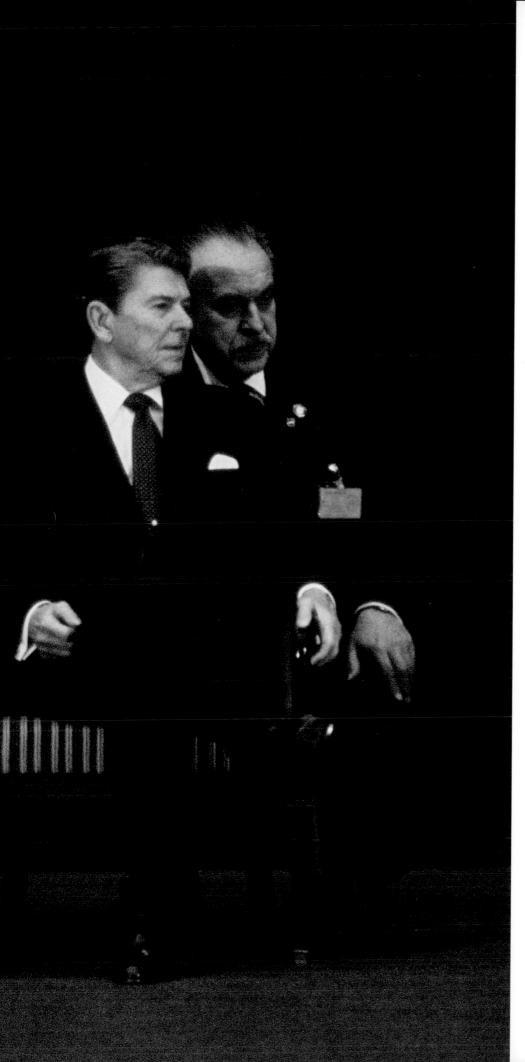

Summit Conference
DAVID BURNETT
Fall 1989

"I like the distraction between the two of them," says David Burnett. "They could each have been in their respective capitals. No one printed the picture in 1987 because everyone wanted to make the point about Reagan and Gorbachev being *together* for the first time. But sometimes things betray themselves. When you look through the camera, you see things people at the scene may not."

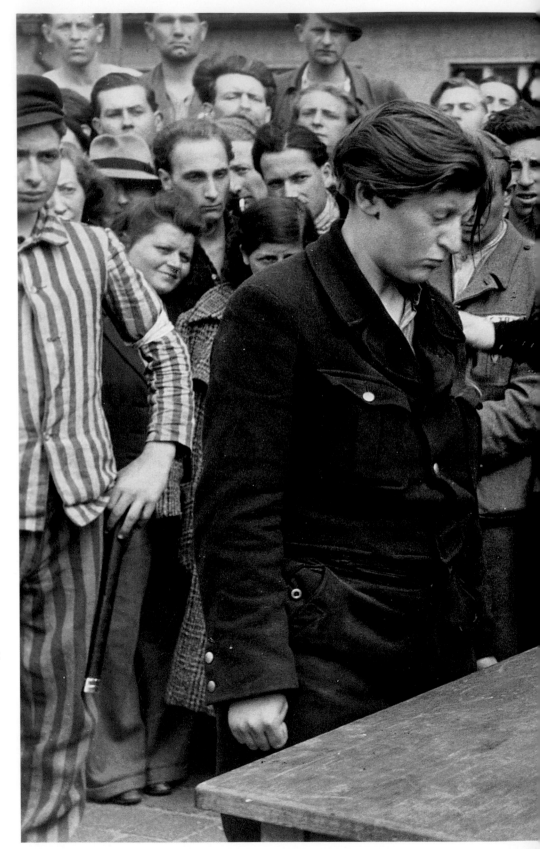

Dessau
HENRI CARTIER-BRESSON
March 3, 1947

In 1945, two years after his escape from a German POW camp, Henri Cartier-Bresson directed a documentary film, *Le Retour,* sponsored by the American Office of War Information and the French Ministry of War Prisoners. It recorded the return of French soldiers and civilians from German captivity.

Those imprisoned in Eastern Europe were processed in the German city of Dessau, on the border of the American and Soviet zones of occupation. Cartier-Bresson placed a U.S. Signal Corps cameraman high in a guard tower overlooking a compound, and he filmed this scene of one displaced person identifying another as a Gestapo stool pigeon.

In the movie the motion of the woman's slap passes in a blink, scarcely noticed. "However, I always kept a Leica with me," says Cartier-Bresson. Standing among the prisoners, he used it to freeze her expression of contempt and hatred forever.

"Sometimes there is a unique picture," Cartier-Bresson noted later, "whose composition so radiates outward from it that the single picture is a story in itself."

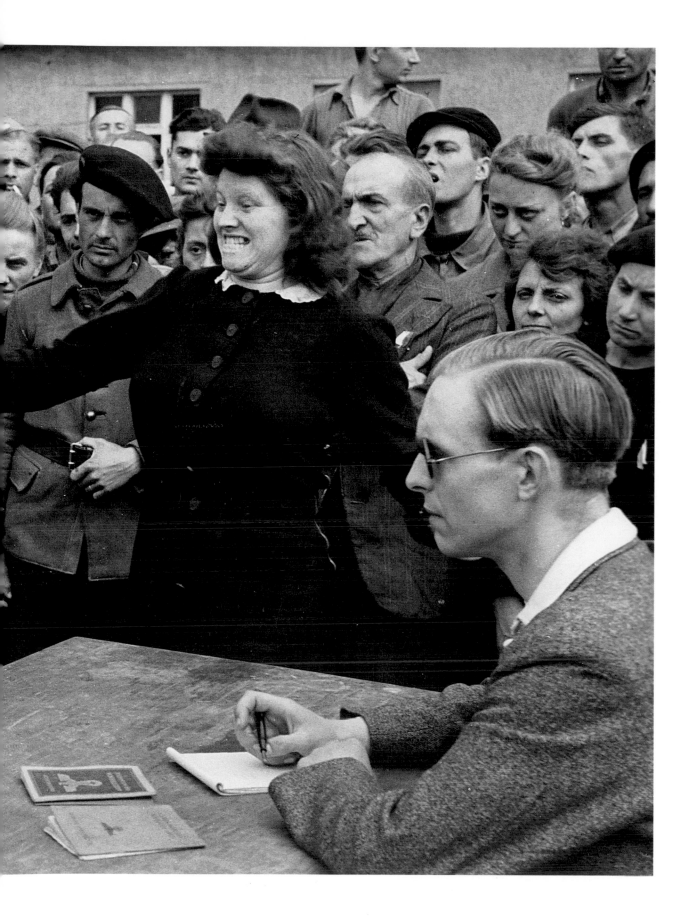

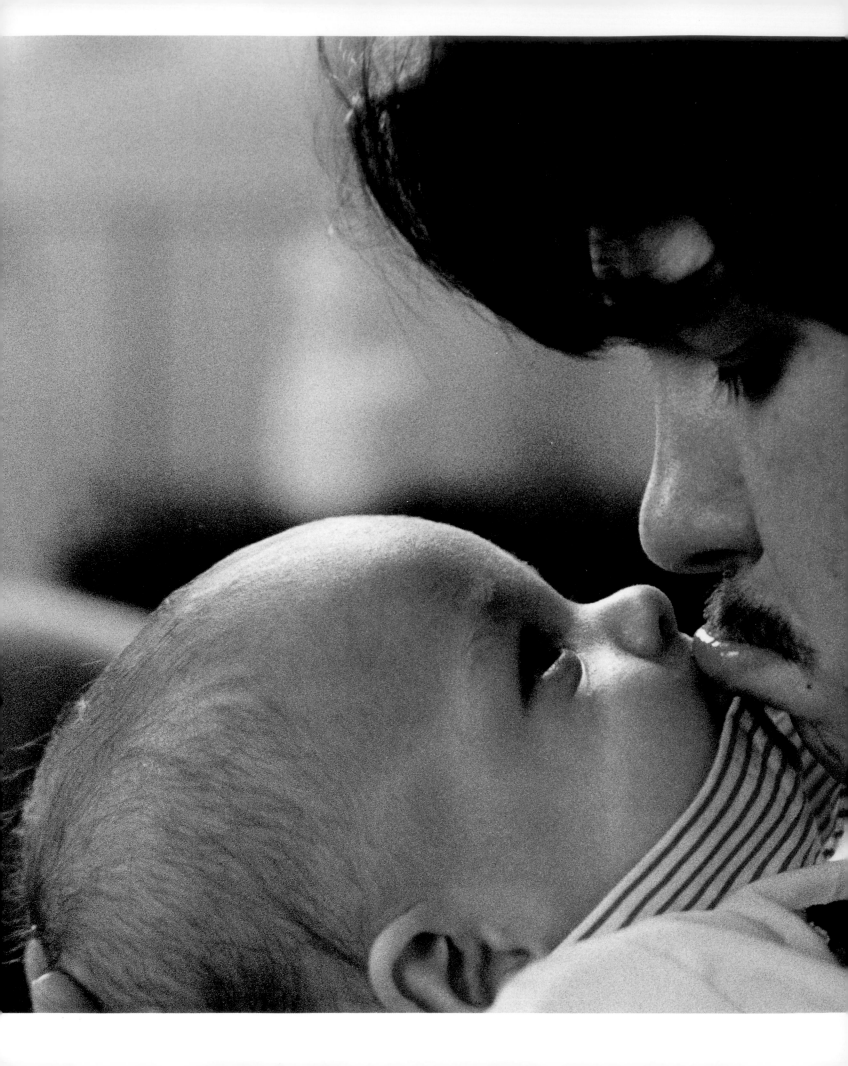

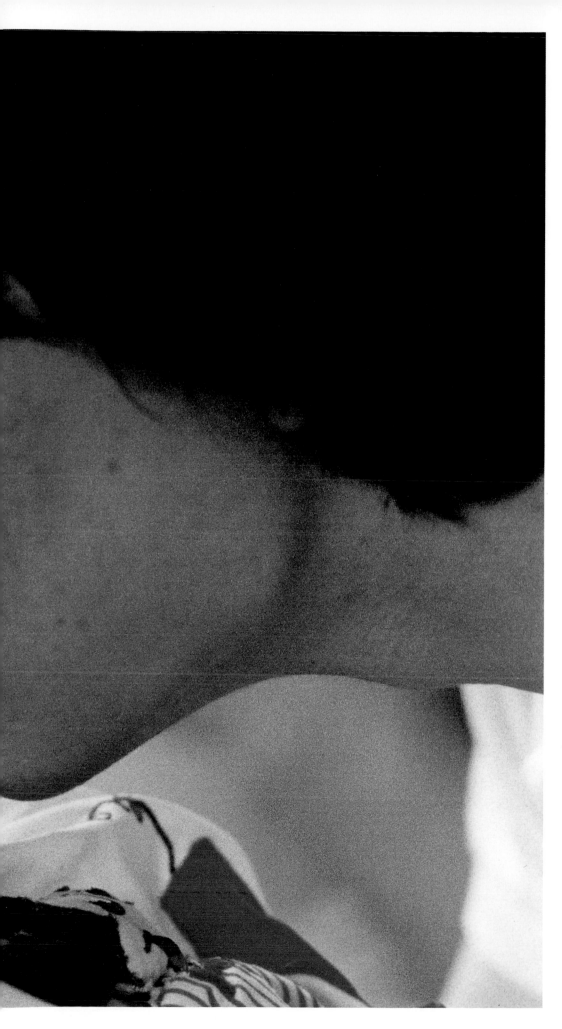

Teenage Father
BRIAN LANKER
June 1984

Ernie Desrosiers, 19, took part in a Portland, Ore., project that taught teenage boys the basics of diapering, burping and, most especially, nurturing their children.

"He seemed like a kid relating to a kid," says Brian Lanker, who photographed Desrosiers with his three-month-old son Zane (the mother was 16). "I don't suppose that he was bargaining for a baby."

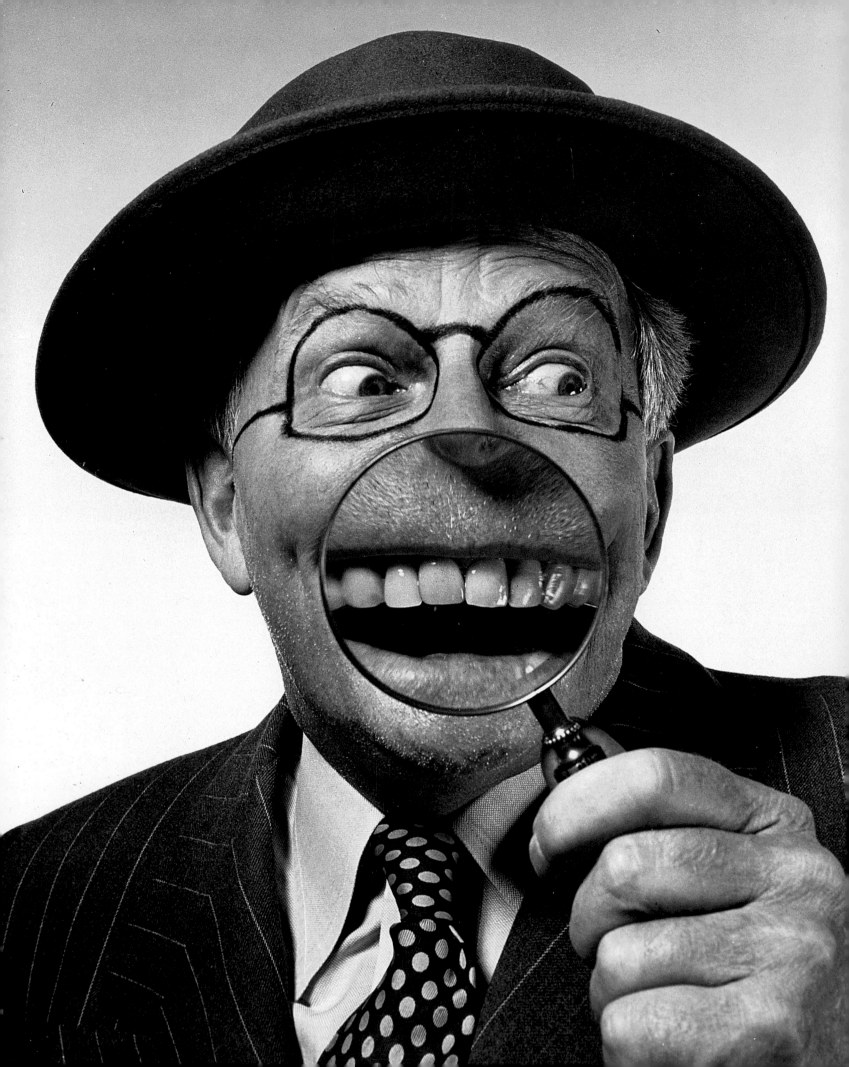

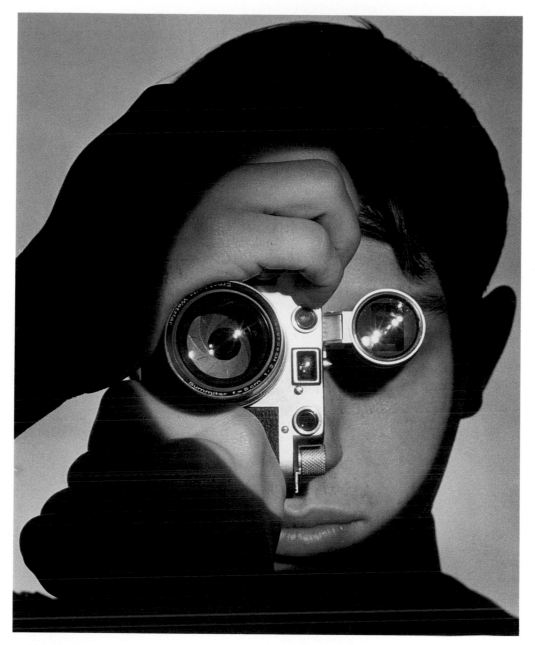

Bobby Clark
PHILIPPE HALSMAN
October 23, 1950

The Photographer
ANDREAS FEININGER
June 27, 1955

Comedian Bobby Clark horsed around from the moment he arrived at Philippe Halsman's studio on West 67th Street in New York City, at one point grabbing a magnifying glass. This was fortunate, because it provided an obvious picture opportunity for Halsman. It was even more fortunate that the glass was there in the first place. A common enough object in many photographers' studios, where it is used for looking at contact prints, it is a tool that Halsman, who had keen close-up vision without his glasses, never used.

When Dennis Stock won a contest for young photographers in 1951, *Life* asked Andreas Feininger to photograph him. "I don't know why," says Feininger, who is famous for his cityscapes and photographs of shells and skeletons. "I normally don't photograph people. We went to a studio where there were lots of lights handy and sort of fooled around. Actually this started a series of photographs I would do: I became fascinated with the strange things people put in front of their faces as part of their professions."

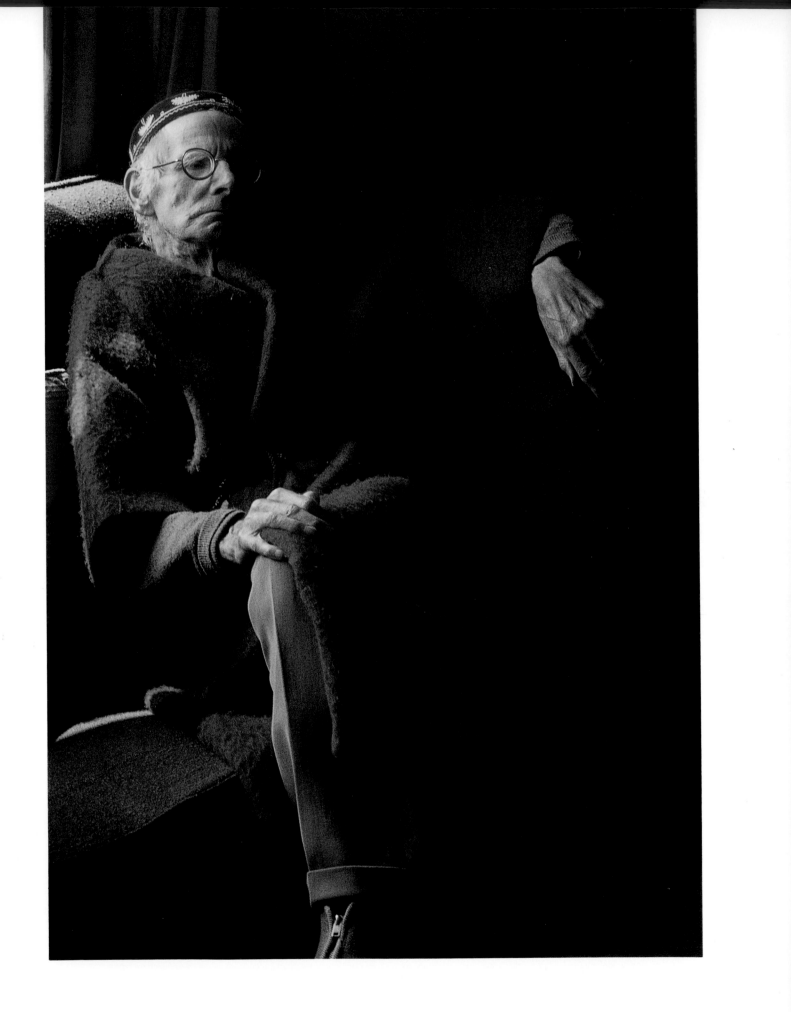

Sean O'Casey
GJON MILI
October 9, 1964

Gjon Mili visited his friend Sean O'Casey, the 84-year-old author of *Juno and the Paycock,* shortly before the playwright's death in Torquay, England.

"I raised my eyes and stopped," Mili wrote. "There at the top of the stairs stood Sean with his arms outstretched, like a tree with two branches. 'Is it you, lad?' he said. 'Is it you? I don't see very well now. In fact I hardly see at all.' I was so moved I was at a loss for words to answer.

"Next morning I found him once again, on the couch in the living room, decked out in a red, monklike robe which his daughter Shivaun had made.

"Though he had completely lost sight in one eye, and there remained only a last glimmer of vision in the other, he would place a photograph very close to his good eye, almost touching, and then by scanning he somehow brought all the details together and he would make a wry comment like, 'Oh, that's an experience! I couldn't have been very happy when you took *that* one, could I?'"

Samuel Beckett
LÜTFI OZKÖK
February 2, 1968

One photographer who photographed the author of *Waiting for Godot* described his session this way: "Samuel Beckett would meet visitors in a café near his home in Paris. He smoked small black cigars and drank small cups of coffee. He was always reluctant to have his picture taken. Every time I clicked the shutter, he sort of ground his teeth. I felt terrible. I could see something in his eyes, like an animal—he was just ready to bolt. I had wanted to take pictures as he interacted with others, but I had the feeling he didn't like candid pictures. If he posed, he expected to sit there and look at you, and that was that."

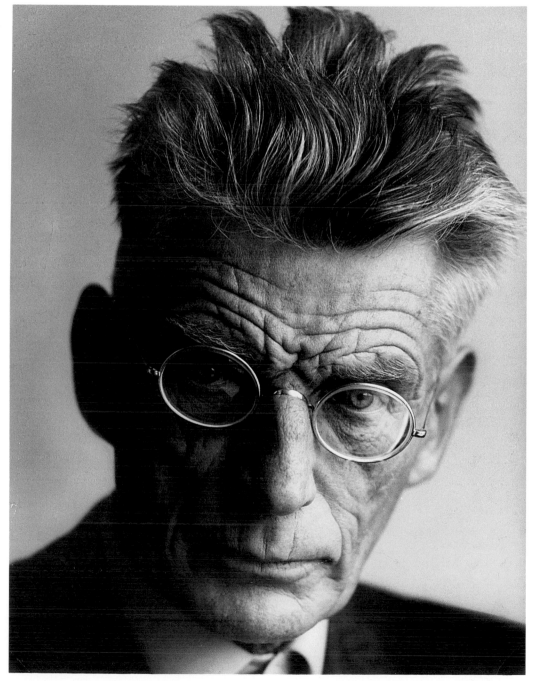

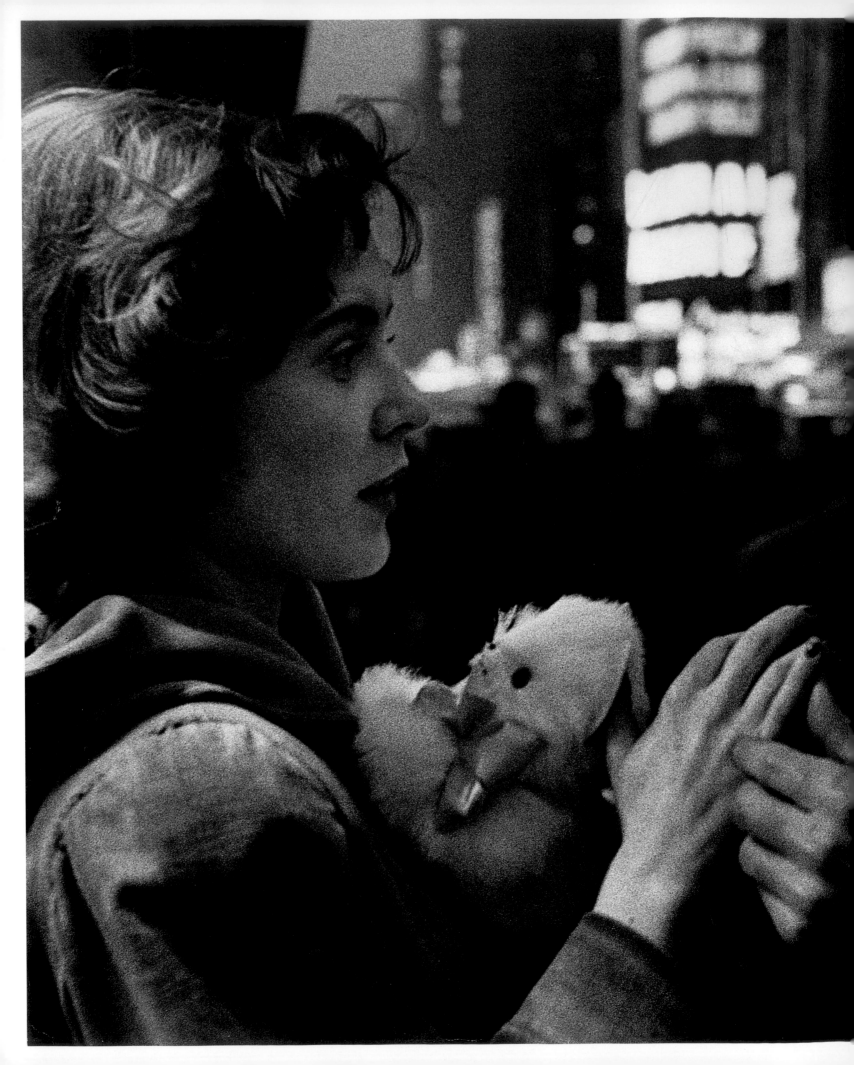

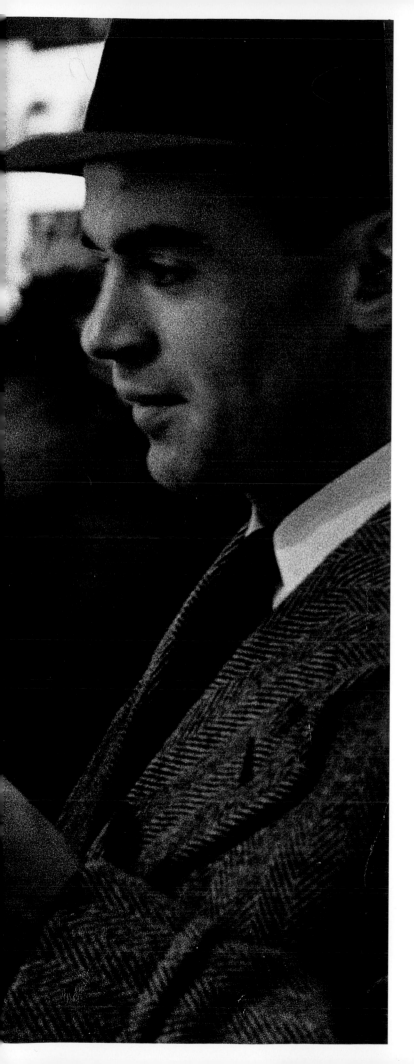

Career Girl
LEONARD McCOMBE
May 3, 1948

Gwyned Filling, 22, came to New York City from the Midwest, got a job as a copywriter with an advertising agency, lived with a girlfriend in a rooming house, and for the better part of a month was photographed by Leonard McCombe. The result was an intimate look at the life of a young career woman in the big city.

On a date with Carl Nichols, one of her two boyfriends, Gwyned spotted a toy cat in a shop window, and Carl bought it for her. She remembered that evening, *Life* wrote, "not so much because of what Carl said or how he looked, but because it was the night she acquired the cat." Gwyned—small surprise after we've read that—married the other fellow.

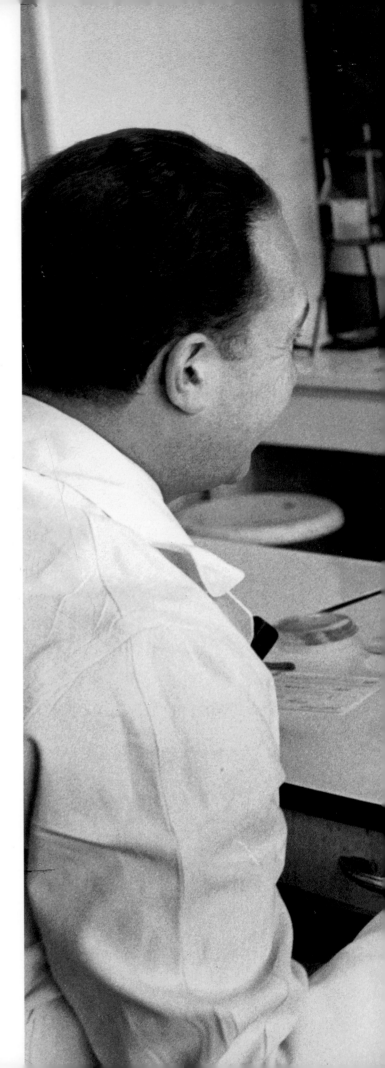

"Ooh! It's a Girl!"
WALLACE KIRKLAND
May 17, 1954

In Chicago, Mrs. Jane Dill, four months pregnant, reacted to the news that her next child was going to be a girl: "Oh, I'm so glad! I have one little girl already. Now I'll have two."

Mrs. Dill had put a tiny paper wafer soaked in a secret formula on her tongue. When the paper was treated with another secret chemical and didn't turn purple, its promoters claimed that no male hormones were present in her saliva. The process, which had proved 98% accurate in France, according to its backers, left "most scientists profoundly skeptical," *Life* reported.

In fact, Mrs. Dill did have a girl a few months later, but the wafer proved correct for only two of the other four mothers in *Life's* story, suggesting that a wafer held on a tongue is no more accurate than a coin flipped on a finger.

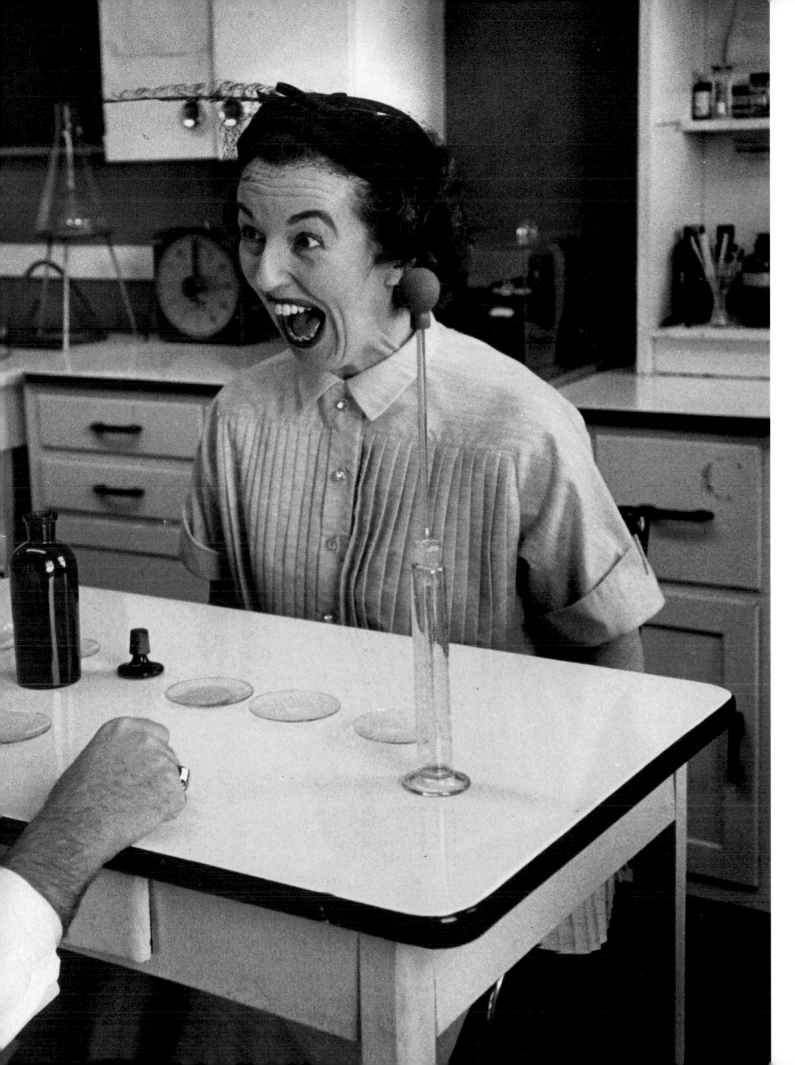

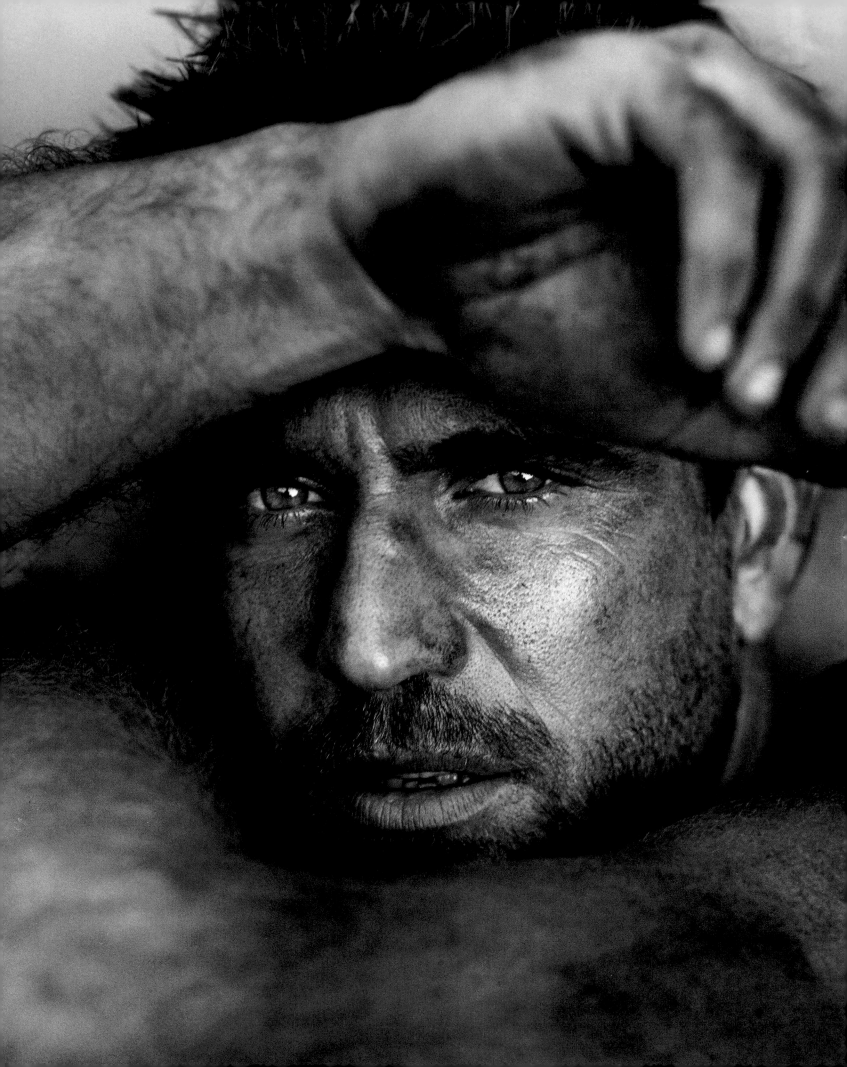

Mel Gibson
HERB RITTS
Fall 1988

"I told Mel Gibson I wanted to take some pictures of him alone," says Herb Ritts, "and we went outside my studio to a small parking lot.

"It was toward sunset. We'd worked all afternoon with Tina Turner on pictures to promote their movie *Mad Max Beyond Thunderdome*.

"'Just go over to the wall,' I said. Gibson squatted down on his haunches. He'd had a few beers during the afternoon. I think he was mellow. The picture is of the man, not the star. It's unglamorous glamour. It's the crooked teeth. The eyes so piercing. I think 50 years from now, when no one remembers Gibson or me, this picture will be just as good as it seems now."

Larry King
MICHAEL O'NEILL
March 1983

"I like to look at details," says Michael O'Neill. "I want to look into people's eyes. Of course, some people try to keep their distance. Andy Warhol kept backing away every time I'd move close.

"I watched Larry King during his broadcast. He'd let the smoke roll out of his mouth, then inhale it through his nostrils. When I had my camera set up, I asked him to do it a dozen times, hoping I'd catch it right. When I saw the results I worried maybe it was too powerful—too much like the dragon of the airwaves. He isn't that. But he does set them on fire."

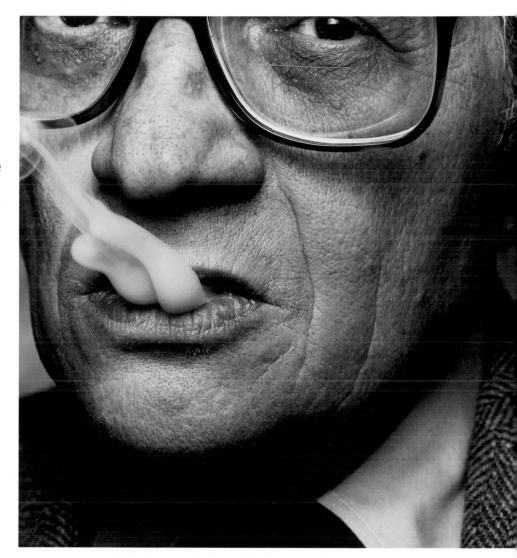

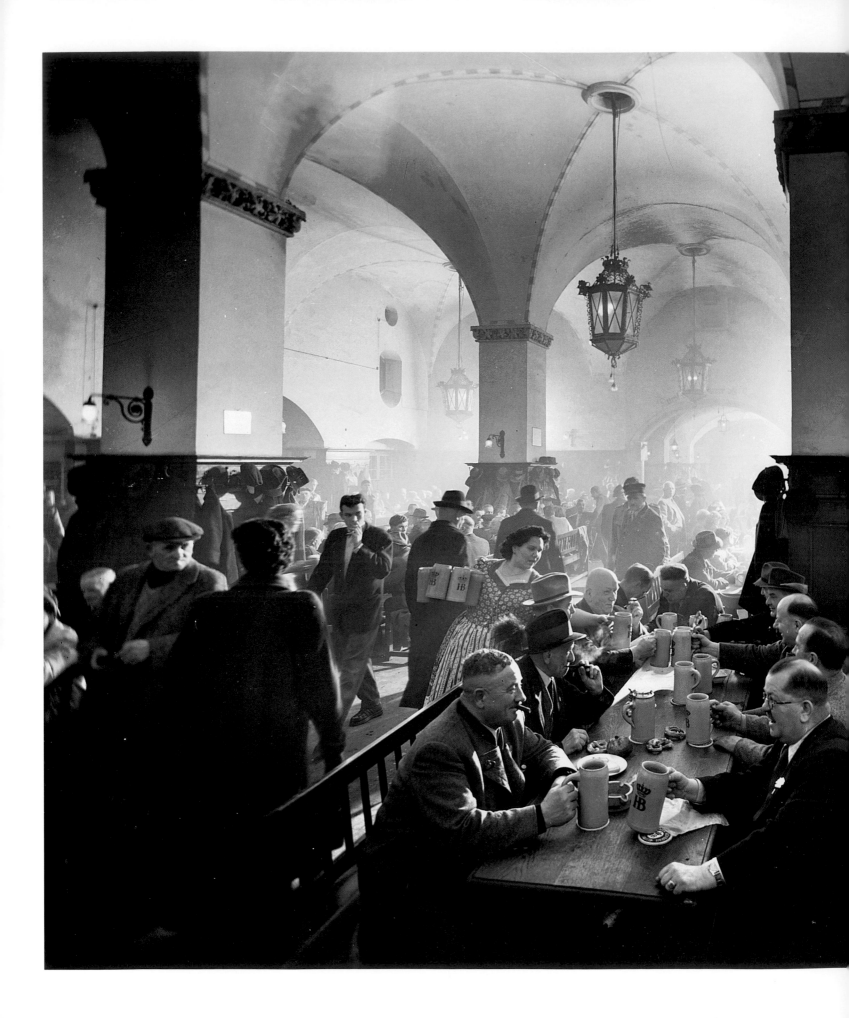

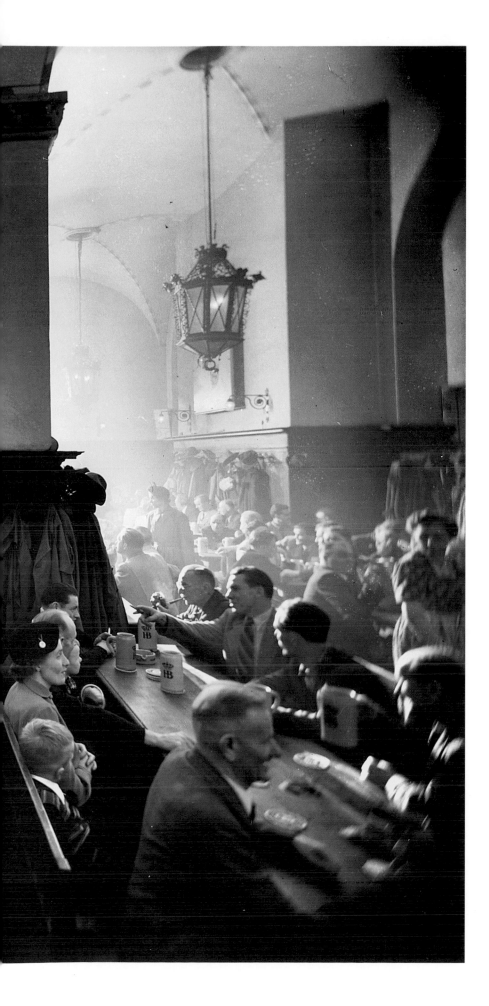

Gemütlichkeit
RALPH CRANE
May 10, 1954

Adolph Hitler first preached the doctrine of his new Nazi Party in open meetings at the Hofbräuhaus in Munich, which first opened for business in 1589. Oddly, *Life* reported, its 5 million customers in 1953 consumed only a bit more than a pint of beer apiece on the premises, hardly enough to wet their whistles. In Bavaria at the time, per-capita beer consumption was three quarts a day.

M. and Mme. Henri Bergeron
JOHN PHILLIPS
October 19, 1942

John Phillips was born in Algeria, making him a French citizen. His father was Welsh, which made him a British citizen too. His mother came from Troy, N.Y., which under the circumstances did *not* make him an American citizen. So two years after joining *Life's* staff in London in November 1936, Phillips came to the United States and got himself naturalized. Perhaps this background made him seem a good choice, in 1942, to photograph the French Canadians of Quebec, many of whom supported the French government at Vichy and considered General Charles De Gaulle a traitor.

Phillips worked alone, concentrating on the small town of Saint-Fidèle, where he found a conservative couple, Monsieur and Madame Henri Bergeron. "Having grown up in France," says Phillips, "I thought they were wonderful peasant types." From notes Phillips made, *Life* wrote that the Bergerons were "thrifty but not stingy, carefree but conscientious, full of laughter and piety." The photograph was later used in 1955 in the "Family of Man" exhibition at the Museum of Modern Art, where a legend under the picture read simply, "We two form a multitude."

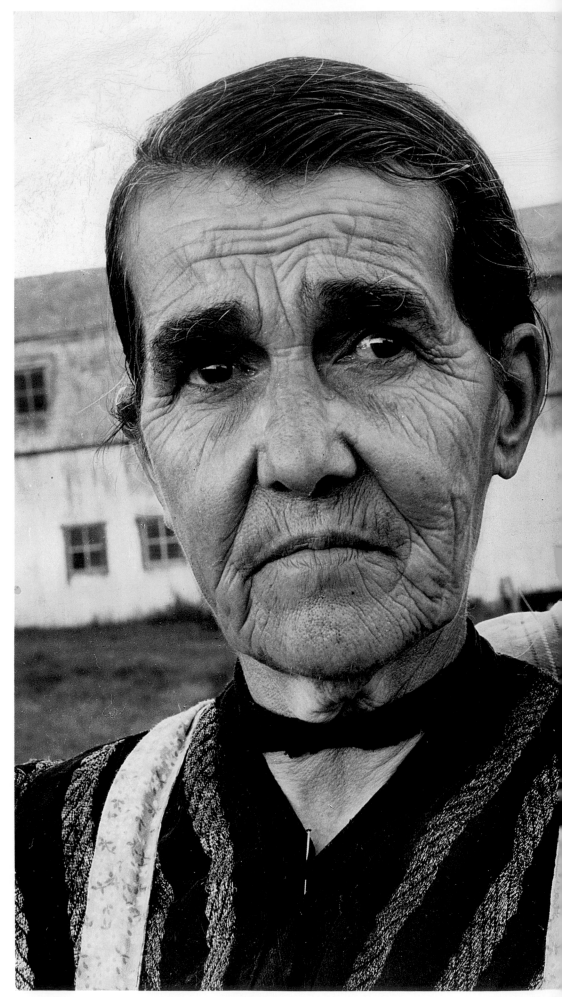

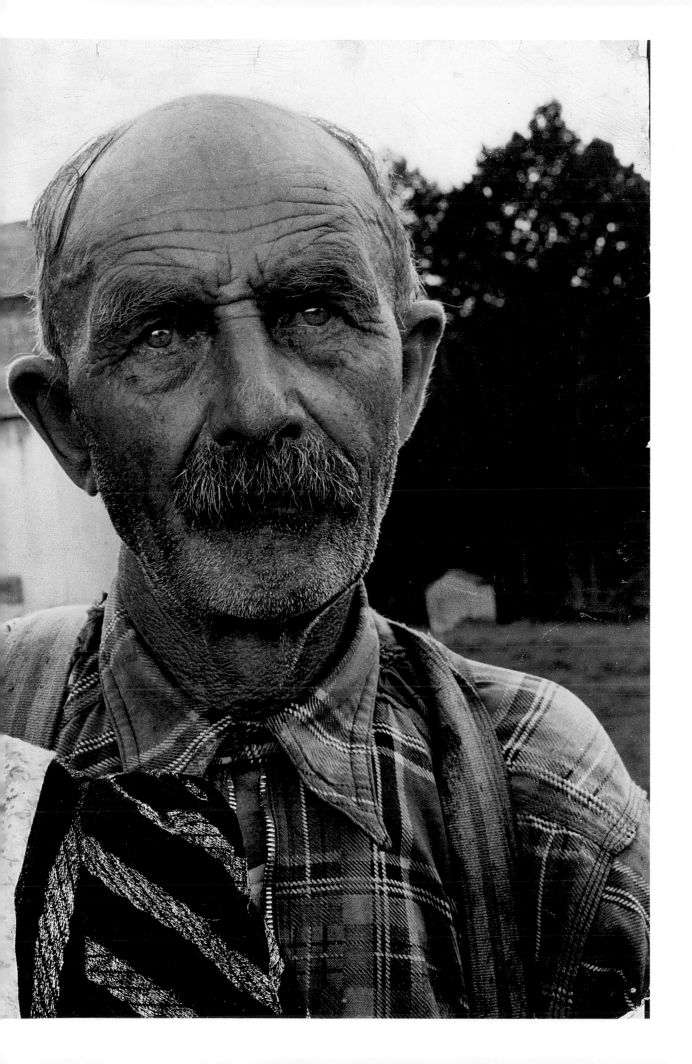

Mutiny
APRIL SAUL
June 1990

"Ring bearer Keith Walkowitz, 5, kept his dad waiting at the altar as his siblings and stepmother-to-be failed to persuade him to march down the aisle," reported *Life.* "Two months later," *Life* continued, "Keith was out of sorts again—at his mother's remarriage—but saved his protest for after the nuptials."

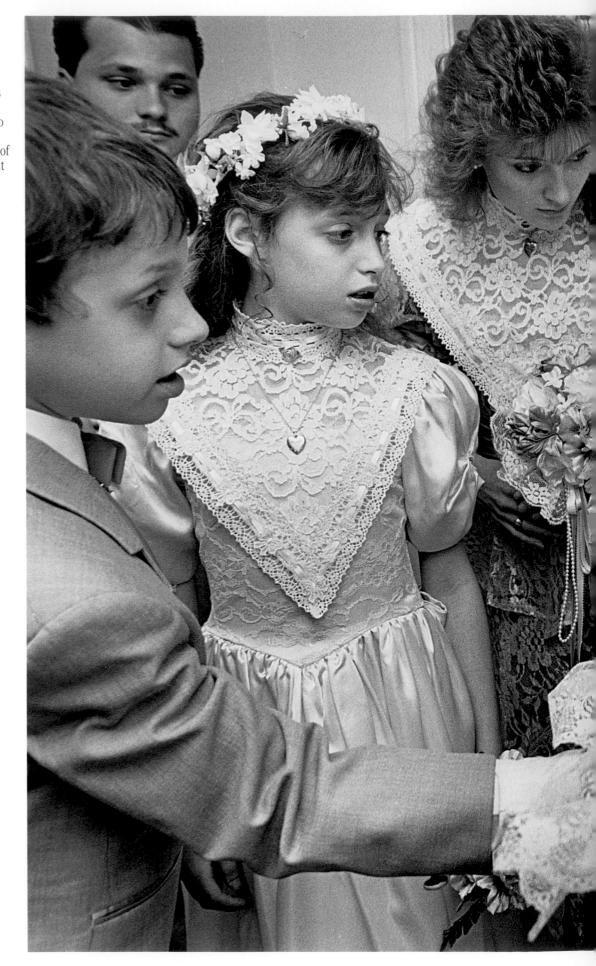

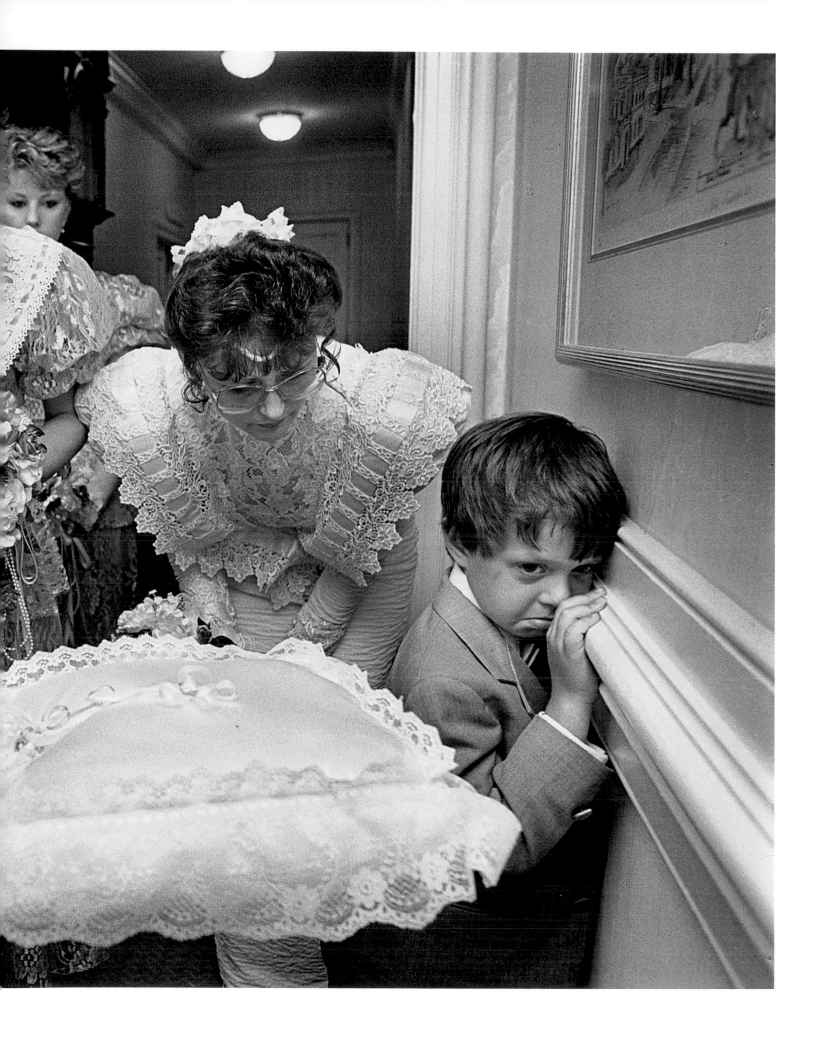

On Sunday, after church, two wire-service photographers sat in the White House Press Room waiting for the "lid" (an announcement that the President would make no more news that day and everyone could go home). Suddenly they were told to bring their cameras and were ushered into the Cabinet Room.

"We had about 30 seconds, and I made half a dozen exposures," says Stan Stearns of United Press International. "Afterward I said, 'That's a great picture, but what's all this about?'"

"Take your film to the office. Develop it. Print it. Then sit on it," answered Lyndon B. Johnson's press secretary. When the time for the President's televised address that night was fixed, the wire-service pictures were released.

Ostensibly, Johnson was working on his first major speech about Vietnam after the Tet offensive. But there was more. When a White House speechwriter told the President that a revision of the speech's ending was being worked on, Johnson replied with a smile, "I may have a little ending of my own."

He did: "I shall not seek, and will not accept, the nomination of my party for another term as your President."

Lyndon B. Johnson
STAN STEARNS
April 12, 1968

Spencer Tracy
J.R. EYERMAN
January 31, 1955

In 1930, when Spencer Tracy made his first screen test, his wife Louise wrote her sister to say, "Spencer does not photograph very well... For the present we are just forgetting talkies."

Before the year was out, however, Tracy had co-starred with Humphrey Bogart in *Up the River.* He would go on to win Oscars in consecutive years, 1938 and 1939, for *Captains Courageous* and *Boys Town,* respectively. To celebrate 25 years of proving Mrs. Tracy wrong (and to plug his 64th film, *Bad Day at Black Rock*), Tracy sat for his only *Life* cover.

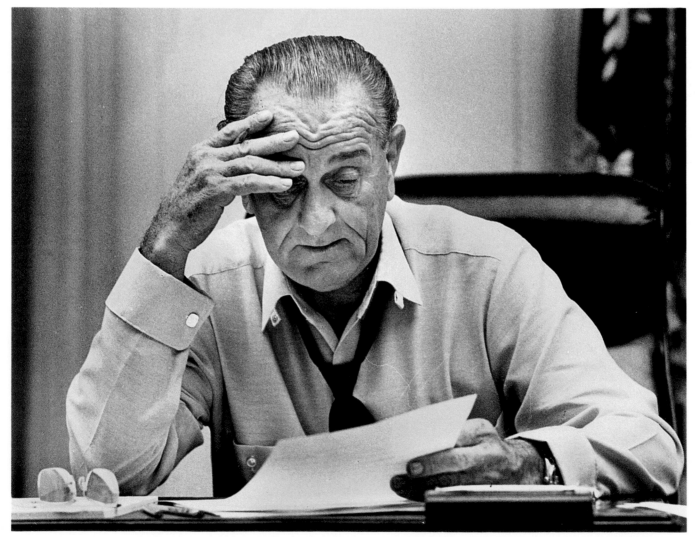

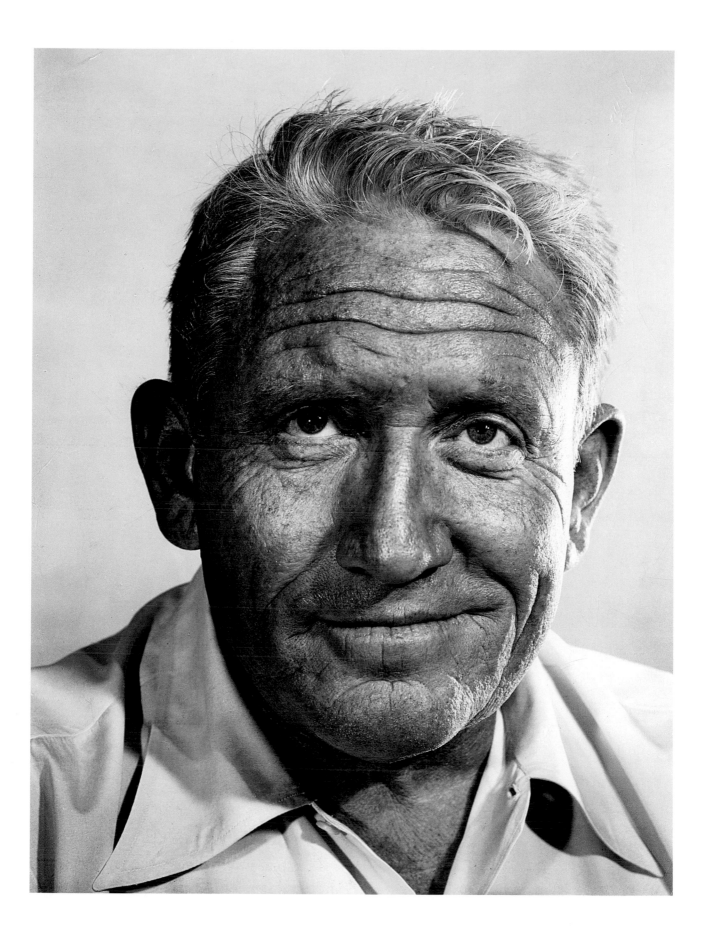

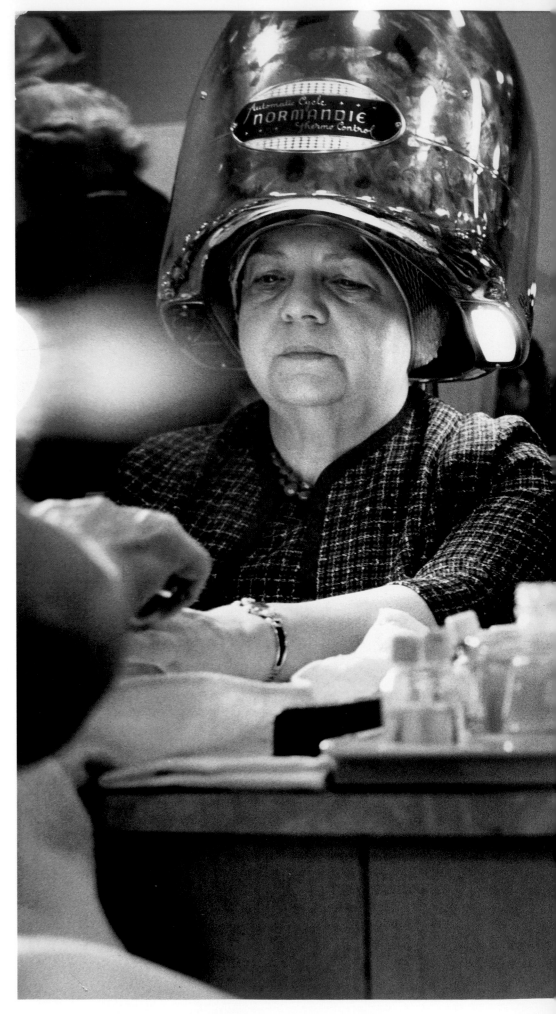

Preteen '62
BURK UZZLE
August 10, 1962

ooking a little ill at ease in the customarily adult world of the beauty parlor," wrote *Life,* "12-year-old Darlene Schaller of Chicago waits with the rest of the ladies while her 'New York cut and style' hairdo dries." This was a monthly treat paid for by her mom.

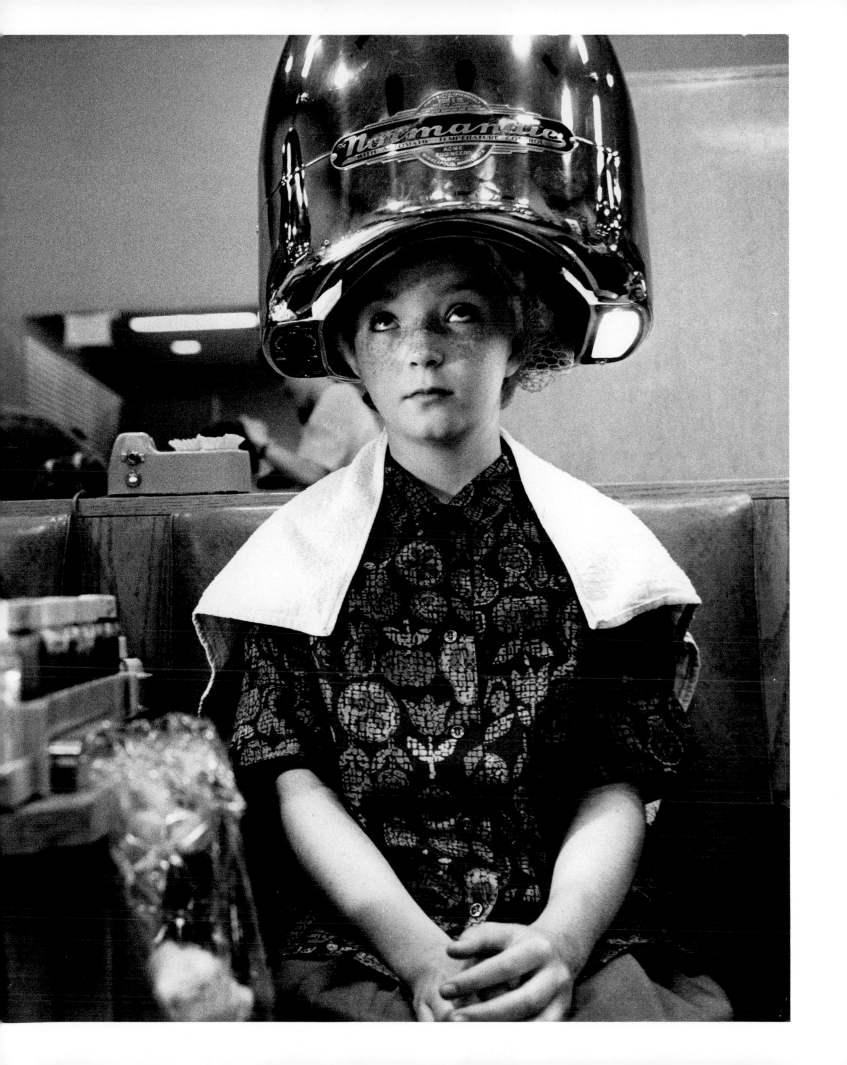

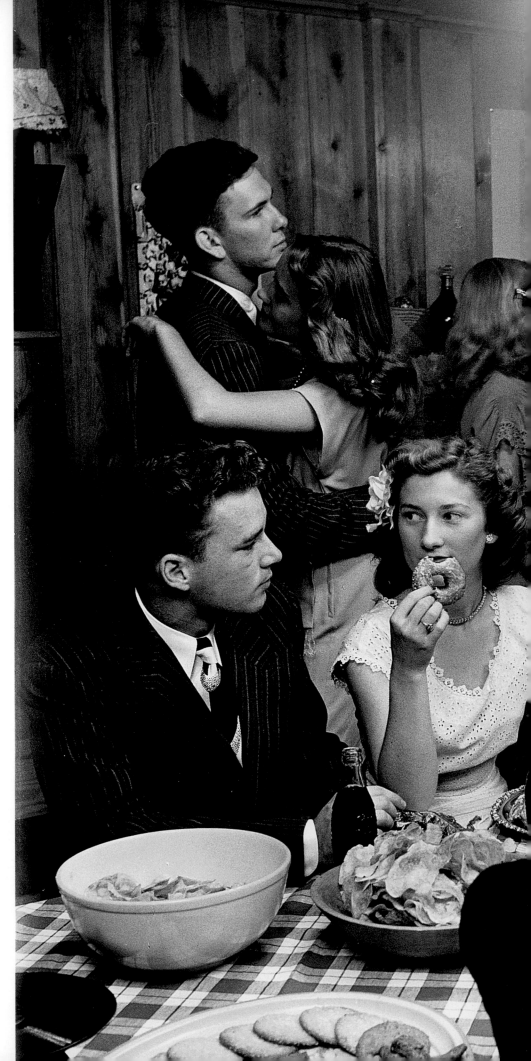

Teenage '47
NINA LEEN
August 4, 1947

In Tulsa, Okla., where identical twins Betty and Barbara Bounds were wearing identical flowers in their hair, teenagers danced to records of dreamy tunes like *Night and Day,* and generally everyone got home by just past midnight.

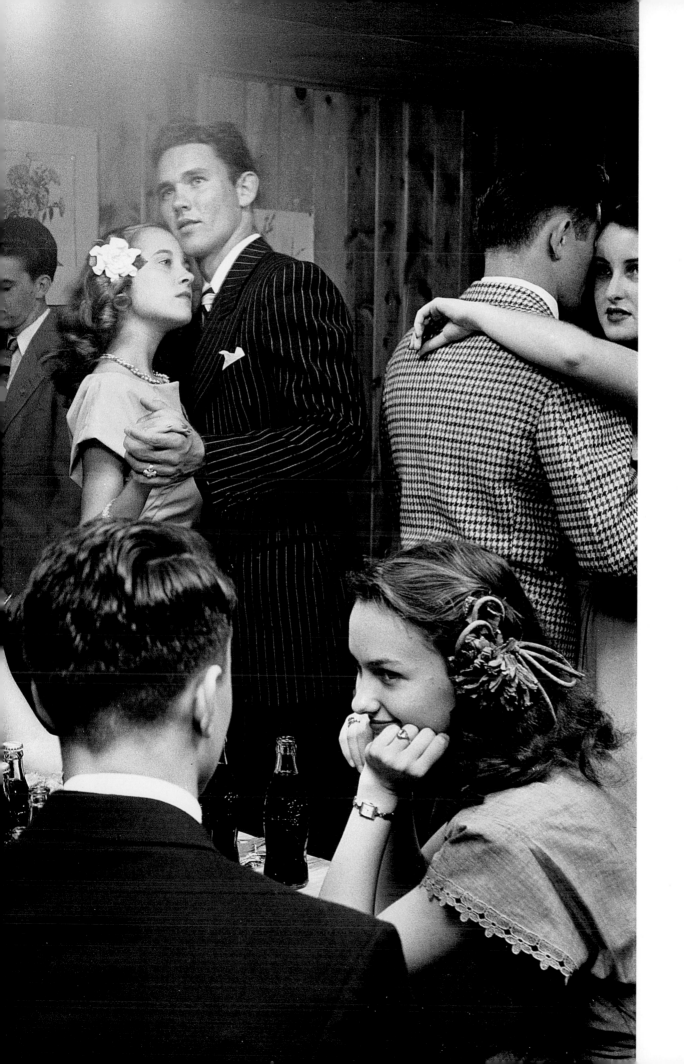

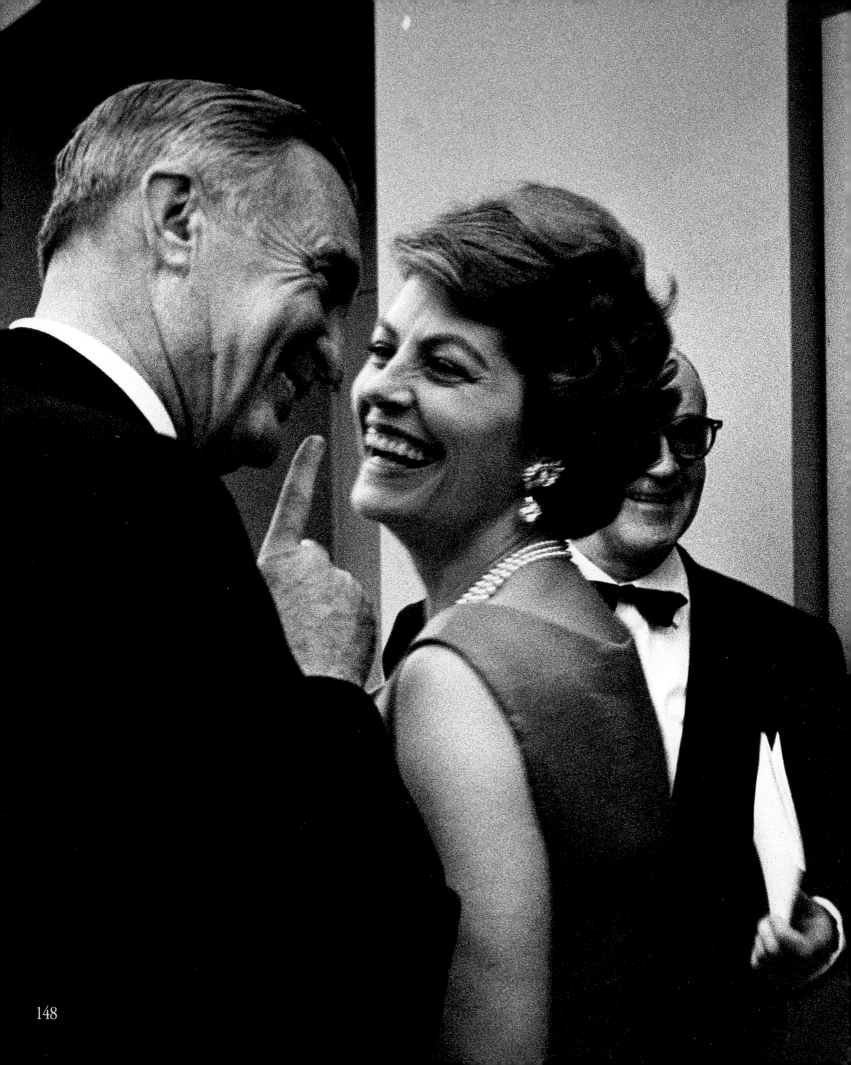

Nicole Alphand
EDWARD CLARK
July 13, 1959

"**N**icole Alphand," reported *Life*, "has proved herself almost everything that an embassy hostess should be: charming, intelligent, poised, friendly."

When she was shown Ed Clark's photograph of herself chatting with Missouri Senator and presidential hopeful Stuart Symington, the French ambassador's wife described the scene: "Here I watched a young girl go up and ask for his autograph. And so after she had gone, I went up to him and said, 'Oh, Senator, may I have your autograph too?' He laughed and said, 'Now don't you pull my leg.'"

Syngman Rhee
HOWARD SOCHUREK
October 30, 1950

"**T**he end of the war loomed as plain as the mustache on Stalin's face," *Life* wrote mistakenly when U.N. troops had captured North Korea's capital, Pyongyang.

On the veranda of his home in Seoul, South Korea's President, elderly Syngman Rhee, wore what *Life* described as "a victory smile as wide as the Han River."

By then, 3,800 Americans had died in Korea, a tidy price for a four-month police action. A few weeks after Howard Sochurek photographed Rhee, China would enter the fighting and prolong the conflict. When the war was finally over, $2^{1}/_{2}$ years later, U.S. dead totaled 54,000.

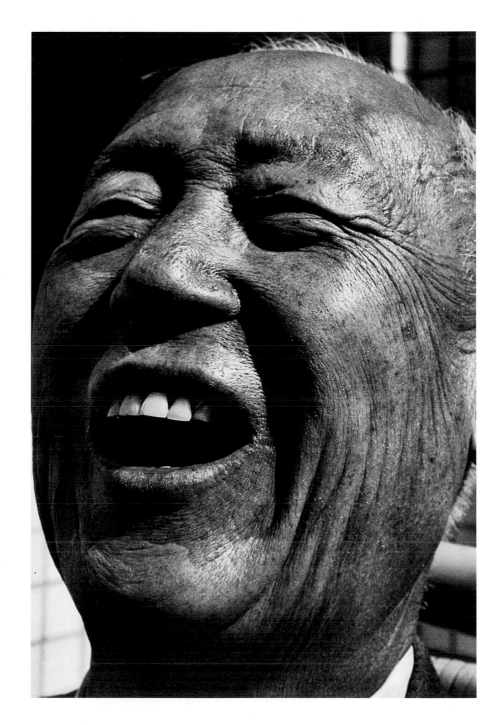

Survivors
UNKNOWN
May 19, 1941

Survivors from the English ocean liner *Britannia,* sunk by the Germans in the South Atlantic, landed on an island off Brazil after spending 23 days in a lifeboat. Photographed soon after reaching the mainland, several of the 13 British officers and men pictured here described the ordeal, during which 44 of the 82 men jammed into a lifeboat built for 50 had died.

"We took turns squatting and standing up. Our daily ration was a cracker and a teaspoon of condensed milk. For two weeks it never rained. When we sighted land, our navigator mumbled, 'I have done my duty. You are all safe.' Then he collapsed and died. At the sight of the Brazilian fishermen who found us, some of us fainted with happiness."

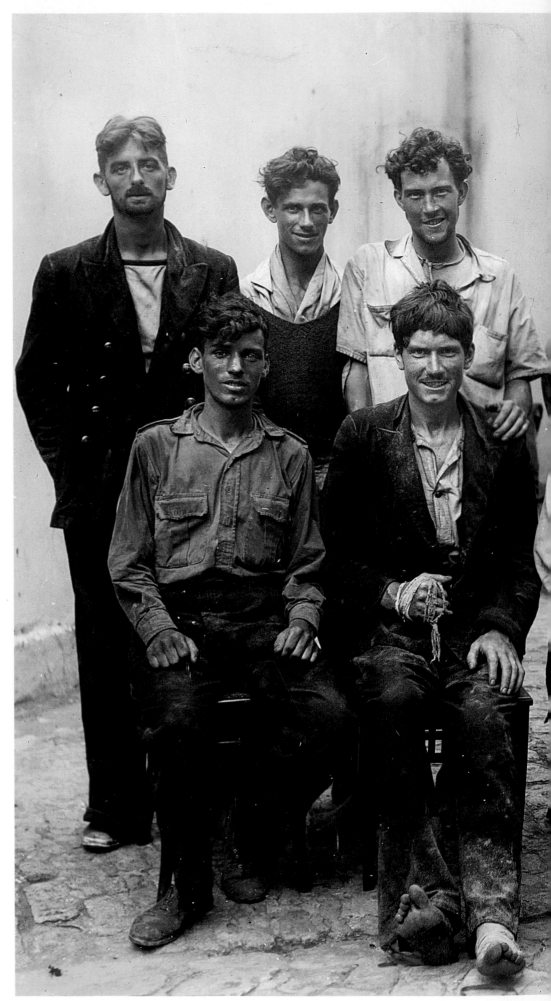

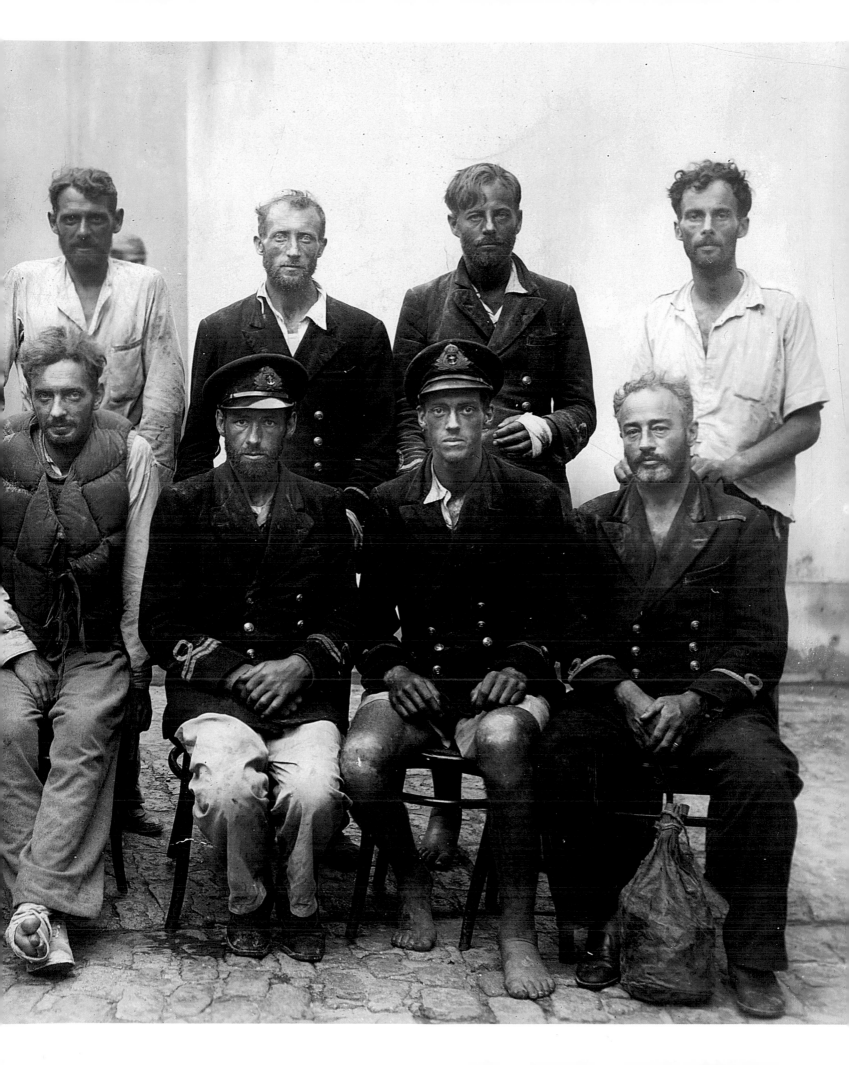

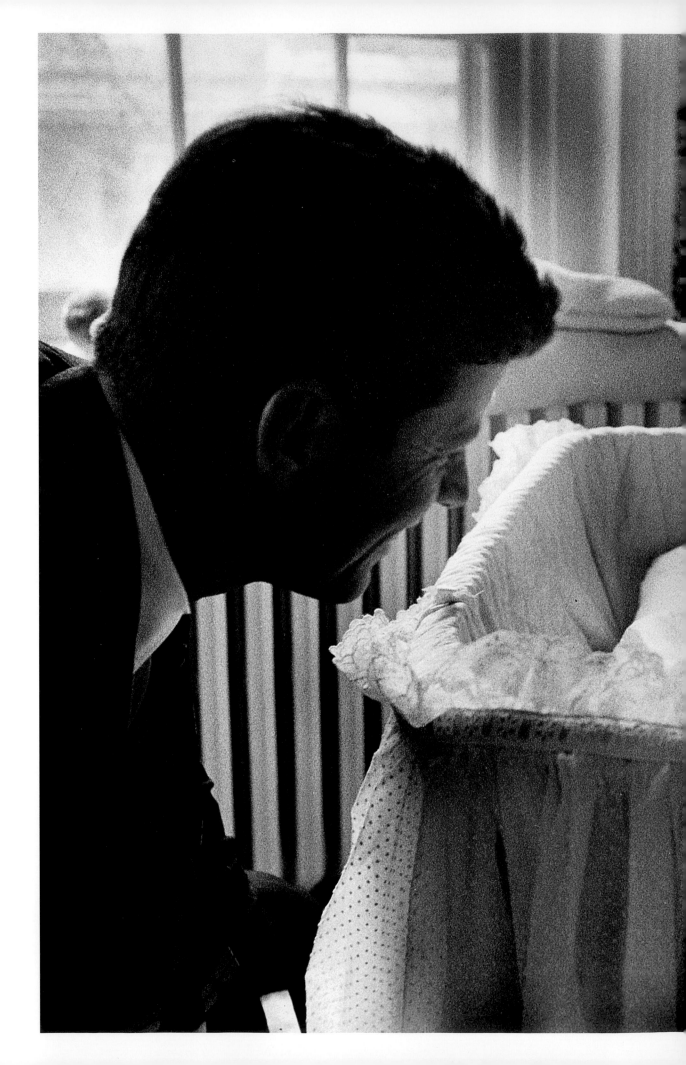

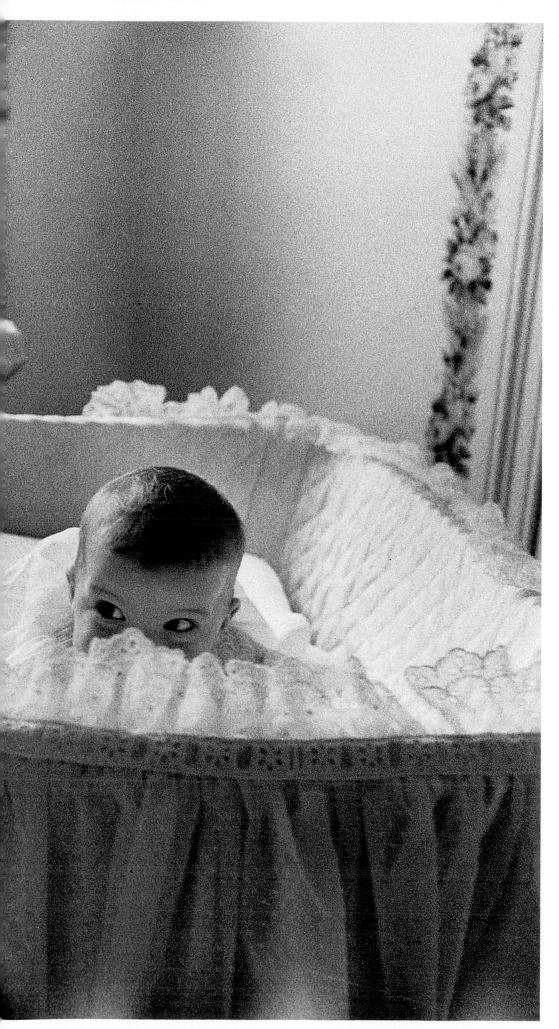

J.F.K. and Caroline
EDWARD CLARK
April 21, 1958

"I was doing a story on Jack Kennedy when he was a Senator, and after lunch at his home in Georgetown, I said that I'd love to take a picture of the baby," Ed Clark recalls. "'Oh, no, she's sleeping,' said Mrs. Kennedy. But Jack said, 'Let's see.'

"I still remember the way Jackie's heels clicked on the stairs as she came up behind us to the third-floor nursery, whispering, 'Please, don't bother her.'

"As her father came into the room, Caroline looked up—and that was the picture. When it ran, Jackie sent me a four-page handwritten note saying how much she liked the photograph and asking for 75 copies."

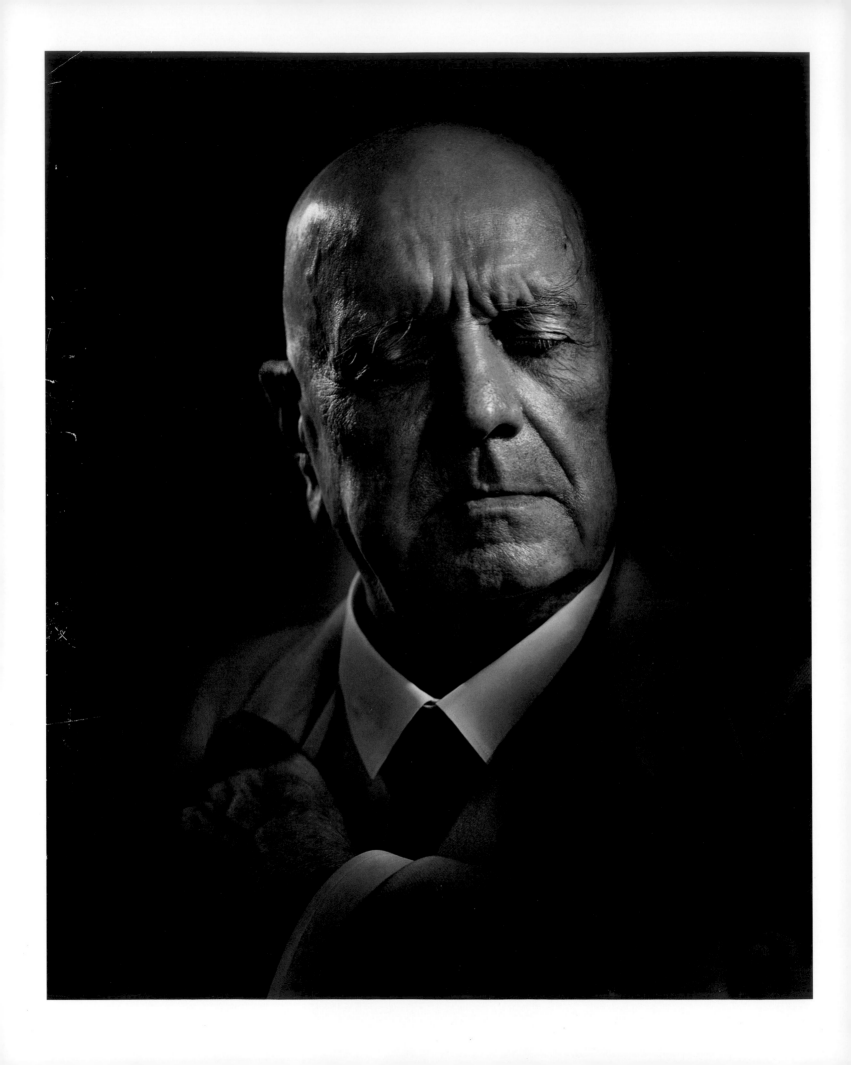

Jean Sibelius
YOUSUF KARSH
November 30, 1959

In 1949 Yousuf Karsh arranged to photograph the 84-year-old Finnish composer Jean Sibelius at his home 30 miles north of Helsinki. "For me," wrote Karsh in his autobiography, *In Search of Greatness,* "the strong somber strains of *Finlandia* resound from the portrait. And yet, the physical reality of the moment was rather different.

"The old gentleman's hand was shaking all the time I was with him, and the frailty of age was apparent in his voice and bearing. But the camera has almost limitless power of selection, and although the signs of age and the ebbing of life were there, it could still capture, in a fleeting second, the noble soul and immortal music of one of the world's finest composers."

Georges Rouault
ARNOLD NEWMAN
February 24, 1958

"Glowing like windows in a cathedral," *Life* wrote, "the paintings of Georges Rouault have shed their somber beauty across the world for nearly half a century." Arnold Newman visited the 85-year-old Rouault in Paris a year before the painter's death.

"Rouault came into the room, very feebly, with a little tiny stutter step, and sank into his chair," says Newman. "Since I could not ask him to move, I moved my camera and tripod around taking pictures from different points. Finally he said something, and his niece began giggling. 'What is it?' I asked.

"'He's photographed all around me, he says,' explained the niece. 'Does he want to photograph my derrière?'"

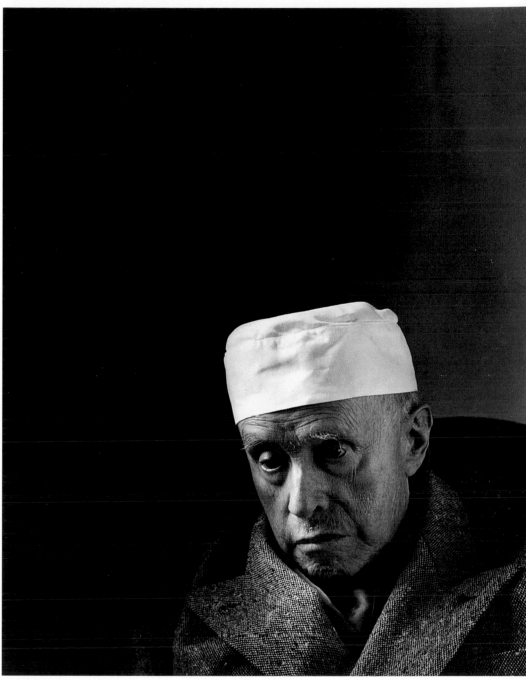

© *Arnold Newman*

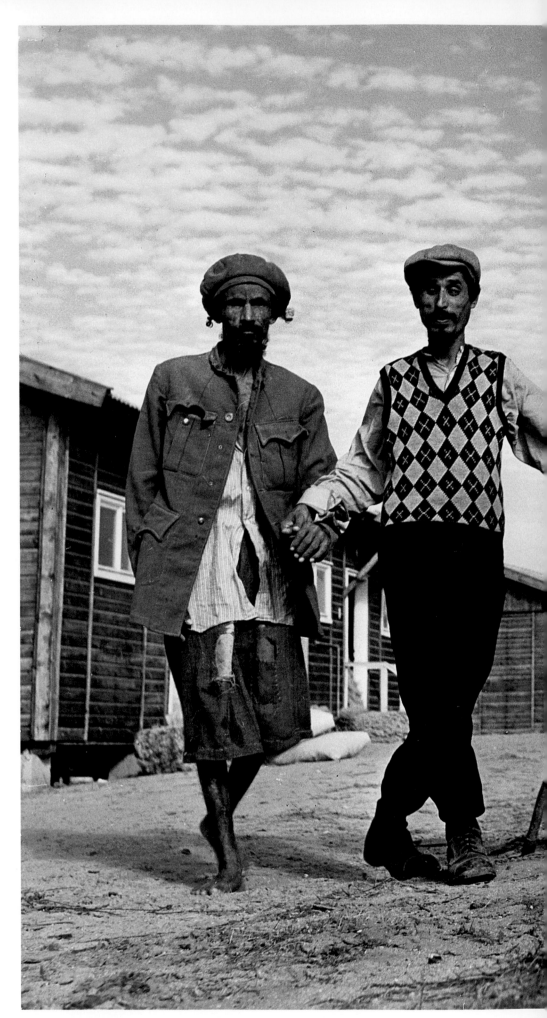

Israel
ROBERT CAPA
May 14, 1951

Robert Capa photographed three blind Yemeni emigrants in Israel as they were led to the dining hall by one of their daughters. Blinded by trachoma, a destructive conjunctivitis for which they could receive no treatment in Yemen, they lived in Gedera, a village for the blind established by a Polish lawyer.

Three years after Israel was created as a national haven for Jews and simultaneously attacked by its Arab neighbors, *Life* observed, "Israel continues to think first of its army, and probably will do so despite the terrific cost until the shaky and often violated armistice is strengthened into a permanent peace."

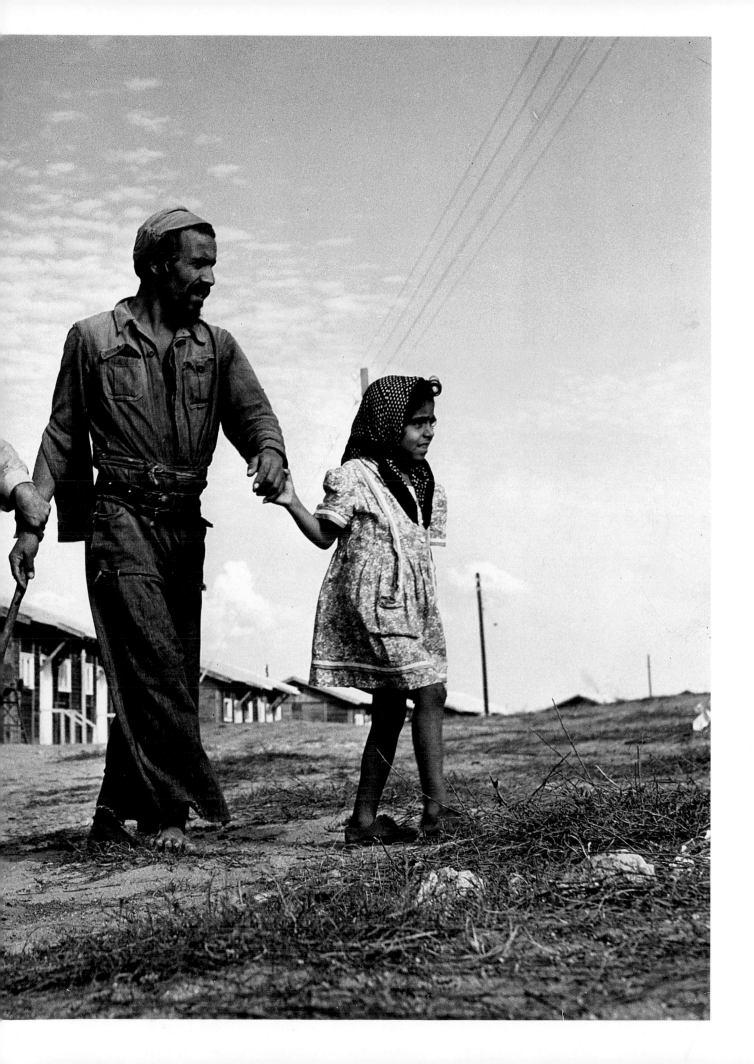

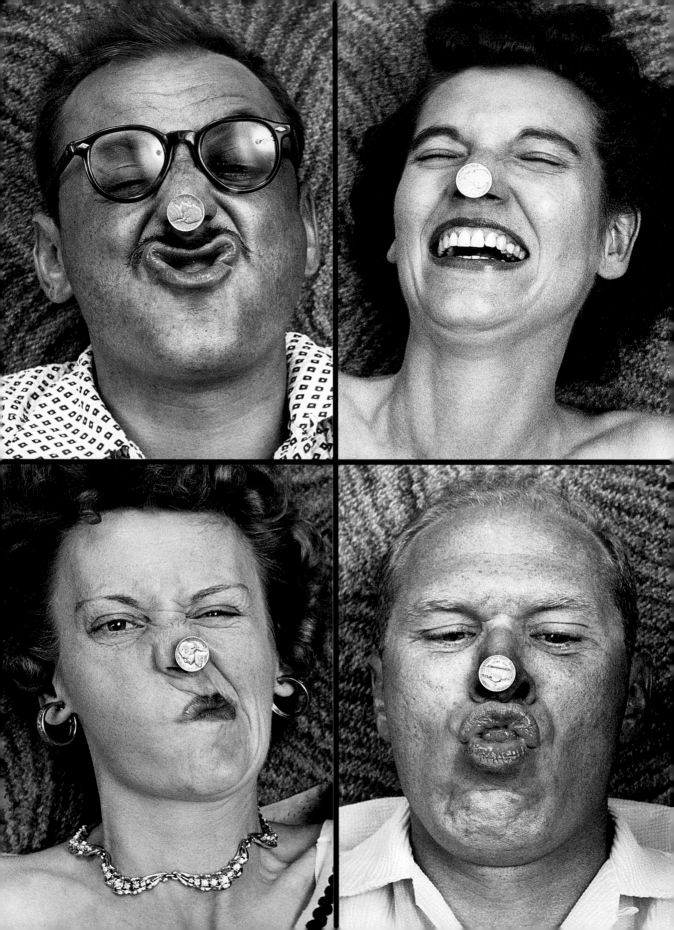

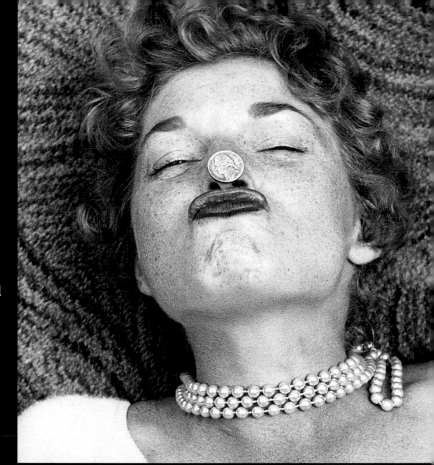

f you were in Waukesha, Wis., in the summer of 1954, you might have been invited to Angus and Betty McDougall's. They liked nonsense games, like the one where you lie on the floor and put a nickel on your nose. According to the rules, you have to get the coin off without shaking your head, or using your hands, or blowing it off your nose. Everyone went wild trying, but no one except Betty McDougall (top row, second from left) could do it. Her trick? She could reach the nickel with her tongue. Betty later admitted that hers was a pretty "dubious talent."

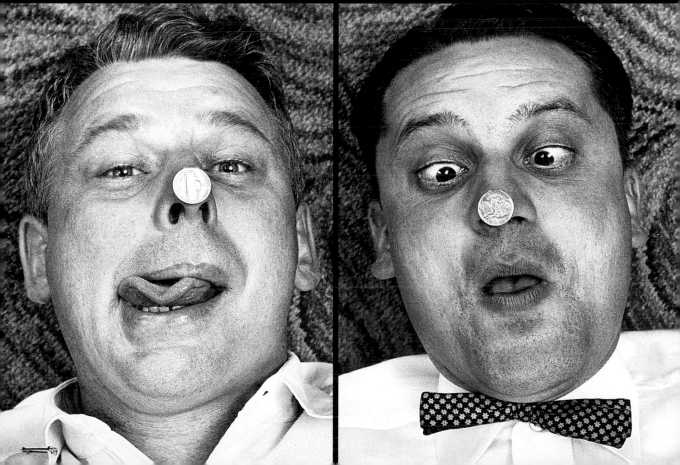

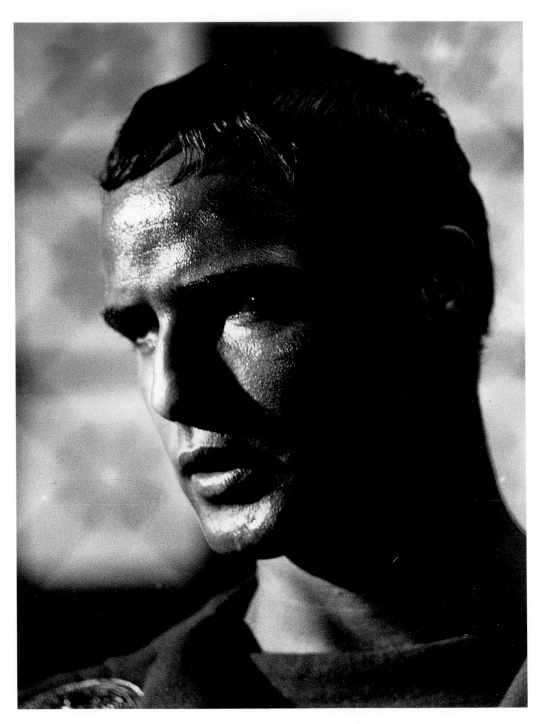

Marlon Brando
JOHN SWOPE
April 20, 1953

During the 20 years after he graduated from Harvard, John Swope did a bit of acting onstage with friends like Henry Fonda, Jimmy Stewart, and Margaret Sullavan. But photography, not performing, proved to be his true interest. Comfortable of manner, Swope moved through the temperaments of Hollywood with ease.

On the set of *Julius Caesar* he found a slender Marlon Brando playing Mark Antony. Brando, *Life* noted, suspended his famous mumble and spoke Shakespeare's lines with clarity.

Swope's widow, actress Dorothy McGuire, describes her husband's love of photography simply: "Light was a part of his body—there, that says it, doesn't it?"

Elizabeth Taylor
PHILIPPE HALSMAN
Fall 1988

In 1948, 16-year-old Elizabeth Taylor arrived alone at Philippe Halsman's New York studio in the middle of the afternoon carrying a green evening dress. Halsman thought the dress needed something more, and Yvonne, his wife, provided a pendant. For the young actress, about to be kissed onscreen for the first time (by Robert Taylor), the afternoon was memorable. Describing it in 1987, she wrote that Halsman "was the first person to make me look at myself as a woman...he had no interest in making my figure appear childish. 'You have bosoms,' he would shout, 'so stick them out!' In one day I learned how to look sultry and pose provocatively. In short, I developed sex appeal."

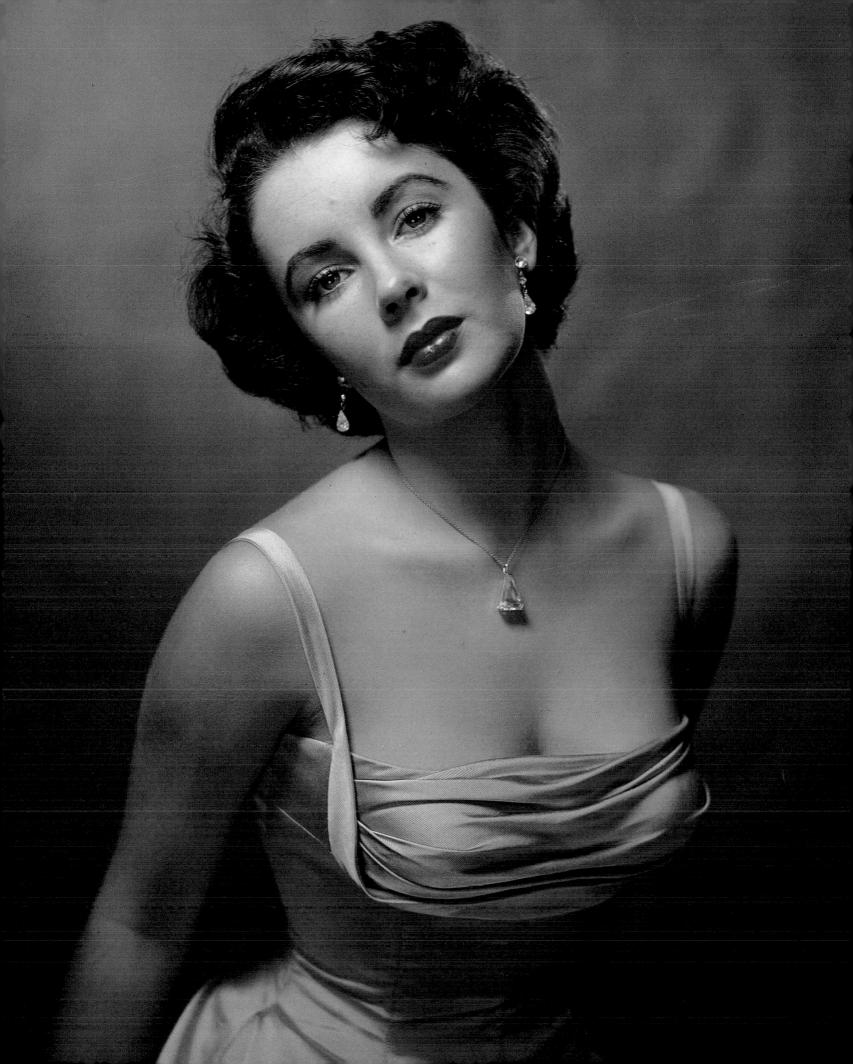

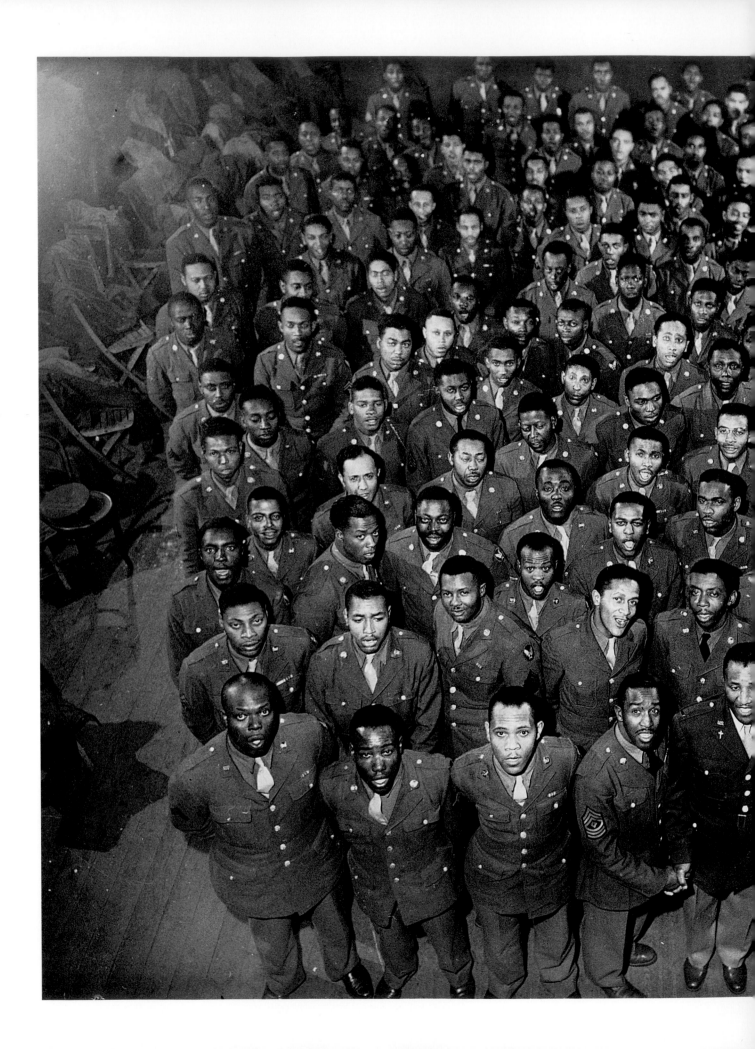

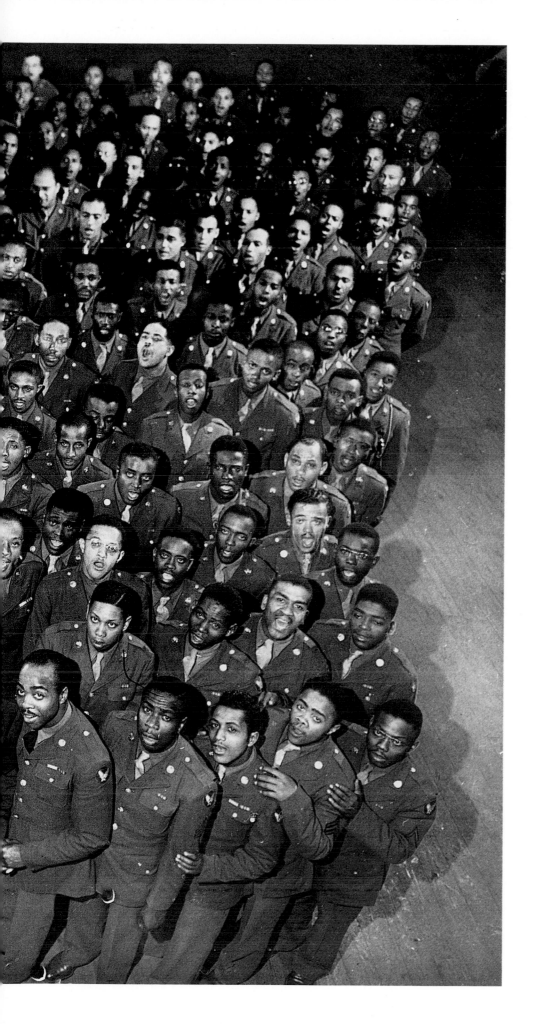

Army Chorus
DAVID E. SCHERMAN
August 8, 1943

"To the slow roll of drums and the swelling applause of a huge audience, a chorus of 200 American Negro soldiers from the Air Force Engineers marched single file onto the stage of London's famous Albert Hall," wrote *Life,* at a time when the armed forces were still segregated.

"Accompanied by the London Symphony Orchestra, the soldiers started to sing a memorable program of folk songs and spirituals. When they were finished, the audience surged off its chairs in applause, and even the orchestra members stomped and clapped their approval."

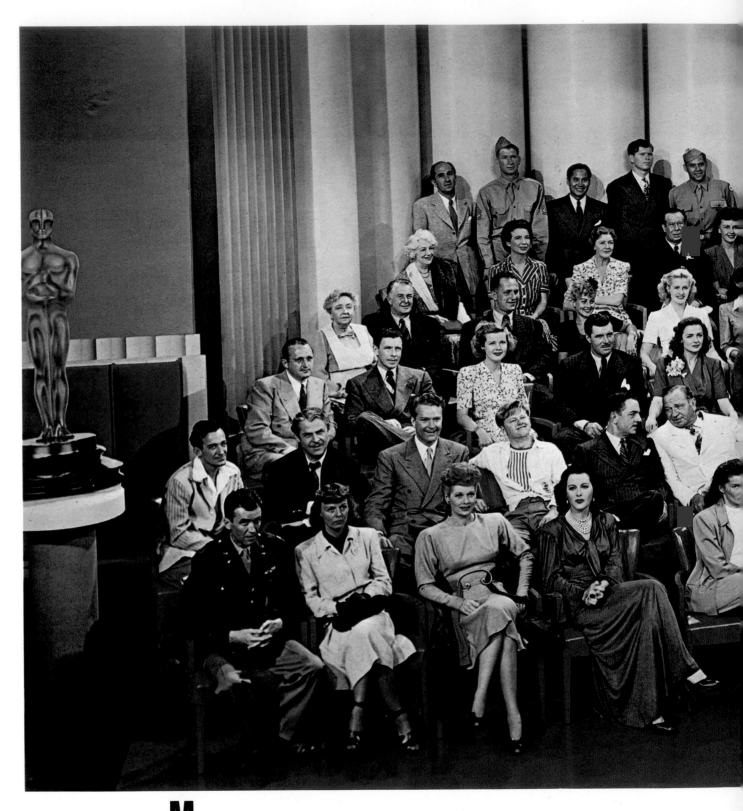

MGM
WALTER SANDERS
September 27, 1943

Metro-Goldwyn-Mayer was about to celebrate its 20th anniversary, and Louis B. Mayer arranged to bring his stars together for *Life*. He seated them roughly according to their earnings at the box office, with his more lucrative players toward the front. The studio was so impressed with the gathering that it filmed Walter Sanders taking the picture.

First row (left to right): James Stewart, Margaret Sullavan, Lucille Ball, Hedy Lamarr, Katharine Hepburn, Louis B. Mayer, Greer Garson, Irene Dunne, Susan Peters, Ginny Simms, Lionel Barrymore. *Second row:* Harry James, Brian Donlevy, Red Skelton, Mickey Rooney, William Powell, Wallace Beery, Spencer Tracy, Walter Pidgeon, Robert Taylor, Jean-Pierre Aumont, Lewis Stone, Gene Kelly, Jackie Jenkins. *Third row:* Tommy Dorsey, George Murphy, Jean Rogers,

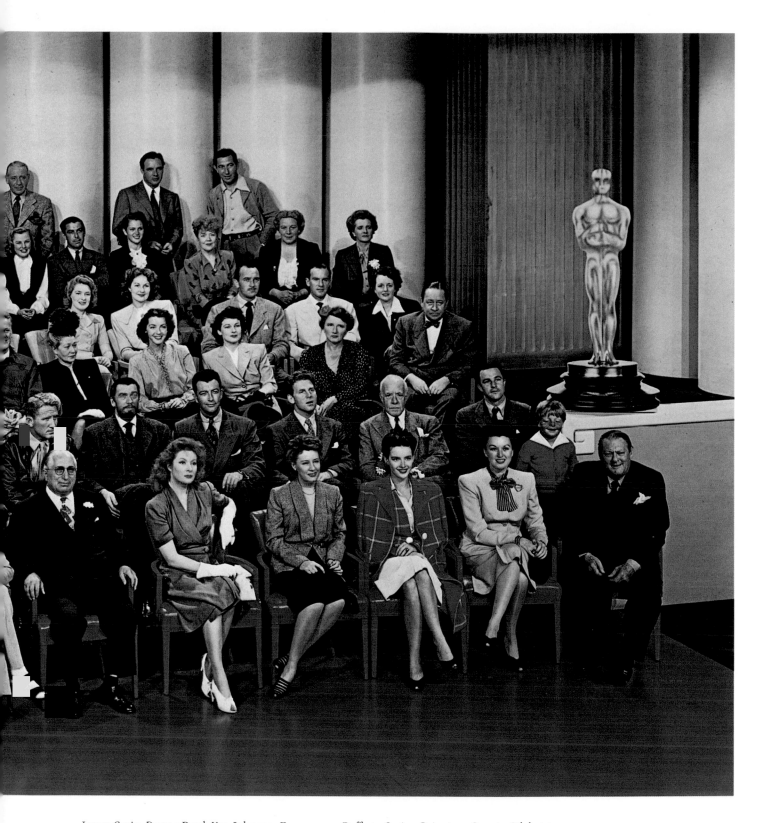

James Craig, Donna Reed, Van Johnson, Fay Bainter, Marsha Hunt, Ruth Hussey, Marjorie Main, Robert Benchley. *Fourth row:* Dame May Whitty, Reginald Owen, Keenan Wynn, Diana Lewis, Marilyn Maxwell, Esther Williams, Ann Richards, Martha Linden, Lee Bowman, Richard Carlson, Mary Astor. *Fifth row:* Blanche Ring, Sara Haden, Fay Holden, Bert Lahr, Frances Gifford, June Allyson, Richard Whorf, Frances Rafferty, Spring Byington, Connie Gilchrist, Gladys Cooper. *Sixth row:* Ben Blue, Chill Wills, Keye Luke, Barry Nelson, Desi Arnaz, Henry O'Neill, Bob Crosby, Rags Ragland. *Absent:* Lana Turner, Judy Garland, Charles Laughton, Laraine Day, Robert Young, Ann Sothern, Margaret O'Brien, Herbert Marshall, Robert Walker, Clark Gable, Robert Montgomery, Melvin Douglas, Lew Ayres. Greta Garbo had retired two years earlier.

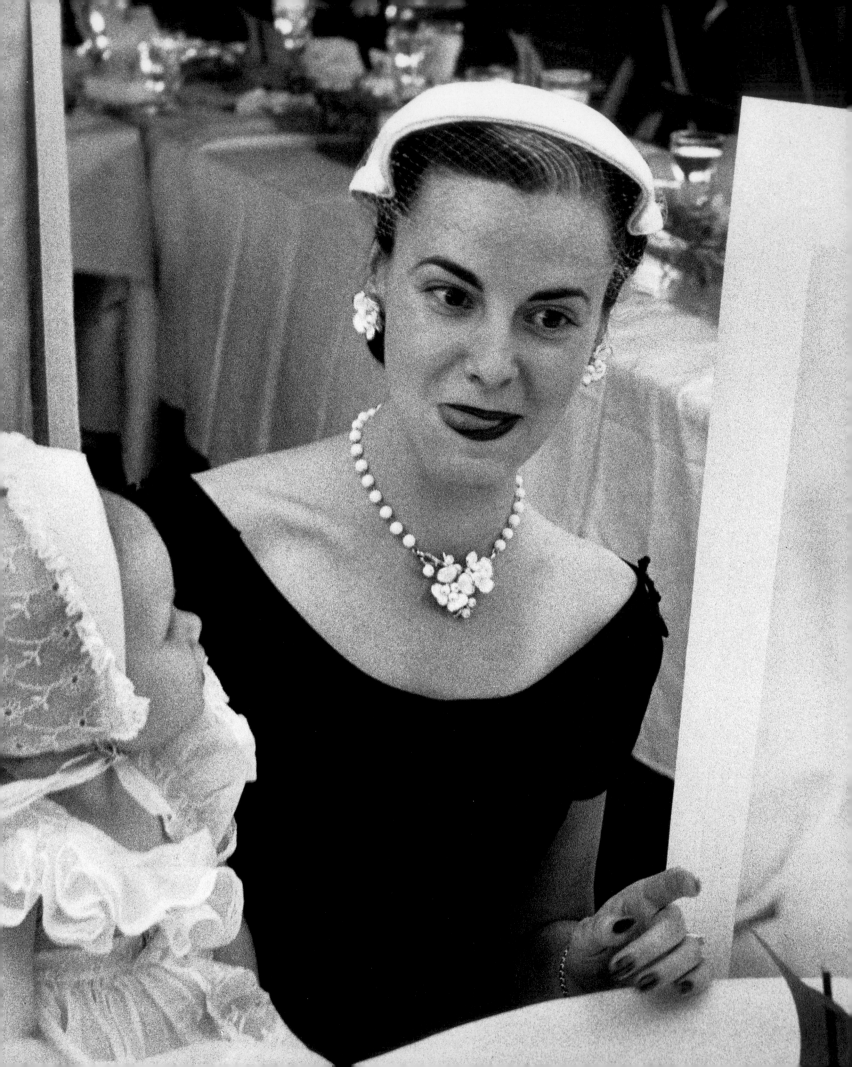

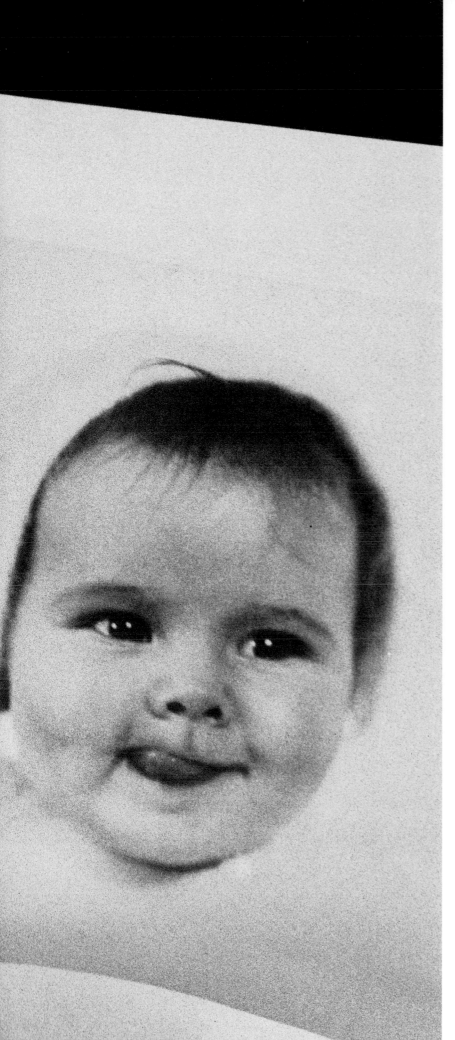

Ivory Soap
GREY VILLET
July 19, 1954

The anniversary, as *Life* described it, was this: "Just 75 years ago in the Cincinnati plant of Procter & Gamble Co., an obscure workman forgot to turn off his machine, walked out to lunch —and thereby made soap history. His machine, accidentally beating air bubbles into the creamy mixture, produced the world's first floating soap. The company did not learn what its careless workman had wrought until weeks later when dealers kept asking for 'the soap that floated.' P&G soon began making it under the name Ivory. Of over 15 billion cakes of Ivory made, only seven are known to have sunk."

On hand at a press conference to celebrate all this was the first photographed Ivory baby, Marjorie Munn, by then 28—who could still delight photographers by simply licking her lips, thereby upstaging her successor, Candice DeGruchy, left.

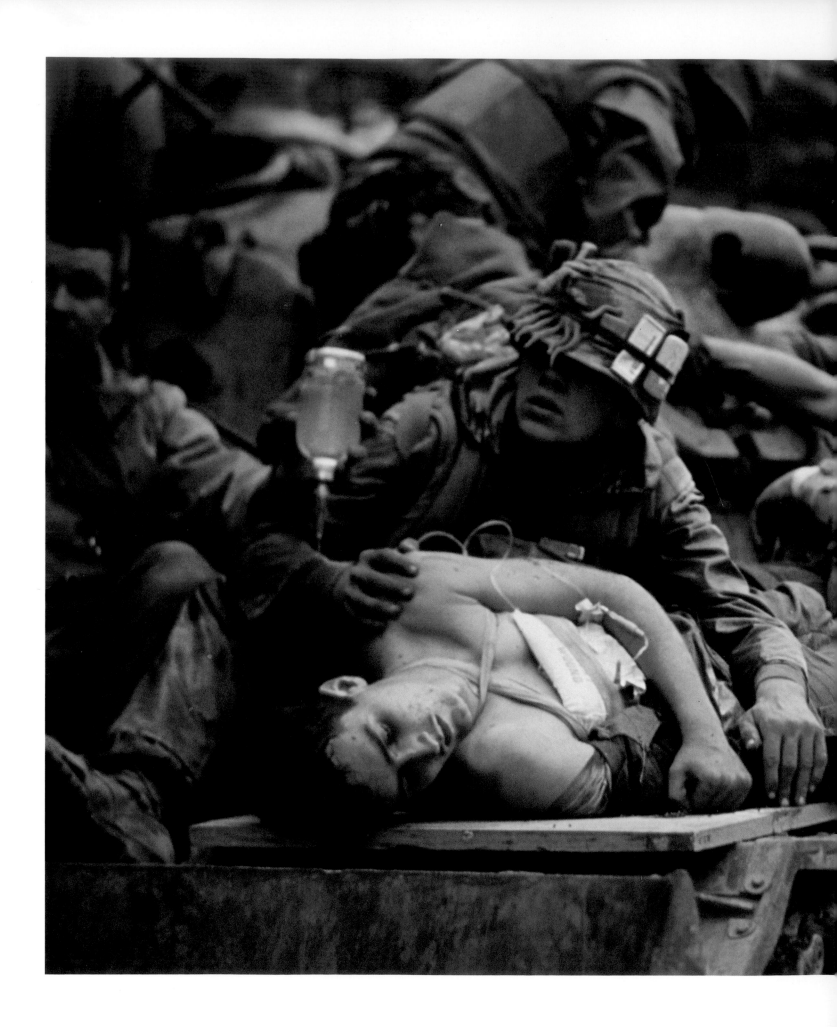

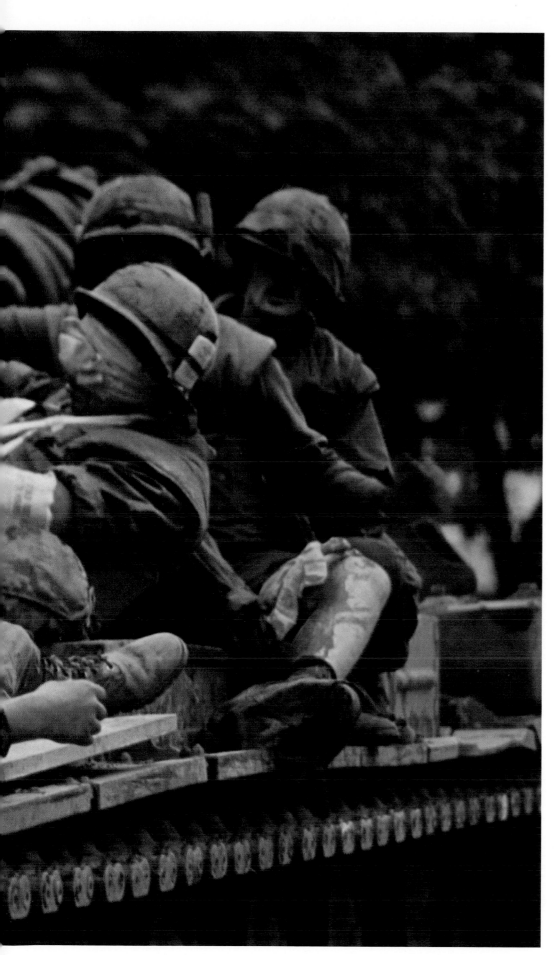

Hué
JOHN OLSON
March 8, 1968

"I recall when I first saw the magazine, I couldn't remember taking this photograph," says John Olson, then a 21-year-old soldier working for the servicemen's newspaper, *Stars and Stripes.* "The fighting in Hué was vivid in my mind. I remember this scene. A tank had come up the street and stopped. I was in the middle of the street taking pictures. I guess I didn't realize how strong the image would be, and, of course, it was all very quick."

At times during the Tet offensive, bad weather prevented helicopters from evacuating the wounded, so tanks were used. In 25 days of fighting in Hué, 490 Americans were killed, 2,252 wounded. The ancient city was severely damaged.

"More than anything else in Vietnam thus far," wrote *Life,* "the fate of Hué demonstrated the sickening irony into which the war has fallen—the destruction of the very things that the U.S. is there to save."

169

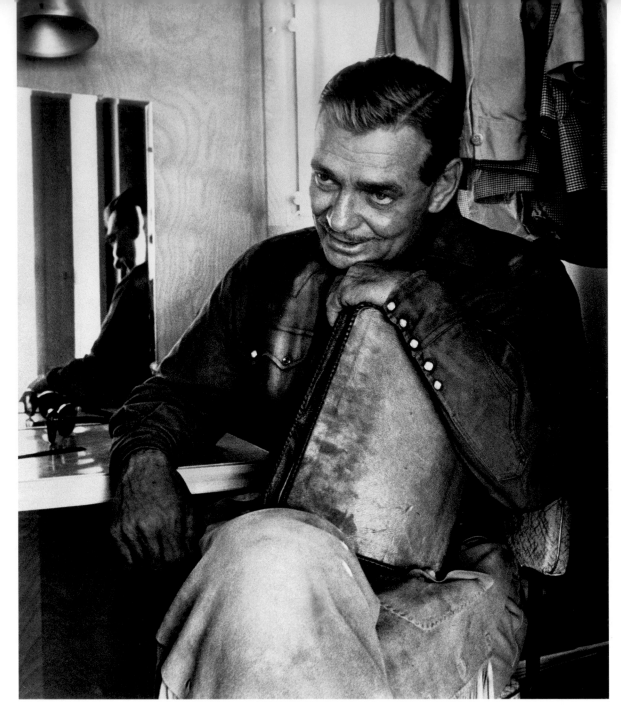

Clark Gable
EVE ARNOLD
November 21, 1960

The Great Profile
BOB LANDRY
September 30, 1940

"Clark Gable was in a surprisingly expansive mood waiting for Marilyn Monroe to arrive on the set of *The Misfits*," says Eve Arnold. "He invited me into his dressing room and mixed himself a can of grapefruit juice with vodka. Then he started talking about his early days acting on Broadway, before he'd ever gone to Hollywood. Without moving I brought out my camera and began to photograph."

Several days later, just before the birth of his first child, the 59-year-old actor suffered a fatal heart attack.

Outside Grauman's Chinese Theater in Hollywood and beside imprints of Tom Mix's horse's hooves, Harold Lloyd's glasses, and Mary Pickford's footprints is "The Great Profile"—or, more specifically, John Barrymore's left. Impressed in cement by Sid Grauman himself, Barrymore could only say, "I feel like the face on the barroom floor."

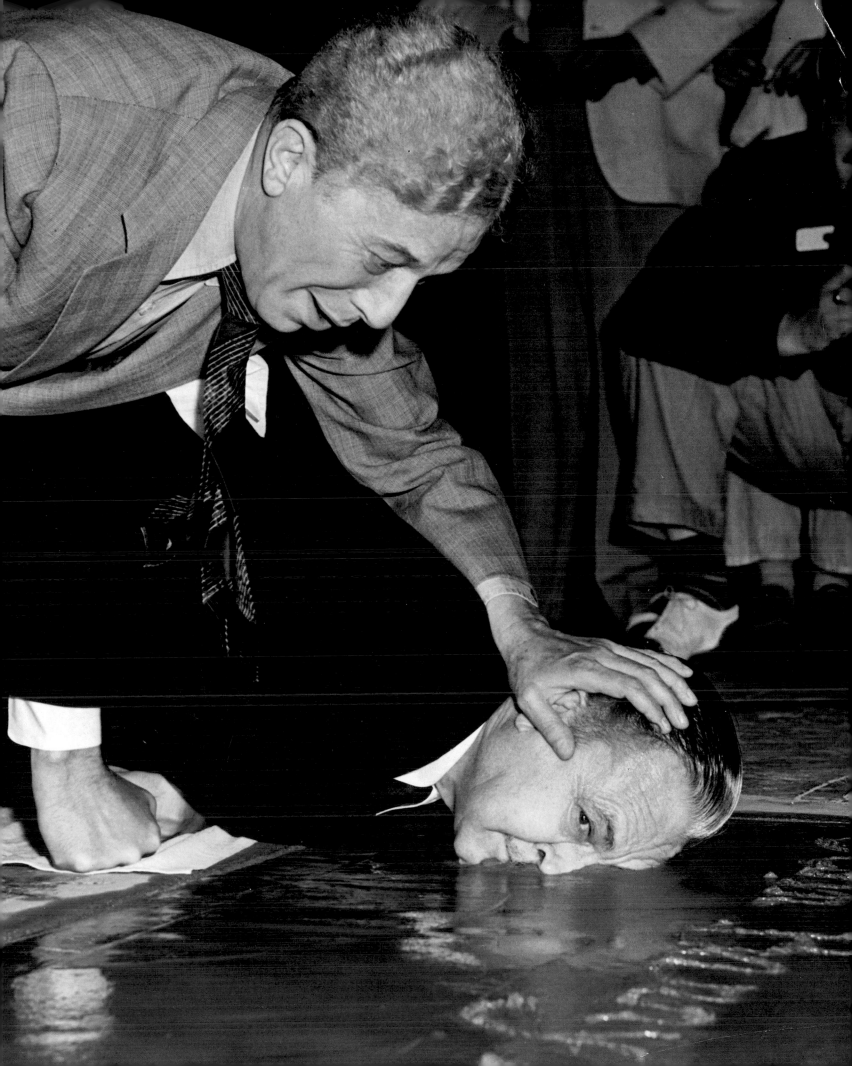

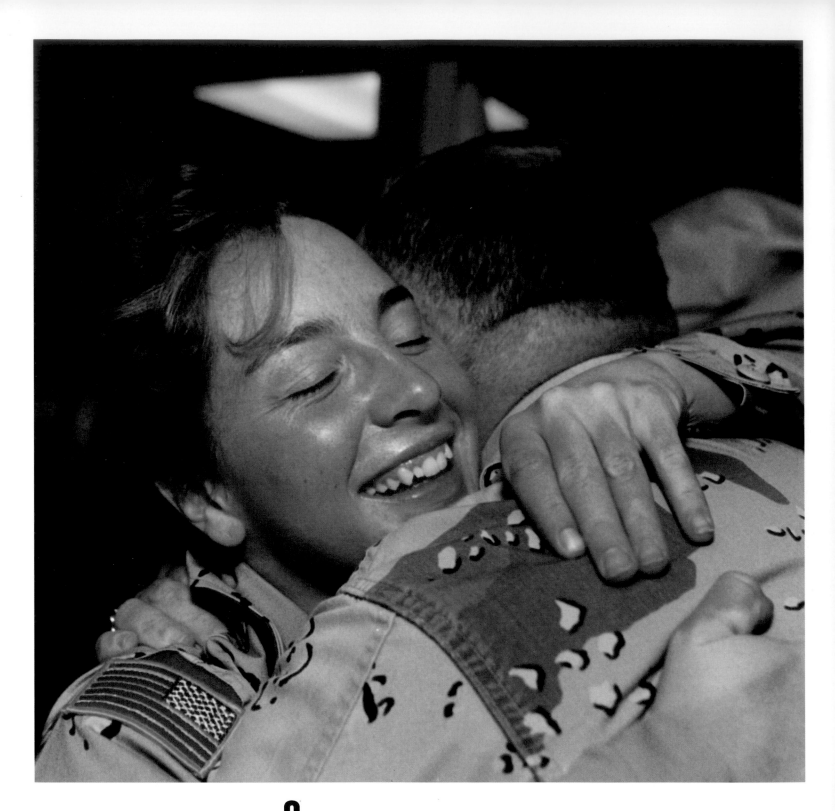

Schwarzkopf and Rathbun-Nealy
HARRY BENSON
March 18, 1991

General H. Norman Schwarzkopf strode into a ward on the hospital ship *Mercy* two days after the cease-fire in the Persian Gulf. Harry Benson was the only reporter on board, having flown to Bahrain from the central command headquarters in Riyadh with the general.

After shaking hands with several pilots who had been shot down and imprisoned, Schwarzkopf approached Melissa Rathbun-Nealy, the first female American soldier ever captured.

"How wonderful to see you in front of me. I prayed for you every night," said the general. "There's something I'd like to do—I hope you don't mind—I'd like to give you a hug."

As reported by Benson in his book *People* (Chronicle Books; 1991), the startled Rathbun-Nealy made a little sound between a laugh and a cry. "Oh no, sir," she said. "I don't mind."

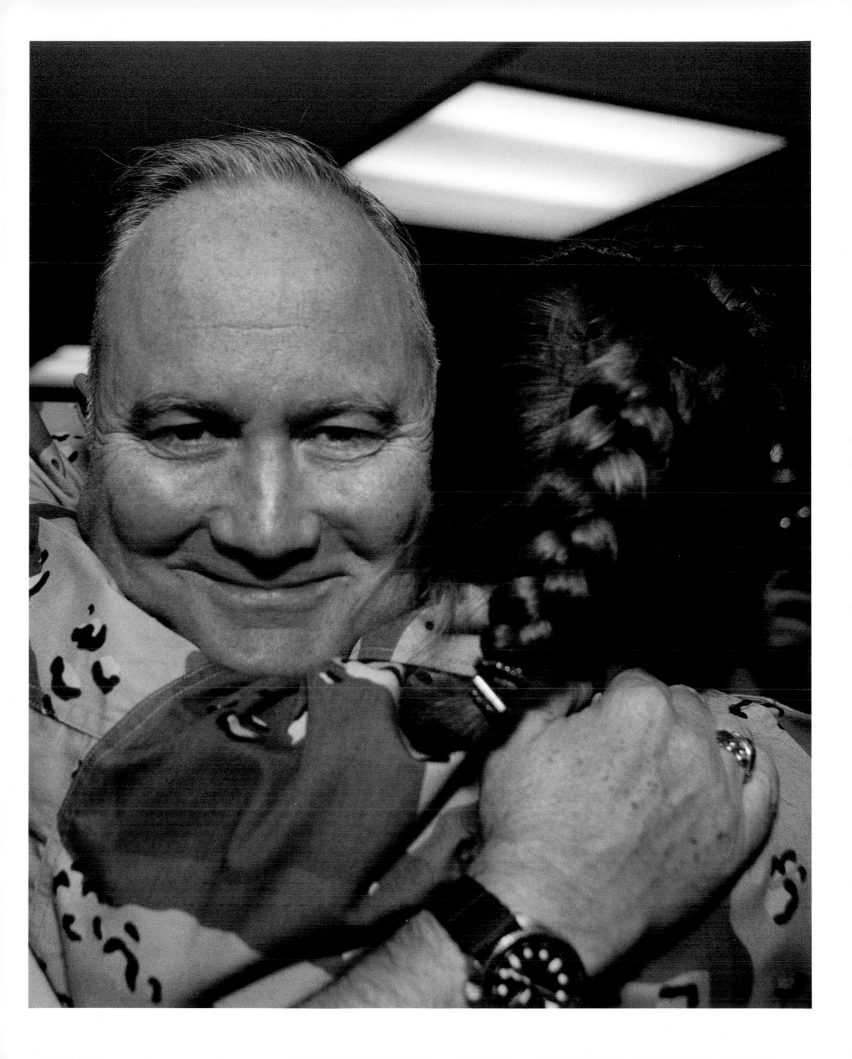

Clemency
GUY HAYES
December 8, 1941

Six members of the Ku Klux Klan were in jail in Georgia for flogging pro-union millworkers. Hearing an appeal for clemency in his office, Governor Eugene Talmadge watched public prosecutor Dan Duke wave a "man whip" and shout, "These are whips you could kill a bull elephant with!"

Unfazed, the Governor recalled he had once helped flog a black himself: "I wasn't in such bad company. The Apostle Paul was a flogger in his life, then confessed, reformed, and became one of the greatest powers of the Christian Church. That proves to me that good people can be misguided and do bad things."

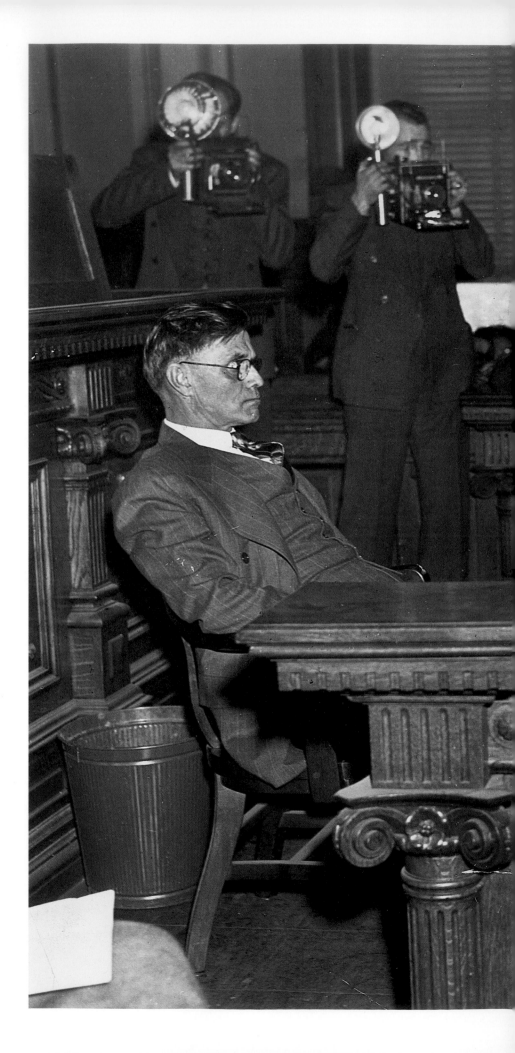

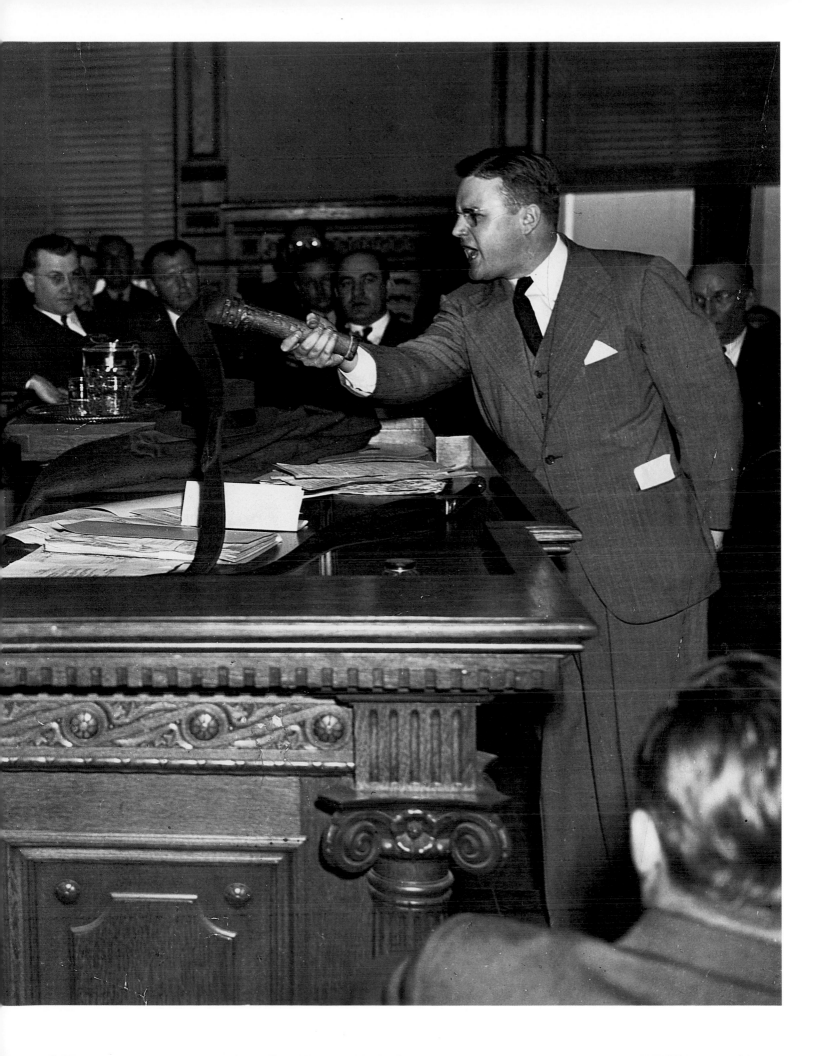

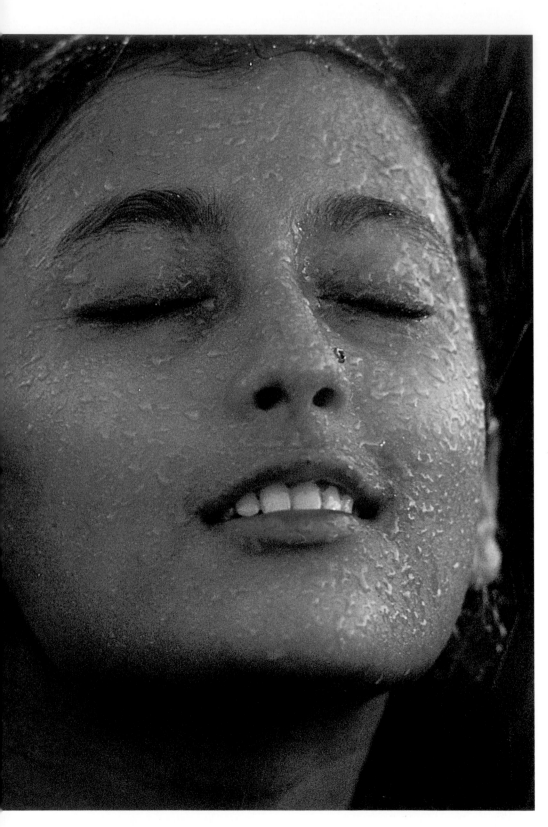

Monsoon
BRIAN BRAKE
September 8, 1961

New Zealand–born Brian Brake took it upon himself to record the annual monsoon rains as they swept across India's parched land. He studied the storms one year and photographed them the next, producing a moody, evocative essay that conveyed both the torpid pace of life in scorching heat and the joy and relief brought by the rain.

Solange
JACQUES-HENRI LARTIGUE
Fall 1988

Jacques-Henri Lartigue took memorable photographs, starting when he was seven years old. His boyhood work is filled with action shots of his wealthy cousins leaping, driving, and flying across France. When he grew up, Lartigue became a painter, and soon his photographs tended to be as still as they once had been active, as beautiful as they once had been vigorous. Most of them were of women: "Everything about them fascinates me," he wrote at 16. He married three of his subjects and photographed many others, including his friend Solange, a striking example of his credo: "I do the flowers. I don't do the weeds."

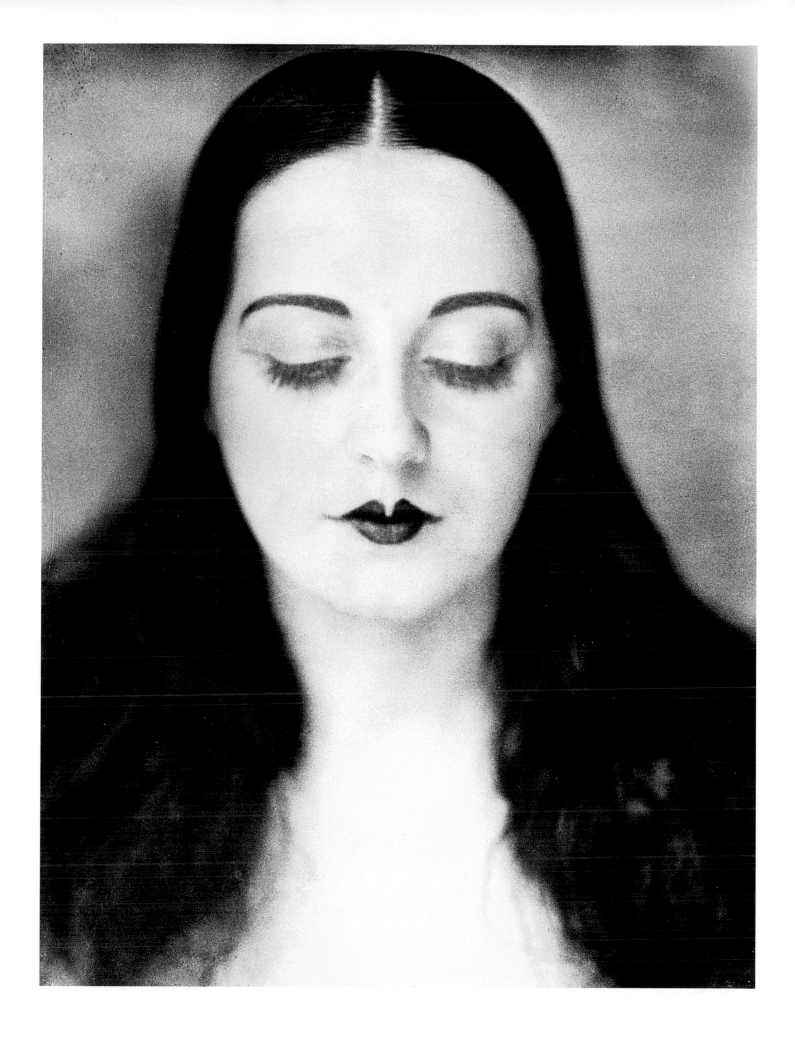

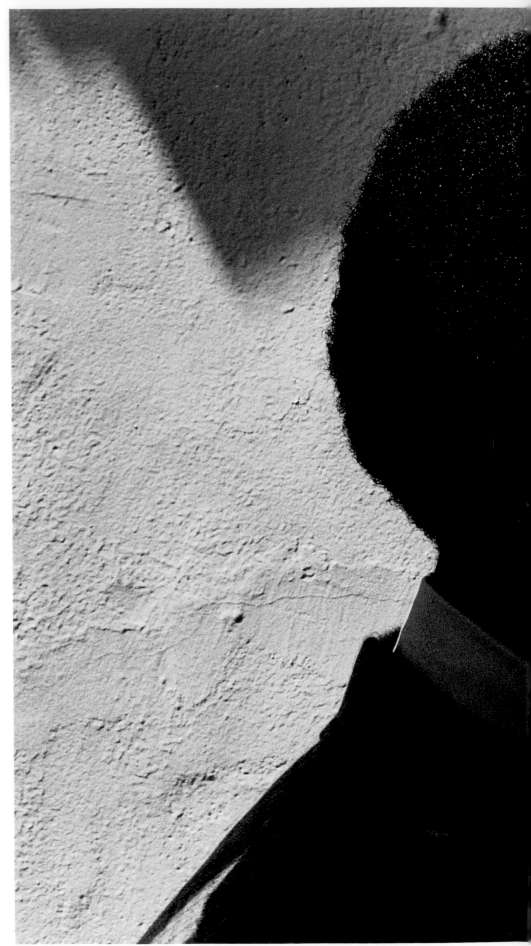

Bill Cosby
JOHN LOENGARD
April 11, 1969

Etienne de Silhouette, Louis XV's finance minister, was so stingy that his name came to denote an inexpensive version of an object, for example a portrait cut from paper showing a person's profile. Less costly than miniature oil paintings, portraits *à la Silhouette* became the rage at French and German courts around the time of the American Revolution.

Nearly 200 years later, Bill Cosby stood in the shady backyard of his house in Beverly Hills while his business manager held up some documents to keep a bit of sunshine off the comedian's shoulder. Cosby's cigar makes his silhouette more complex, but it is the bright wire-framed eyeglasses that give the portrait its full dimension.

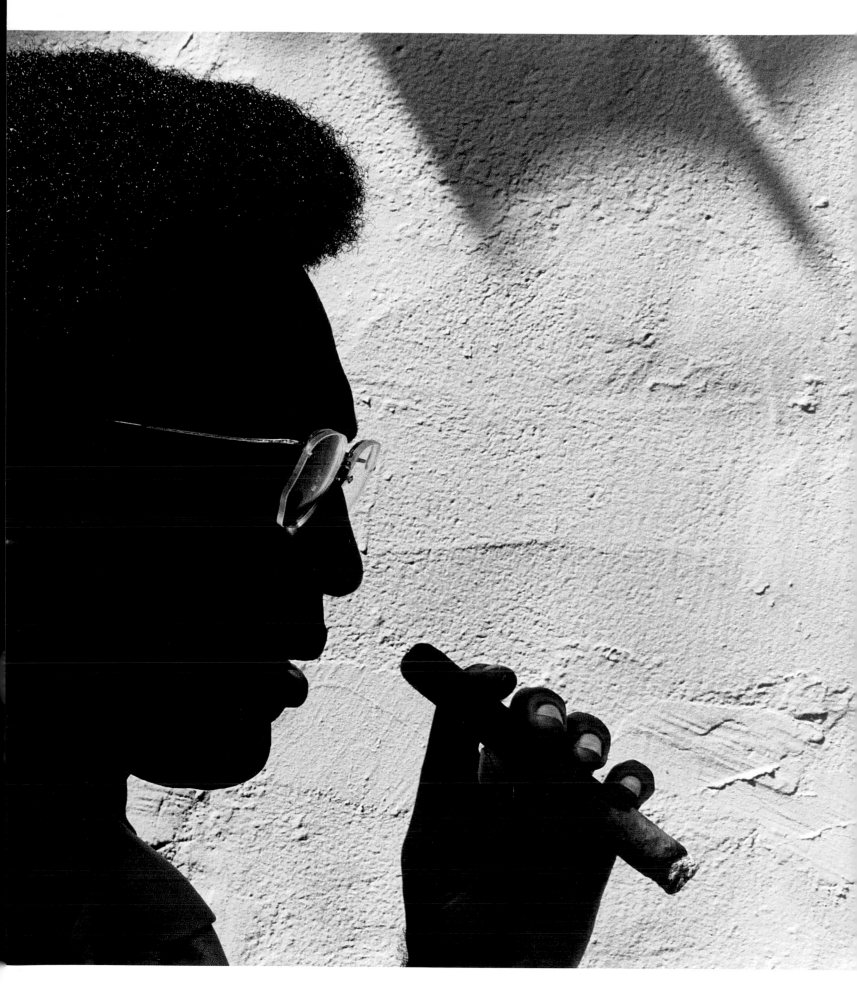

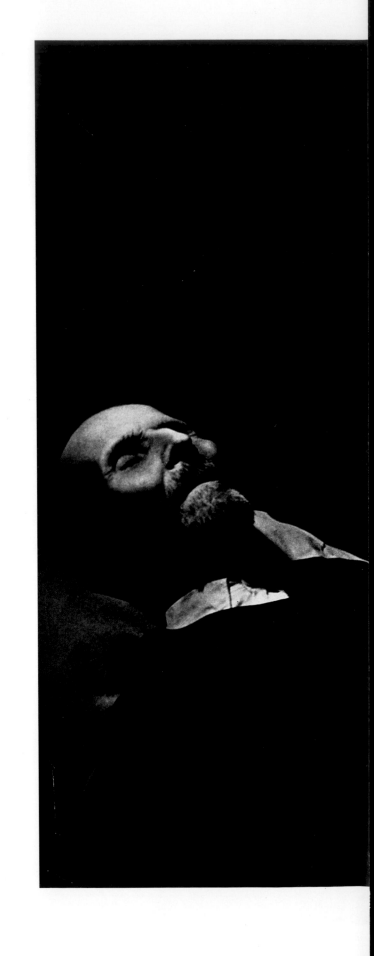

Spanish Wake
W. EUGENE SMITH
April 9, 1951

Age 75, Juan Larra died early one morning in the old Spanish village of Deleitosa. According to W. Eugene Smith's biographer, Jim Hughes, Señor Larra's son asked Smith for a ride to the provincial capital in order to get the papers necessary for a burial. On their return, Smith stood outside the house.

"It was a very moving scene, but I couldn't bring myself to go in, to just walk in. I just couldn't do it," Smith recalled.

Finally the son came out, and Smith, through an interpreter, asked, "Sir, I do not wish to dishonor your father, but would it be permissible to enter your home and to photograph?"

"Please come in. I would be honored," the son replied.

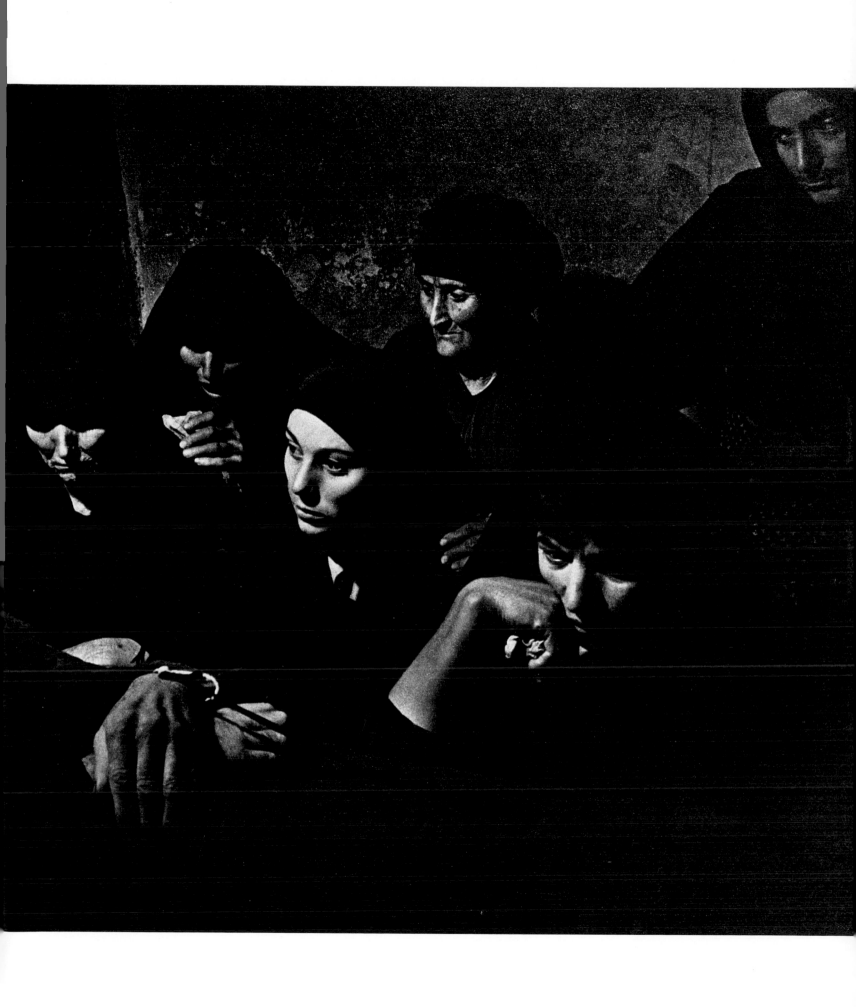

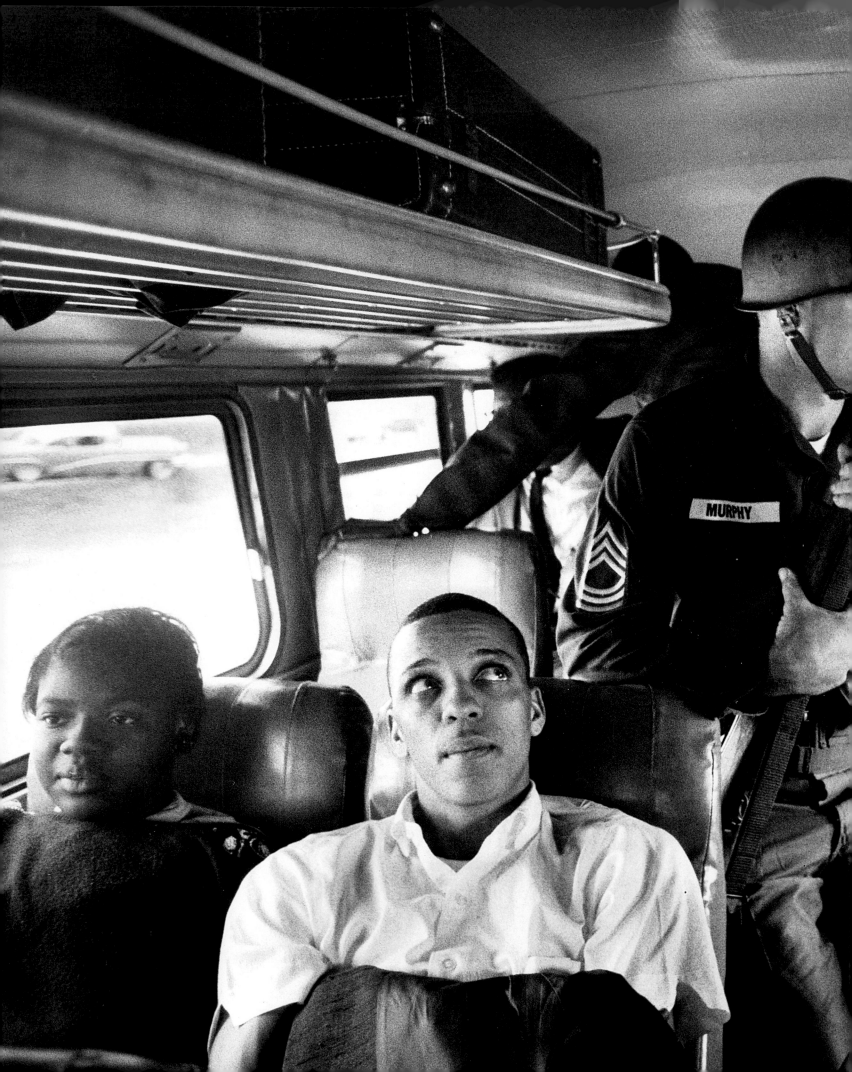

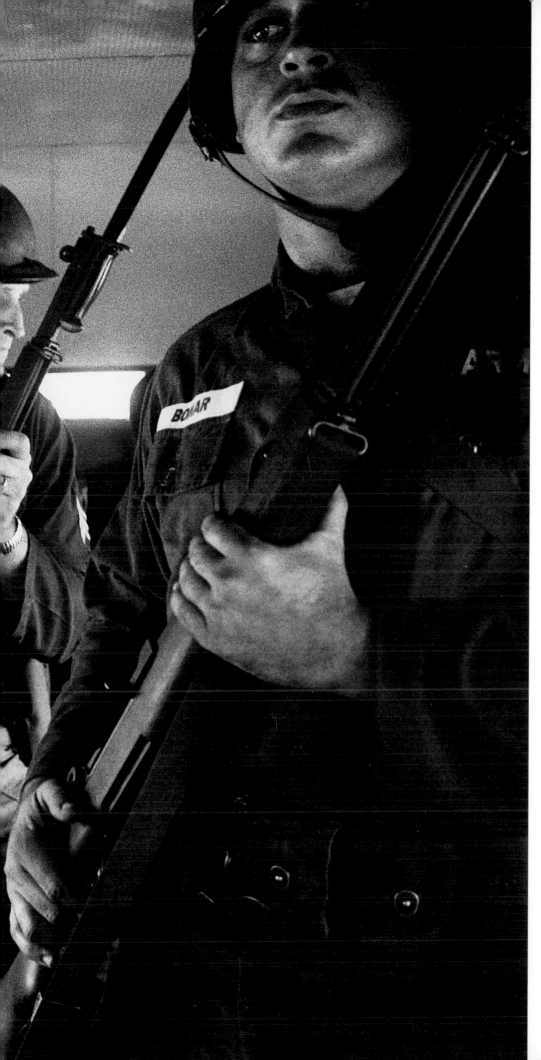

Freedom Riders
PAUL SCHUTZER
June 2, 1961

In the spring of 1961, despite Attorney General Robert Kennedy's pleas for "a cooling-off period," Freedom Riders continued to take buses through the South, demanding enforcement of a federal law prohibiting segregation on vehicles and at bus stations serving interstate travelers.

Two buses, loaded with 27 Riders and 20 members of the media, left Montgomery, Ala., protected by 1,000 Alabama National Guardsmen. At the Mississippi border, a passenger, David Dennis, watched apprehensively as Mississippi Guardsmen boarded the bus.

In Jackson, having been asked twice to leave the white waiting room at the bus depot, all 27 Riders went to jail rather than pay $200 each in fines. Reported *Life:* "Mississippi offered the incoming Freedom Riders safe, swift escort service from the border right into the city courts, where they were convicted for 'disobeying an officer.'"

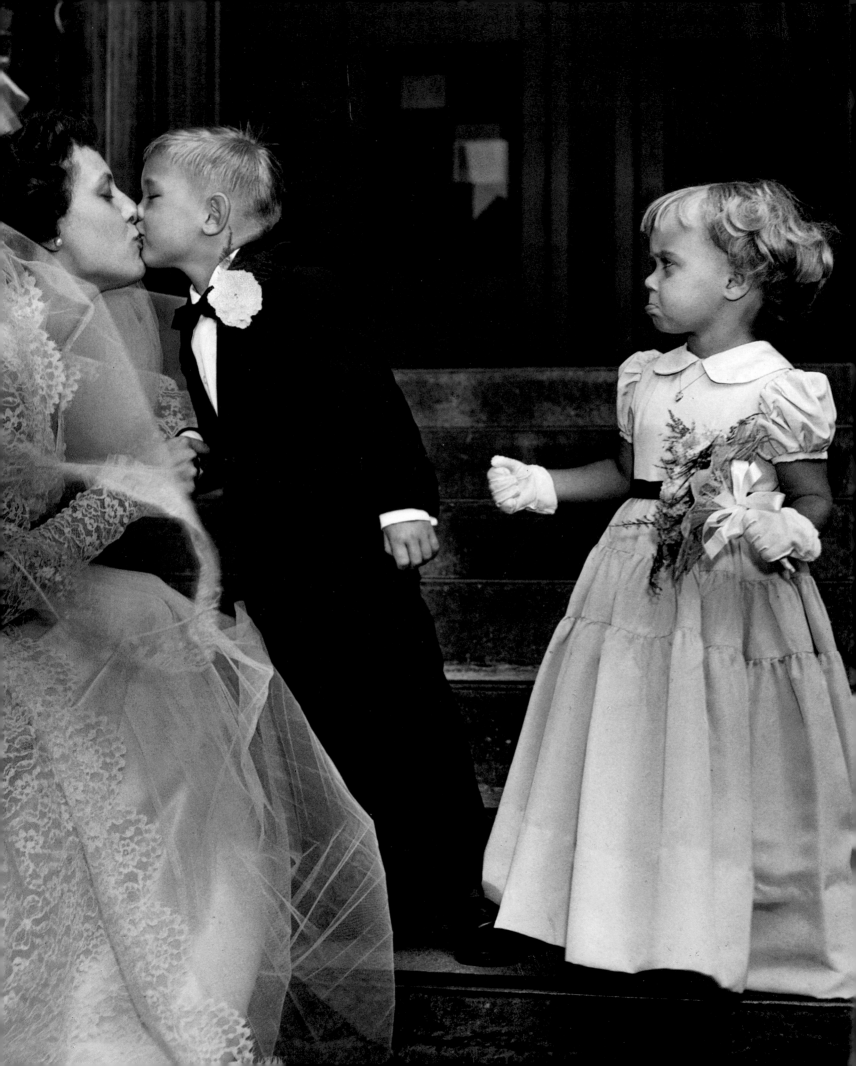

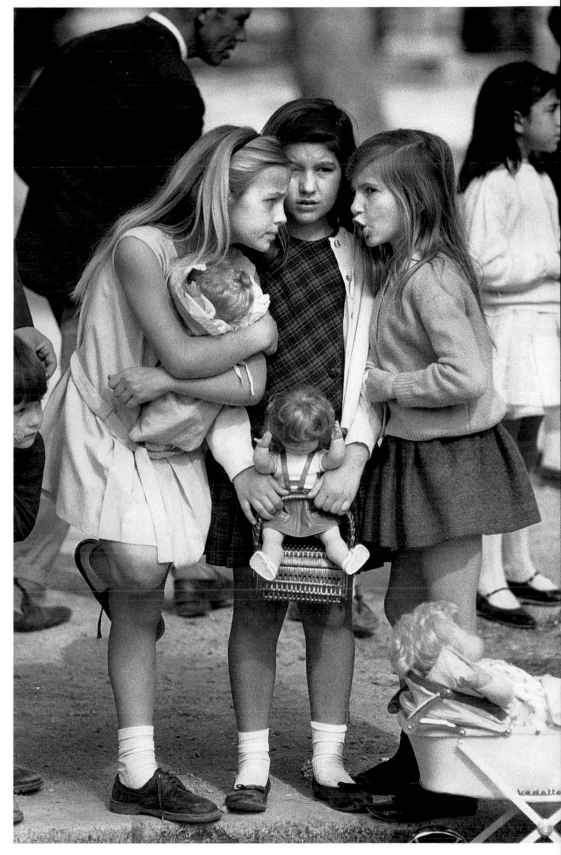

Flower Girl
MILDRED TOTUSHEK
May 31, 1954

Mildred Totushek worked as an industrial photographer in Milwaukee, but she quit. "They didn't pay women that well in those days," she says, "so I set up my own business doing portraits, weddings, and a bit of everything."

Totushek was ready when the bride, Mrs. August Kachigian, left St. Mary's Roman Catholic Church. The newlywed turned to kiss her three-year-old nephew, Ricky Lofy, and flower girl Jan Schlueter reacted.

One of the joys in photography is seeing what comes out of the developing tank. "I had seen *something* happening," says Totushek, "but I certainly didn't know she had her fist tightened up like she was going to pop him."

Gossip
KEN HEYMAN
December 17, 1971

"We see humor in children behaving like adults," says Ken Heyman to explain why his photograph of three daughters of American servicemen talking in Seville, Spain, was for a time the second-best-selling postcard in the U.S.

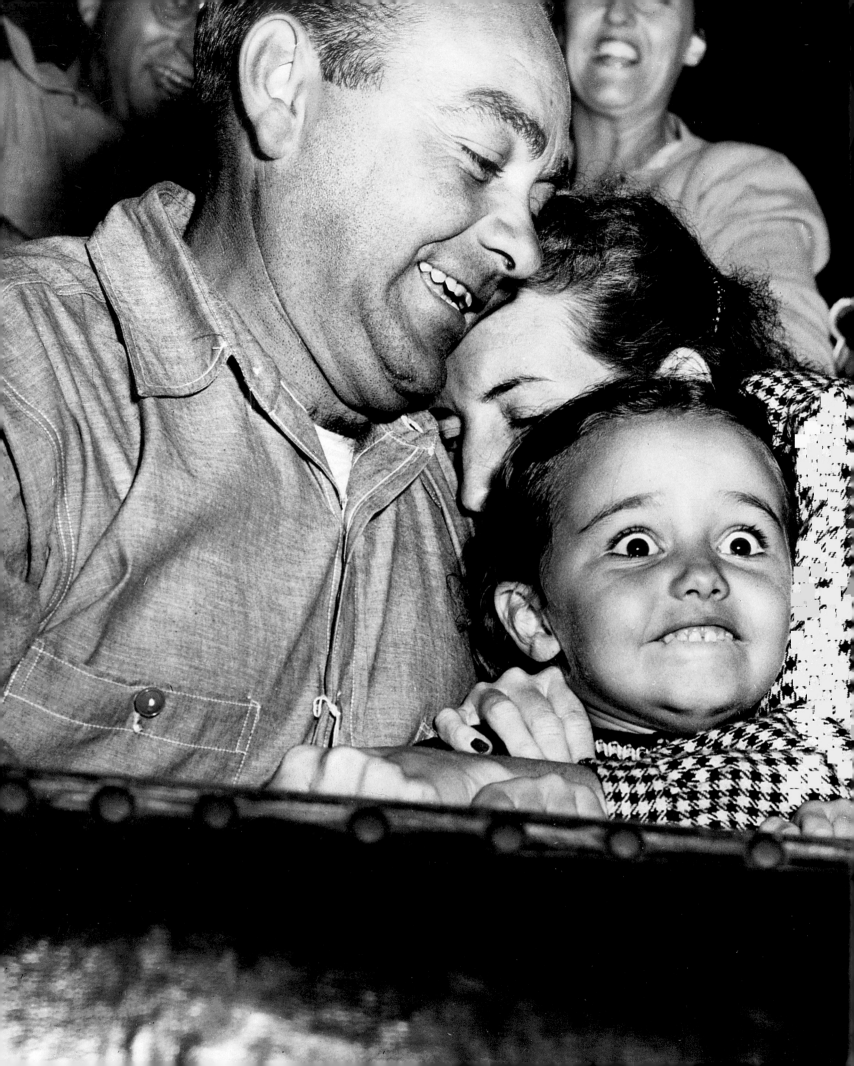

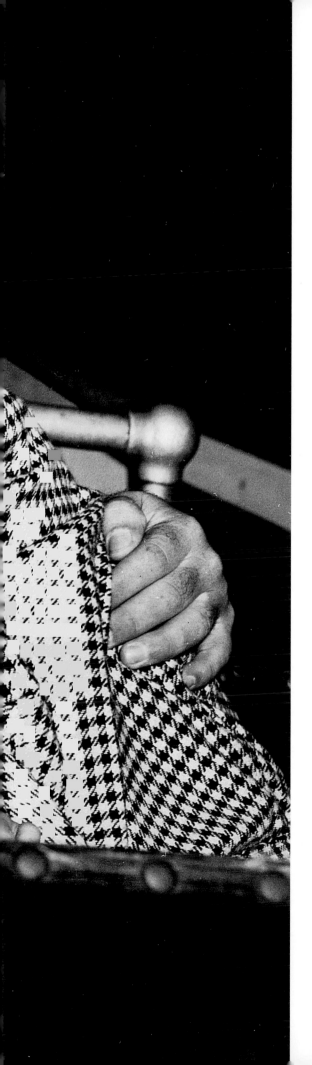

Roller Coaster
RAY SHORR
October 6, 1947

Frank Tilyou, the owner of an amusement park at Coney Island, hired Ray Shorr to produce one publicity picture each day and send it to all the newspapers in New York City.

"I took pictures of the mayor's daughter on a ride—that kind of thing. It took an hour each day. What was I gonna do with the other seven?" asks Shorr. He decided to photograph the passengers on the roller coaster.

Wedging his hip under the safety bar in the front seat of the first car and holding a Speed Graphic camera with a high-speed strobe flash above his head, Shorr remembers taking 100 rides over five nights and documenting the bridgework in a lot of riders' mouths—as well as the expression of terror on the face of a four-year-old from the neighborhood.

"Dropping backward through space isn't bad if you know where you're going," says Shorr, who went on to become a fashion photographer. "I knew."

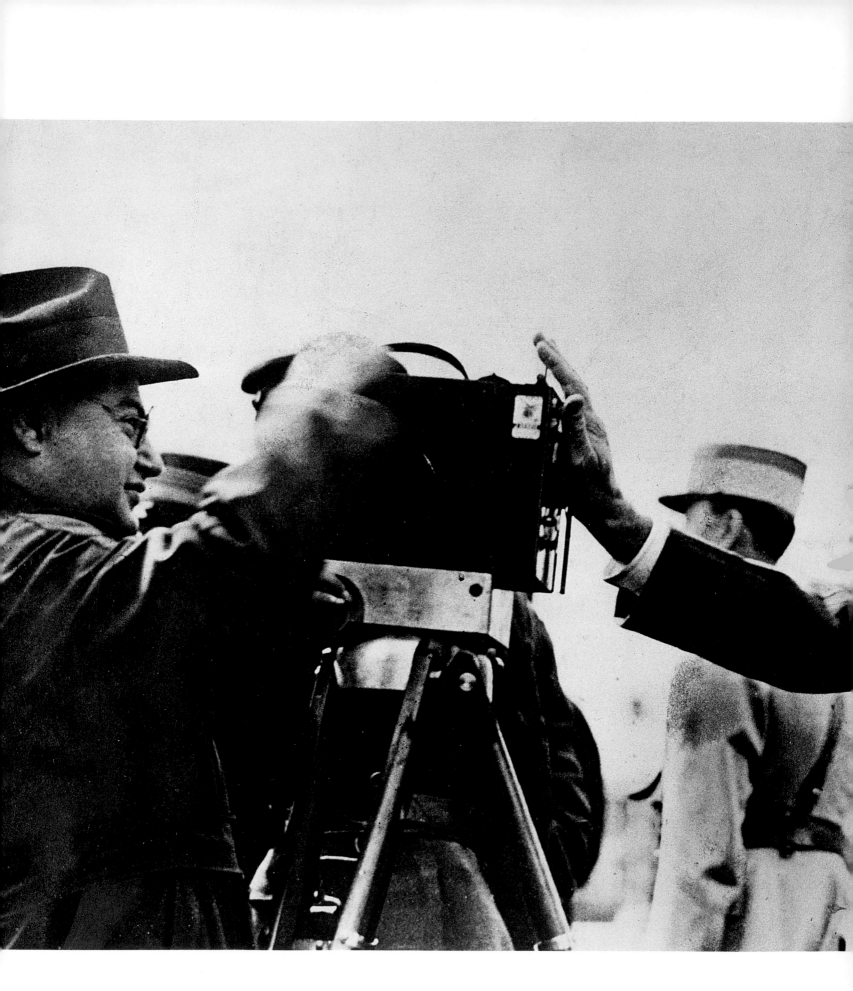

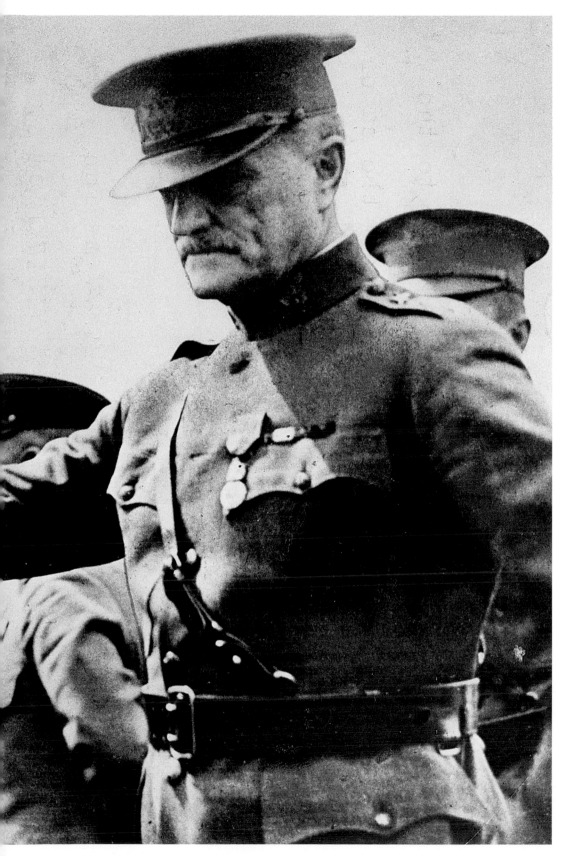

General John J. Pershing
H.M. VAN TINE
July 12, 1937

An army's relationship with the press is often difficult. Generals have their reasons to prefer censorship. They think it's easy to impose (in this case, it was: just reach out and cover the photographer's lens). General Pershing, being a man of action, made his gesture gracefully. His timing was superb. His bearing commanding. But the truth is that at Fort Myer, Va., Pershing made the same mistake that many a general has made in the past. He didn't cover his flank.

INDEX

SOURCES

The *Aegis*, Bel Air, Maryland / 35
Association des Amis de Jacques-Henri Lartigue (Paris) / 177
Black Star / 45, 82, 110, 144
Brown Brothers / 33
Camera Press Ltd. / 73
Columbus (Georgia) *Ledger-Enquirer* / 28
Contact Press Images Inc. / 120
Cook Collection, Valentine Museum, Richmond, Virginia / 38
Culver / 86
International Magazine Service, Stockholm, Sweden / 119
Library of Congress / 14
Magnum Photos, Inc. / 26, 48, 50, 112, 122, 156, 170
New York *Post* / 94
The *Observer* (London) / 74
The Philadelphia *Inquirer* / 140
Photo Researchers, Inc. / 176
Stars and Stripes / 101, 168
UPI-Bettmann / 56, 142
Werek Pressebildagentur / 104
Wide World / 84
Woodfin Camp & Associates / 20, 154

The captions to photographs on pages 50, 98, 122, 130, 140 and 180 originally appeared in the *Life* Special Edition, Fall 1990.

Most photographers are quoted from interviews in the preparation of this book. Others are quoted from the issues of *Life* in which their photograph appeared or books they themselves have written describing their work.

Other quotations are from either *Life* or the following sources:
Kiki (page 36): *Man Ray, American Artist* by Neil Baldwin, Clarkson N. Potter, Inc., 1988, page 150;
Thomas Hart Benton (page 40): *Jackson Pollack, An American Saga,* by Steven Naifeh and Gregory White Smith, HarperCollins Publishers, 1991, page 225;
Ulysses S. Grant (page 102): *Patriotic Gore* by Edmund Wilson, Oxford University Press, 1962, pages 132, 133, 140;
Lyndon B. Johnson (page 142): *Counsel to the President* by Clark Clifford, Random House, 1991, page 522;
Elizabeth Taylor (page 161): *Elizabeth Takes Off* by Elizabeth Taylor, G.P. Putnam's Sons, 1987, page 58;
Juan Larra and W. Eugene Smith (page 180): *Shadow & Substance* by Jim Hughes, McGraw-Hill Publishing Company, 1989, page 256.